CHALLENGING GENDER STEREOTYPES IN THE EARLY YEARS

What does gender equity mean for early years practitioners? What are early years settings already doing to promote gender equality and why is this so important? How can we provide children with a solid basis from which they can grow into people who are not limited by society's expectations of their gender?

This is a manual for every early years practitioner who wishes to expand their knowledge and improve their practice regarding gender stereotyping in the early years. Drawing from the authors' experience developing a public health programme tackling gender stereotypes, it explores the reasons why gender inequality is still an issue, identifies how gender inequality is perpetuated and provides a framework and practical tools to drive change. The framework includes an audit process to celebrate areas of success and to identify areas for development, alongside a host of suggestions on how to navigate tricky situations in creative, respectful and effective ways.

With the voices and experiences of experts and practitioners woven throughout the text, alongside key reflections and scenarios with which the reader can critically engage, *Challenging Gender Stereotypes in the Early Years* challenges readers to consider their own practice, drive staff awareness and make a difference to their setting.

Susie Heywood and **Barbara Adzajlic** are public health professionals with over 15 years' experience working on areas like mental health, gender-based violence, suicide prevention, behaviour change and inequalities.

Together, Susie and Barbara co-created the Gender Friendly Nursery, a programme of training and accreditation supporting early learning and childcare establishments to address gender equality as part of their roles with NHS Greater Glasgow & Clyde. They now work together to offer guidance, support and training to organisations that wish to improve their practice in relation to gender inequality.

CHALLENGING GENDER STEREOTYPES IN THE EARLY YEARS

Changing the Narrative

Susie Heywood and Barbara Adzajlic

Routledge
Taylor & Francis Group

LONDON AND NEW YORK

Image Credit: © Fiordaliso / Getty Images

First published 2023
by Routledge
4 Park Square, Milton Park, Abingdon, Oxon OX14 4RN

and by Routledge
605 Third Avenue, New York, NY 10158

Routledge is an imprint of the Taylor & Francis Group, an informa business

British Library Cataloguing-in-Publication Data
A catalogue record for this book is available from the British Library

Library of Congress Cataloging-in-Publication Data
A catalog record has been requested for this book

ISBN: 978-0-367-76652-8 (hbk)
ISBN: 978-0-367-76650-4 (pbk)
ISBN: 978-1-003-16792-1 (ebk)

DOI: 10.4324/9781003167921

Typeset in Interstate
by Newgen Publishing UK

Access the Support Material: www.routledge.com/9780367766504

CONTENTS

ACKNOWLEDGEMENTS

We would like to thank the following people who agreed to be interviewed and have their voices included in this book: Dr Rosie Baruah (Consultant in Intensive Care Medicine), Julie Cameron (Mental Health Foundation), Nicky Coia (NHS Greater Glasgow & Clyde), James Cook (Educator), Graham Goulden (Cultivating Minds), Anita Le Tissier (Educator), Dr Nancy Lombard (Glasgow Caledonian University), Thomas Lynch (Dads Rock), Margrét Pála Ólafsdóttir (Hjalli Nurseries), Professor Gina Rippon (Aston University), Shaddai Tembo (Critical Early Years) and Davy Thompson (White Ribbon Scotland).

Thanks also to the numerous people who gave their time, their thoughts and their support as we worked on this book. These include Susie Bennet, Linz Connell, Francesca Mallen, Dr Robyn Muir, Sue Palmer, Cara Richardson, John Wadsworth and Alison Whelan.

Massive thanks to our patient and understanding families, who supported our passion and commitment to this work.

We would also like to acknowledge NHS Greater Glasgow & Clyde and their Gender Friendly Nursery project; they supported us to develop our passion for this topic area and provided the initial inspiration for this book.

AN IMPORTANT NOTE ON SAFETY AND SELF-CARE

Part of finding your "why" is about connecting with the issue. Throughout this book we will explore various issues and explain their connection to gender stereotypes. These include domestic abuse, rape and sexual assault, other forms of gender-based violence, homophobia and transphobia, racism and other forms of discrimination, suicide, mental illness, eating disorders and poverty.

Many of you may have experienced some of these – whether it's something that has affected you personally or something that has touched the lives of your family, friends or community.

Please take care as you read about these things. If you find you are being affected and if you need to, please find someone to talk to. Talking always helps. There are also organisations that can provide advice, support or a listening ear. We have included details of some of these in the Appendices.

Introduction

In 2014 we attended a conference. Although we worked as part of the same wider team within NHS Greater Glasgow & Clyde, we were attending for quite different reasons. The conference was being organised by respect*me* – Scotland's anti-bullying organisation – and the title of the conference was "Gender is Everyone's Agenda". Susie was undertaking work looking at how men's mental health could be supported, and at how to build connections with other men, as part of the suicide-prevention work she was undertaking at the time. For Barbara, who was working on the prevention of violence against women in school and community settings, it was an opportunity to find out about how issues of gender were impacting other walks of life and what other people were doing to address it.

In what would turn out to be quite a fortuitous move, both of us had signed up to attend a workshop being delivered by Zero Tolerance (Scotland's campaigning charity working to eradicate violence against women and girls), promoting its recently produced guide to reducing gender stereotypes in the early years, *Just Like a Child*.[1] During the workshop, we heard about the importance of reducing gender stereotypes in the early years as a preventative action against gender-based violence.

During the workshop, we both had our own "lightbulb moments", where we realised that gender stereotypes, and the resulting gender inequality that they produce, are part of a narrative that is provided to children and adults about the way we "should" and "shouldn't" be, think and act. This narrative, we realised, lay at the root of many of the public health issues that we, and various members of our wider team, were working so hard to reduce. Zero Tolerance was on to something here: looking at how we could get in early to reduce these stereotypes!

Over lunch, at the end of the day and in the days following the conference, we kept on chatting about this. *Just Like A Child* was full of useful tips for early years professionals wanting to take action, but we both knew from our work with schools and educational settings, and relating to public health issues generally, that most effective change happens when an issue is tackled at various levels and across all areas of a setting and its practice. What might be useful for early years settings that were serious about tackling the issue of gender stereotyping? And so the seeds of the Gender Friendly Nursery project (which we developed as part of NHS Greater Glasgow & Clyde), and the resulting work we have done around championing and promoting gender equitable practice, were sown.

DOI: 10.4324/9781003167921-1

The content of this book has been partly inspired by the work that we did in developing the Gender Friendly Nursery programme, which really was quite groundbreaking in its approach. Since then, we have spent many hours undertaking reading and research, and engaging in deeply passionate discussions – rich and varied conversations with practitioners and topic experts that have deepened and developed our knowledge and understanding even further. While we have written this book with early years practitioners in mind – nursery staff and managers, childminders, early level primary education teachers – and will refer to "practitioners" throughout, the majority of the learning, strategies and approaches are applicable to anyone who comes into contact with children in these early years. For example, we have delivered training to voluntary sector staff involved in supporting children and families, who have found it extremely relevant.

Our personal experiences as mothers, daughters, sisters, partners and women have helped us to deepen our understanding of the issues; however, we understood the need to look to others in order to learn new perspectives. So, as we wrote this book, we returned to some of the experts whose work we had read and to whom we had chatted, who kindly agreed to be interviewed so we could share their words directly with you. We spoke with practitioners from across the United Kingdom to gain a better understanding of working in the early years.

We have been delivering training to early years childcare professionals for well over five years now. One of the things we like to say about our approach is that it takes participants on a journey, from the "what?" through to the "why?" and finally to the "how?" We have followed this principle in structuring this book.

It might be that you have decided to read this because of the "what?" ("What is this all about?" "What do I need to know?") or the "how?" ("How can I become a better practitioner?" "How can I do better for the children I work with?"). So you may be quite surprised at the length of time that we will spend on the "why?"

But there's a reason why we believe it's so important for practitioners to develop a sense of "why" doing this work and making these changes are so important. There are many "why" questions that we will attempt to answer:

- Why do we need to improve our practice in relation to gender stereotypes?
- Why is the early years one of the most important times to start?
- Why and in what way are gender stereotypes limiting the opportunities and aspirations of children?
- Why are gender stereotypes a problem for pretty much everyone?
- Why do those seemingly harmless phrases, beliefs or jokes need to be continually challenged?

We haven't yet had a conversation with a childcare practitioner who doesn't agree that we should ensure children are not in any way limited because of gender. Many already have a really good understanding of, and experience in, ways in which they can adapt their practice to create equal opportunities for all children across the nursery. It is important to recognise and celebrate this good practice. Well done! Hopefully this book will provide you with more ideas, suggestions and a structure for how you and your setting can not only minimise gender stereotyping, but also begin to compensate for the messages that children will already be receiving about gender roles from society in general. But we also hope that, through reading this, you will develop a broad understanding of the myriad "whys" - that you will have your own lightbulb moment.

We have seen these moments in the training we have delivered. We have heard scepticism change to determination. Seen people becoming more curious, more animated, more aware. We have listened to the conversations around the table - the plans being made for change. We have seen people connect with their "why?"

We found our "why" at that conference, and have continued to find more and more "whys" through reading, conversations and our experiences as women and mothers. Through this book, we hope to demonstrate that gender inequality is having an impact on us in so many ways, often without us even realising it. Sometimes it's only when it is all presented to you in the one place that you can really understand the very real harms associated with these seemingly "harmless" beliefs and behaviours.

We will explore the links with gender-based violence and its impact, particularly on women and girls. We will look at men's violence against each other and to themselves, and the ways in which the need to conform to masculinity is harming our men and boys. We will talk about how the messages we are being given in the media are putting pressure on us all to conform to idealised body images. We will discuss how women are over-represented in the caring professions and men are over-represented in the science and technology industry, why this matters and how the messages we give to children may be funnelling them down particular career paths. We'll explain the role that gender stereotypes play in promoting homophobia and transphobia, and look at some of the mental health impacts of all of the above. And much, much more.

We will also provide you with practical tools, suggestions and ideas for how you can make changes to your practice and setting. How you can incorporate "equitable approaches" that change the narrative about what it means to be a boy or a girl, and that teach children there are limitless possibilities open to them that are not tied to being either a boy or a girl. You'll find these throughout the book, towards the end of each "why" chapter, in order to help you relate the action to the specific issues we are outlining - and you can bring them together using the tools at the end of the book.

Not every action will work for you or in your setting. The children with whom you work may need a unique response based on their own circumstances and needs. Our hope is that these suggestions will inspire you. We have included an audit table to help you consider your strengths and areas for development. We have also provided an action checklist, which you can use as you work your way through each chapter to note down any actions that you feel are important and any ideas that jump into your head as you go, or following the audit.

Our approach is a proactive one, which takes thought, planning and constant reflection. It is much more than a checklist exercise. It's not easy! So for us that's why the "why" is important, because without the "why", will we really do our best to make it happen?

We are excited to share this with you. It has been a labour of love, fuelled by our passion to make a difference for the next generation. It has also been a nerve-wracking prospect - committing to paper something we have been living and breathing for over five years is no mean feat. We have had to be brave and bold, knowing that some people may disagree, and knowing that our approach is far from perfect. We too are still learning. We understand that we come to this from a position of privilege. And we are willing and ready to listen and keep

Susie and Barbara

learning – so do let us know what you think, because as the inspirational Maya Angelou once said, "I did then what I knew how to do. Now that I know better, I do better."

We believe we can all do better. And we hope that after reading this you will feel that you know a bit better too. We can't wait to see what we can all do together!

Note

1   Zero Tolerance, *Just Like a Child: Respect Gender Equality in the Early Years – a Guide for Early Years Professionals* (2013). Available at www.zerotolerance.org.uk/resources/Just-Like-a-Child.pdf

PART 1

1 Key Concepts and Definitions

Barbara Adzajlic and Susie Heywood

To help you get the most out of the book, this chapter defines some of the key concepts and terms that will be used throughout and that underpin our approach. Meaning and usage of words can change over time and between people, so it's useful to lay out what we mean when we use certain terms in this book. We do this with a full understanding that some readers may disagree, or see things differently – and that's okay. Hopefully attempting to define them will make your journey through the book a bit easier.

Sex and Gender

It is probably pretty vital from the outset to define what we mean when we talk about gender, and to understand how this differs from sex. When we started reading into this a bit further as we prepared to write this chapter, we found ourselves getting caught up in the complexities of some of the arguments and science around the terms, to the extent that we began to doubt our own understanding at times, and many long conversations (often over wine) ensued. Defining sex and gender is complex, and there are areas where people can't seem to agree. Our approach is to keep an open mind, to be ready to listen, learn and adapt – something we do regularly, which explains why committing these definitions to print has felt so difficult.

   When we started working around this topic we were keen to keep our working definitions simple, while acknowledging these complexities and differences. The definitions we tend to use are:

Sex: Either of the two main categories (male and female) into which humans and most other living things are divided on the basis of their reproductive functions.
Gender: A spectrum, within which a person identifies as boy/man, girl/woman, anywhere in between or neither. Refers to social and cultural differences rather than biological ones.

So think of sex as being primarily about biology, chromosomes, body parts and having babies. It determines whether you are biologically male or female or (for a small minority) intersex. "Intersex" is the term used to describe people who are born with body parts or a physiology that do not fit into what we typically categorise as male and female.[1] It has been estimated that between 1 and 2 per cent of the population are intersex.[2]

   Gender, on the other, hand is socially constructed. It is less rigid and more complex, and it includes both a person's own feelings about how they identify, and the societal expectations

DOI: 10.4324/9781003167921-3

and stereotypes associated with being masculine or feminine. Many people reject these stereotypes and expectations because they can be unrealistic and harmful in a variety of ways that we will discuss in this book. People may not identify as masculine or feminine at all (they may be non-binary and there are also many different terms used to self-identify).

Some people think of gender as a spectrum, with the binary categories of masculine and feminine at each end, although it is important to acknowledge right away that what people see as masculine and feminine can differ, and trying to define this too much can take us down the path towards stereotypes.

We can also think about gender as an identity. People can "feel" male (masculine) or female (feminine), or anything in between, or neither. Our behaviours, our physical characteristics and the choices we make may lead others to make assumptions about our gender identity. However, as a society we are beginning to better understand that gender identity is more complex than this, and it is now being seen as more fluid and less fixed.

While as a society we share a general understanding of the characteristics and qualities that typify masculinity and femininity, it's important to note that definitions of masculinity and femininity, and therefore gender, can vary considerably between different cultures, and have changed throughout history. So, for example:

High Heels
In the United Kingdom today, wearing high heels is strongly associated with women, femininity and glamour (and occasionally very, very sore feet), but it hasn't always been that way. Did you know that high heels first made an appearance in fifteenth-century Persia (now Iran); they were used by soldiers to help secure their feet in stirrups as they rode their horses? Then, as people travelled and cultures mixed, they made an appearance among the seventeenth-century French aristocracy, with male aristocrats wearing skyscraper heels as a demonstration of their social status and masculinity.

Pink and Blue
It feels like nobody can escape the pink and blue mania that seems to dominate pretty much every arena relating to children these days. But did you know it wasn't actually like this until relatively recently? Historically, pink was seen as a variation of military red, and was strongly associated with boys. And as the colour of the Virgin Mary's clothes, blue was more commonly associated with and worn by girls.

So gender is both something that is assumed based on how closely someone conforms to the characteristics and behaviours (and stereotypes) associated with the two main gender categories, and also an identity with which a person associates. What is seen as typical of the male and female gender categories can change over time and place.

Gender Equality and Gender Inequality

If what we ultimately hope to achieve is gender equality, it feels as if defining exactly what we mean by gender equality is also pretty important. Gender equality is the state in which access to rights or opportunities are unaffected by gender; it does not mean an end to gender or gender identity. As we will see, our approach is not an attempt to eradicate gender from our early years settings, but rather an attempt to ensure that children aren't being limited because of it.

It is important to note here that some people may talk about "sex-based equality". Gender equality is a well-accepted term. Certainly in this book we are concerned primarily with cultural and societal stereotypes, attitudes and problems that tend to be associated with gender. That is why we have chosen the term "gender equality". We do, however, recognise that some of these issues are sex based, and may refer to this from time to time.

Gender inequality (the state in which the access to rights or opportunity is unfairly affected by gender) is very real and problematic – we need only look around us to see evidence of this.

- We see gender inequality in the high levels of violence against women across the globe.
- We see it in the increased levels of completed suicide among men compared with women.
- We see it when we look at the lack of female representation in boardrooms, political parties and other power structures.
- We see it when women feel guilty about returning to the workplace after starting a family, or are penalised professionally for taking time off work.
- We see it in men feeling unable to comfortably pursue a career in childcare for fear of what other people might think.

Gender inequality remains a problem that affects almost all of us in some way, and that seems very difficult to solve. If we are ever going to achieve gender equality, though, we have to believe it is possible. A couple of years ago, we were invited to attend a conference with an audience made up of women who were working in a variety of ways to reduce gender inequality. A speaker asked us all to raise our hands if we believed that at some point in the future we would achieve gender equality. It was quite an eye-opener to look around the packed room and see that the number of people with their hands up barely reached double figures. The response of the speaker was something of an admonishment – if we don't believe we can achieve gender equality, then we never will.

You may have heard the saying, "A journey of a thousand miles begins with a single step". We know that this book, and changing the practice of everyone who spends time with children in the early years alone, will not bring about gender equality. However, we do believe that it can make a difference – particularly when gender inequality is being tackled in other areas too.

(Gender) Equity

If gender equality is the goal, then we would argue that gender equity is the approach that is needed to get us there. The aim of the Gender Friendly Nursery programme, which we were involved in creating, was always to create environments where children were not in any way limited because of gender. Of course, eliminating all talk of gender would be one way of trying to achieve this. However, this is not the world in which we live. Like it or not, we live in a highly gendered world.

From the day we hear the answer to the question "Is it a boy or a girl?", as adults we begin to adjust our behaviour, our choices, our assumptions and our expectations of children. So our approach takes this into account and works within a context where the vast majority of children will be being raised knowing that they are either a boy or a girl, and understanding what this means for them: what society tells them about how they should look, how they should act and what they should do with their lives.

An equitable approach to gender inequality acknowledges that children already experience differences based on their gender. In order to achieve equality, we have to understand these differences and what they mean for each child (or group of children). Once we have this understanding, we can then put things in place that will mean they are not disadvantaged in any way because of this difference. While we will explore what this might mean in practice with gender differences and young children in more depth in a later chapter, it is useful at this point to ensure that there is a shared understanding of equity.

Figure 1.1 – and the many versions of it that you can find online – demonstrates why an equitable approach is fairer: it takes into the account the differences in opportunities people begin with (whether due to gender, poverty or discrimination) as well as the different barriers they may have to overcome in order to achieve the same thing.

If we treat everyone in the same way (in other words, *equally*) and give each person exactly the same thing to help them to see over the fence or reach the branches of the apple tree (as some versions have it), then because of the level of disadvantage some people face, they will still not have the same opportunities or access. However, if we recognise disadvantage, and treat people *equitably*, or fairly, giving each exactly what they need, then the end result is equality. One version we have seen includes a ramp in the second image that not only means a wheelchair user can get onto the block, but also makes it safer and easier for anyone to get up and stay up there. Taking a fair and equitable approach means addressing the needs of the most disadvantaged – and in doing so often making things better for everyone.

So if we think of this in the context of an early years setting, where we know that some children will require extra support in order to access the same experiences and opportunities, we can see that it is not enough to treat every child in the same way. When it comes to gender, we know (and will demonstrate in later chapters) that by the time they are attending pre-school, boys and girls will be absorbing messages about what is and is not acceptable, achievable or desirable for them because of their gender. Our equitable approach encourages practitioners to consider this in their day-to-day planning and practice, and to provide opportunities that will allow children to move beyond these limitations.

Our work to develop and refine our approach has been a massive journey for us – we are learning all the time, refining our ideas based on new information, research and the experience of our colleagues and friends working in early learning and childcare. We're not afraid to admit that some of the early iterations of our training include things that we're not sure

Figure 1.1 a and Fig. 1.1b Equality and Equity

we would stand by now, in the light of new knowledge. It's important to always be open to learning and adjusting – we are sure this will continue.

One such journey for us was a move towards this "equitable" approach to gender inequality. We had read about the Egalia preschools in Sweden, and tried desperately to find the funds to visit. (I can assure you that the desperation was wholly due to a desire to see this unique model of early years education in a country which is held up as a gold standard when it comes to public health and social equality, and not at all to do with the chance to escape two young kids and hang out with a cool colleague!) For those of you who aren't aware, the Egalia preschool attempts to create a gender-neutral environment – or an environment where gender is minimised as a concept and a reality for children in an attempt to ensure that children's experiences are not diminished because of what is expected of their gender. We will learn more about this model in Chapter 16, but for now it's sufficient to say that over time we have moved our approach away from one of gender neutrality to an approach that recognises that our children are born and raised in a gendered society, and that our approach has to be rooted in this context if it's going to be effective. We would still love to visit Sweden and the nurseries, though!

Intersectional Inequality

It is also exceptionally important to note that gender is far from the only inequality impacting children. Income inequality, educational inequality, racial inequality and health inequality are among the inequalities that affect the extent to which children progress, achieve and thrive in early childhood. The Equality Act that covers most parts of the United Kingdom,[3] and the duties it places upon us, mean that we need to be aware of a variety of inequalities, and we are legally bound to ensure that the effects of many of these inequalities are addressed.

For example, the attainment gap between children who grow up in affluent households and those who don't is widely acknowledged. We know that the ability to buy school uniforms, complete homework at home on IT equipment, eat a decent breakfast, attend school trips and have cultural experiences outside of school have a huge impact on children's chances of academic success. Recognising this, in Scotland Pupil Equity Funding is allocated to every school on the basis of how many of its pupils qualify for free school meals. The funds have to be spent in ways that address the attainment gap. Similar schemes exist across the United Kingdom. But we won't address the issue properly unless we consider those intersecting issues that compound the disadvantages experienced by children.

We know that Black children are significantly more likely to be excluded from school[4] and that children in lower income households, when compared with those in higher earning households, are significantly behind in their knowledge of vocabulary and problem-solving ability.[5] When we combine these two characteristics, the likelihood of Black children from lower income households having poorer educational outcomes is compounded by unfair external factors of racism and poverty that have nothing to do with those children's abilities. Racism and poverty intersect in the same way roads intersect at a crossroads, with an increased likelihood of collisions and injuries. The more types of discrimination a person faces, the higher the likelihood of disadvantage or harm.

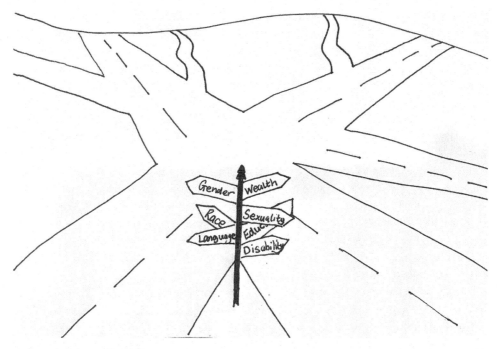

Figure 1.2 Intersectionality

We are trying to say that gender inequality is no more important or harmful than the other inequalities facing our children. We cannot afford to place all our attention on gender at the expense of these other issues. We must look at gender inequality and how it interacts and intersects with other inequalities if we are to truly begin to make a difference to children's lives. When these inequalities are combined (and they often are), the impacts on children can be devastating. We will reflect on these intersecting inequalities throughout this book.[6]

Stereotypes

Early on in this work, we looked for a dictionary definition of the word "stereotype". One that we found and have worked with since is "a widely held but fixed and oversimplified image or idea of a particular type of person or thing". A simpler definition might be "putting people into a category or group based on a shared characteristic and making assumptions about all people in that group". For example, she is a girl and all girls like pink; therefore, she must like pink.

Stereotyping groups people into categories, assigns characteristics, traits and behaviours to these categories, then assumes that all or most people within these categories must share these. We all do it – it helps us simplify quite a complicated world. In her book *The Gendered Brain*, Gina Rippon suggests that, "Our brains are, in fact, the ultimate stereotypers, sometimes drawing very rapid conclusions based on very little data or based on strong expectations, arising from personal past experience or from the cultural norms and expectations of our surroundings."[7] We are sure that, if asked, you could come up with a fairly lengthy list of common stereotypes. Let us give you a start: French men are romantic; Italians make good lovers; blondes have more fun. These three examples are fairly positive – we are sure you have thought of many more that are not. Stereotypes will also vary between people, locations, cultures and time periods.

Another thing about stereotypes is that it often feels like there is a sort of "ring of truth" about them. For example, the chances are that many of the little girls you know may act in very similar ways, or like very similar things. We will talk later in the book about why that might be, and whether the differences we might see are natural or a result of socialisation. Evidence also suggests that because of the way our brains work, because of our tendency to group people and things, and because of the bias and stereotypes we hold, we are more likely to notice and remember the things that confirm the stereotypes and beliefs we hold, and to miss, forget or misremember the things that don't – the counter-stereotypical examples. As parents, we may be more likely to remember the things our children do that confirm the stereotypes than to notice the things that they do that don't.[8]

One key point, however, is that stereotypes are a misrepresentation and can be extremely harmful. For example, stereotypes about a marginalised group in society can be reinforced by the dominant group as an expression of power. They can lead to people being treated differently or unfairly based on presumed characteristics. A very obvious example of this is racial profiling by police officers; however, often the impacts of stereotyping are less obvious. For example, anecdotally we have heard that some midwives, when tasked with asking pregnant women about domestic abuse, are less likely to ask women from middle-class families, working on an assumption that domestic abuse is something that only happens in working-class families. This kind of stereotyping leads to people not getting what they need because of assumptions being made about them. Stereotyping can also lead to people being excluded from particular groups or categories because they do not share these common characteristics or traits. It is useful to note that people can self-identify with a stereotype about their group, and that's okay. It's absolutely alright for a little girl to like pink – we just can't assume that every little girl does!

Which brings us to the focus of this book: gender stereotyping. These are the assumptions that we make about a person based on their gender. Throughout this book, we will explore examples of gender stereotyping, how these stereotypes are perpetuated throughout society and how they are reinforced across the lifespan. We will demonstrate that these stereotypes, many of which may at first glance seem innocuous and harmless, are actually limiting all children in a number of ways.

Some Final Definitions

A Public Health Approach

We will touch on these in other chapters in more depth, but it is useful to quickly highlight some other concepts that we believe are vital to our approach. We will explain why our approach is not only rooted in public health, but takes what is often called a "public health approach". Essentially, this means an approach that is rooted in the idea that our focus should be on preventing issues from arising by addressing the root causes. As we will explain in later chapters, we believe that gender stereotypes lie at the root of some of the big public health issues with which we are grappling as a society, so reducing our exposure to these messages can help.

A Whole Setting Approach

Because of the prevalence of these stereotypes, there is no one single action that can make a difference on its own. When it comes to early years settings, we believe it is not only important, but vital, that practitioners examine all aspects of nursery life and consider ways in which gender stereotypes can be reduced. This is what we call a "whole setting approach". We believe the best way to make changes to settings is to involve everyone in the process. Ideally, all members of staff in a setting, from management down, should be aware and should seek to make changes to practice if needed. Not only will this maximise the impact; it will future-proof the setting should staff decide to move on. "Everyone" also includes parents, carers, wider stakeholders and communities, and we will discuss how you might involve them later in the book.

Audit

In order to support settings to take this whole setting approach, we have provided an audit tool. The word "audit" might sound a bit intimidating or bring to mind images of accountants hunched over financial accounts, but all we mean here is a review of those areas of nursery life that we have identified as being crucial to taking an equitable approach to gender stereotyping. Our audit tool, which is included in Part 3, gives you an opportunity to think through these key areas and about what you already have in place that promotes gender equity – or could be used to do this. It then asks you to think about any areas you'd like to change. By the time you have finished reading this book, we would expect that you will already have identified quite a few strengths and a few areas for development. The audit process can really help to consolidate these ideas and support further reflection, thinking and planning. As we will demonstrate in Part 3, this auditing process, while developed with nursery settings in mind, can be used by anyone looking to examine their individual or organisational practice.

We hope our working definitions will support you as you work your way through this book. We acknowledge here that our explanations do not fully capture the complexity of these terms. There may be elements where people may hold differing opinions, and that's okay. These definitions are the starting point for your journey through this book and you may wish to return to them at various points.

Notes

1 For more information on intersex, see the factsheet from the United Nations at www.unfe.org/wp-content/uploads/2017/05/UNFE-Intersex.pdf. As well as describing better than we could what constitutes intersex, it also highlights the discriminations and violations faced by intersex people, and makes recommendations for action to protect the rights of intersex people.
2 Anne Fausto-Sterling, *Sexing the Body: Gender Politics and the Construction of Sexuality* (New York: Basic Books, 2000).

3   UK Government, *The Equality Act 2010*. Available at: www.legislation.gov.uk/ukpga/2010/15/contents (accessed 2 January 2020).

4   E. Timpson, Timpson Review of School Exclusion (2019). Available at https://assets.publishing.serv ice.gov.uk/government/uploads/system/uploads/attachment_data/file/807862/Timpson_review.pdf (accessed Jan 2022).

5   P. Bradshaw, *Growing Up in Scotland: Changes in Child Cognitive Ability in the Pre-school Year* (Edinburgh: Scottish Government, 2011). Available at www.gov.scot/publications/growing-up-scotl and-changes-child-cognitive-ability-pre-school-years (accessed 2 January 2022).

6   For more information on intersectionality see the work of Kimberlé Crenshaw, who first coined the term. This TED Talk is particularly useful and powerful: K. Crenshaw, *The Urgency of Intersectionality*, TED Talk K (2016). Available at www.ted.com/talks/kimberle_crenshaw_the_urgency_of_intersecti onality/discussion (accessed 16 January 2022).

7   G. Rippon, *The Gendered Brain: The New Neuroscience That Shatters the Myth of the Female brain* (London: Bodley Head, 2019).

8   For a really great explanation of the ways in which our brains work to categorise and sort people into groups, read about the "three mental tricks" described by Christia Spears Brown in her useful book *Parenting Beyond Pink and Blue: How to Raise Your Kids Free of Gender Stereotypes* (London: Ten Speed Press, 2014). She talks about our brains exaggerating between-group differences, exaggerating within-group similarities and remembering information that is consistent with the stereotypes we hold. Remember that this applies to adults and children alike!

2 Gender Inequality

What are We Getting Right?

Barbara Adzajlic and Susie Heywood

It's important to note right at the start of this book that we have come a long way when it comes to our practice around equality, and more specifically gender. We are guessing that there's already lots that you and your setting already do that promotes gender equality. The aim of this short chapter is to capture and celebrate some of this work, and the work of organisations and initiatives that have been doing their bit to ensure children aren't being limited because of gender. It also aims to demonstrate where our approach may differ and why.

Equalities Law

We are, of course, required by law to ensure that our practice is fair and does not discriminate. The Equality Act 2010,[1] which brought previous anti-discrimination Acts and laws together under one single Act, legally protects people from discrimination in the workplace and wider settings. It legislates against unfair treatment on the basis of any of nine protected characteristics.

The Protected Characteristics Under The Equality Act 2010

- Age
- Disability
- Gender reassignment
- Marriage and civil partnership
- Pregnancy and maternity
- Race
- Religion or belief
- Sex
- Sexual orientation

As a result, we all have a duty to ensure that our structures and practice do not in any way impinge on people's rights under the Act. Although the protected characteristics of sex and

DOI: 10.4324/9781003167921-4

gender reassignment may seem most directly relevant to a gender equitable approach, as we will demonstrate throughout the book, other aspects such as sexual orientation, and pregnancy and maternity are also relevant here. In fact, as we have previously mentioned in our key definitions, the protected characteristics can intersect, meaning that some people can face increased risk of unfair treatment.

Guidance for the Early Years Sector

Increasingly, early years educational policy and practice documents are recognising the importance of addressing gender inequality, stereotypes and sexism, and while not always explicit, policies are broadly supportive of actions around these topics. Each of the four home nations has its own statutory and non-statutory guidance documents for the sector – for example, in England the Statutory Framework for the Early Years Foundation Stage (EYFS)[2] sets out the standards and expectations for learning, development and care for children from birth to five years. It highlights equality of opportunity and anti-discriminatory practice, asserting that every child is unique and should be included and supported in an enabling environment, which recognises that children learn and develop in different ways. However, neither it nor the accompanying Development Matters Curriculum Guidance for the EYFS presents any specific practice guidance regarding equalities or equitable approaches.

Recognising the need for more detailed guidance to support the early learning goals, the Early Years Coalition produced *Birth to 5 Matters*,[3] which has been warmly welcomed by the sector. This guidance includes a specific section about inclusive practice and equalities, which can support the sector to develop good practice in these areas. It emphasises the importance of valuing and respecting diversity in early years settings and calls for practitioners to address discrimination, understand their own and other bias and challenge limiting gender (and other) stereotypes. It specifically highlights the importance of equity – recognising the unique barriers for individual children and providing a counterbalance that allows them to thrive.

Another positive example is the Scottish national guidance for the early years, *Realising The Ambition: Being Me*. This builds on the principles included in the earlier *Pre-Birth to 3* and *Building the Ambition* guidance, and really captures the vitally important role of the early years workforce and the central role of play in the early years.[4] The guidance recognises the impact of gender stereotypes and gender bias in the early years. It asks practitioners to challenge their own and others' gender bias and take an equitable approach to their work with children. The centrality of play in the early years and beyond is now firmly part of educational discourse in Scotland and beyond – it is now widely accepted that when it comes to the benefits for children, "play is the way".[5]

For practitioners and settings keen to ensure that their play-based approaches are sensitive to gender stereotypes, the Care Inspectorate in Scotland worked with Zero Tolerance to produce specific guidance around *Gender Equal Play*,[6] which explores the impact of gender stereotypes and supports practitioners who wish to ensure that children's play is not limited by them. It is well worth a look and is particularly useful for unpicking the question that often arises around how we can balance gender-equitable approaches with child-led play.

Good Practice: Organisations and Initiatives[7]

When we started work on this topic back in 2015, as we began developing the Gender Friendly Nursery approach with NHS Greater Glasgow & Clyde (see Case Study 1, below), there were relatively few initiatives (that we were aware of) working on this topic, and even less so with a specific early years focus. Thankfully that has changed! One of the key initiatives that has driven action is the work of the Institute of Physics, which aimed to address the gender imbalance around Physics A-Level uptake by funding a series of pilot projects in schools. As a result, we have seen developments such as the Improving Gender Balance and Equalities initiative in Scotland and the Gender Action in Schools project in England, set up to continue to deliver on some of the findings and recommendations of the Institute of Physics' work.

There is also a range of independent and charitable organisations driving work on this topic. These include Lifting Limits, which is working in some English schools to promote gender equality and reduce gender stereotypes, and the Global Equality Collective, which has developed an app for education and other settings which allows them to audit their practice and make positive changes across a range of equality areas.

The mass reach of the inspirational Let Toys Be Toys campaign continues to highlight the pervasiveness of gender stereotypes across the toy industry, and has had huge success in influencing the practice of some industry big hitters. It has an offshoot campaign, Let Books Be Books, which raises fundamental questions about children's books and the messages they send. Let Clothes Be Clothes campaigns for an end to the stereotypes perpetuated through children's clothing, and more recently has focused on important issues such as uniform policies.

These are just some of the initiatives that are out there – apologies to those we have not included. We have included links to some of these organisations at the end of the book should you wish to explore more.

Case Study 1: The Gender Friendly Nursery programme – NHS Greater Glasgow & Clyde

The Gender Friendly Nursery programme in NHS Greater Glasgow & Clyde (NHSGGC) is an example of a forward-thinking, practical approach to supporting early years practitioners to develop and celebrate good practice regarding reducing gender stereotyping. Of course, as co-creators of this approach through our roles as staff within NHSGGC, we may be slightly biased! The approach incorporates an in-depth staff training, audit tool, action plan and "Gender Friendly Nursery" accreditation, which nurseries go through with the support of NHSGGC staff and materials. Evaluation and feedback showed that the training raised staff awareness of the issues as well as provoking intention for practice change.[8] Those nurseries that continued their journey through to Gender Friendly Nursery accreditation undertook a variety of actions from creating gender policies and sharing programme messages with parents and carers through to auditing nursery environments and resources, investing in new materials and supporting each other as staff to ensure that practice and language use were not reinforcing stereotypes. The programme continues to be rolled out across Glasgow City.

The approach we advocate in this book is partly informed by our experiences of the development and delivery of the Gender Friendly Nursery programme, as well as the ongoing learning, reading and conversations that continue to shape our thinking every day.

Good Practice in Education and Early Years

Reflection: Take a few minutes to consider the positive things that you and/or your setting already do to eliminate gender stereotyping or to ensure that all children are able to fully participate in all activities in the nursery.

We know from the years spent working with staff from across the education sector, the wealth of good practice already happening within early years and education generally. The *Gender Equal Play* guidance mentioned earlier includes case studies of individual nurseries that have taken steps to eliminate gender stereotyping in various aspects of their practice and is well worth a look.[9] Included are examples where staff made changes to language use and to interactions with the children around superhero play and dressing-up to encourage more creative play among the boys; and where nurseries have utilised open-ended and natural play materials including block play, and incorporated child-led outdoor play. We've seen staff who have made changes to the language they use in the playroom, who have used storytelling to gently challenge gender stereotypes with the children, who have developed alternatives to activities that often reinforced the gender binary. It is always inspiring to hear and see these things – things are improving and many, many practitioners now "get it" (many others have for a long time!) and are altering their practice as a result.

Very often, these examples of good practice involve individual initiatives, one-off inputs or great practice in one setting or with an individual member of staff. The huge culture change that's required if we are truly going to achieve gender equality means we need people and organisations at all different levels and in a variety of settings to be promoting positive messages around gender and challenging harmful stereotypes. In order to make meaningful and impactful change across settings it's important to look at all aspects of a setting and explore where change is needed. The education sector has a long history of taking this holistic approach – often called a "whole setting approach" – where we think about every aspect of the "life" of that setting, and about how we can address an issue with all the key players and places in a school or nursery. That means staff (ideally all staff, including administrative, cleaners and janitors), children, families, partner organisations and others who might visit. It also means thinking about all the ways in which we have to interact with those people, including our environment, our learning and play resources, our policies and our overall ethos.

In Scotland, a whole schools approach was followed in the Health Promoting Schools programme in the years leading up to 2009, by which time every local authority school was required to achieve Health Promoting School status. It acknowledged that a school can't become a Health Promoting School solely by changing the school meals, or setting up an after-school walking club, or running an assembly about how to avoid tooth decay. We need planned and sustained actions like these at every level to make sure a school is a physically, socially and mentally healthy environment for everyone in it. This approach is still championed internationally by the World Health Organization.[10] The international Eco Schools programme takes a similar approach.[11]

The Gender Friendly Nursery initiative is an example of an early years-focused approach that attempts to make this holistic approach specific to gender stereotyping. We believe that in order to achieve the culture change that is needed to tackle gender inequality and gender stereotyping, we need everyone on board. At a societal level, this means tackling these issues through changes to governmental policy or structural changes in the ways our huge institutions are run, right down to the attitudes and actions of individuals within communities and families.

There is Still Work to Be Done

While there is much to be positive about, and so many people already drawing attention to the issues, there is still a lot of work to be done. Gender stereotypes are everywhere, and like it or not, they continue to influence our interactions with young children. We know that this book alone won't make much difference, and that collective action is what is really needed; however, we all have a part to play. If our influence in the life of even one child means that they grow up understanding that anything is possible for them, then we think the effort was a worthwhile endeavour.

Notes

1   UK Government, *The Equality Act 2010*. Available at www.legislation.gov.uk/ukpga/2010/15/contents (accessed 2 January 2020).

2   Department of Education, *The Statutory Framework for the Early Years Foundation Stage* (2017). Available at https://assets.publishing.service.gov.uk/government/uploads/system/uploads/attachment_data/file/974907/EYFS_framework_-_March_2021.pdf (accessed 2 January 2022).

3   Early Years Coalition, *Birth to 5 Matters: Non Statutory Guidance for the Early Years Foundation Stage* (2021). Available at https://birthto5matters.org.uk (accessed 2 January 2022).

4   Education Scotland (2020) *Realising the Ambition: Being Me*. Found at https://education.gov.scot/improvement/learning-resources/realising-the-ambition (accessed 2 January 2022).

5   We highly recommend *Play is the Way* (Edinburgh: CCWB Press, 2021), edited by Sue Palmer from Upstart Scotland, for a comprehensive overview of the history of play based pedagogy within Scottish Education.

6   The Care Inspectorate and Zero Tolerance, *Gender Equal Play in Early Learning & Childcare* (2018). Available at https://hub.careinspectorate.com/media/3466/gender-equal-play-in-early-learning-and-childcare.pdf (accessed 2 January 2022).

7   We have included links to these and other useful organisations in Appendix 3.

8 S. Heywood, *An evaluation of the North East Glasgow Pilot of the Gender Friendly Nursery Programme*. Available at www.nhsggc.org.uk/media/250744/nhsggc_ph_gender_friendly_nursery_evaluation_report_2018-10.pdf (accessed 2 January 2022).

9 The Care Inspectorate & Zero Tolerance, *Gender Equal Play*.

10 World Health Organization, *Health Promoting Schools* (2021). Available at www.who.int/health-topics/health-promoting-schools. (accessed 2 January 2022).

11 *Eco Schools*. Available at www.ecoschools.global (accessed 2 January 2022).

3 Young Brains
Gender, Sex and Child Development

Barbara Adzajlic

We can often observe differences in the ways girls and boys play and behave. But are these gendered differences just part and parcel of being born male or female? In this chapter, we'll look at what up-to-date science is telling us about brains: that yes, we do see small differences between the brains of baby girls and baby boys, but that there are two very important points to note about these differences:

- They are less significant and less interesting than the differences between brains within a group of boys, or within a group of girls. In other words, boys come in many different shapes and sizes, and so do their brains; the same applies to girls.
- Our brains have great neuroplasticity, meaning that they are always developing, so these differences can be overcome or exacerbated, depending on the experiences of those children.

We'll also look at how and when children learn about gender and develop ideas about gender roles, particularly in the first five years of life. We will consider how gender roles are learned and reinforced by society and by how adults interact with children, a process that begins right from the moment a woman finds out she is pregnant. We'll include some real life anecdotes, and point you towards our main sources, which you can follow up as further reading to really get a handle on the research and arm yourself with the facts. We'll also give you some areas to think about in relation to your own experience and practice.

Boy Brain/Girl Brain?

What do we already know about the children in your care: about what they know, understand and think about gender, and about what this means for them? Do boys really *naturally* gravitate towards noisy, active and "science-y" toys? Are they really *innately* slower than girls in some aspects of their development, like those fine motor skills that enable them to start writing? Are girls' brains better set up to understand emotions and display caring and nurturing skills? What about those "bossy" pre-school girls: do they just develop this way or is there more to it?

Practitioners and parents sometimes ask us these questions, and it's clear that there is a prevailing belief that some of the differences we observe in the characteristics of boys

DOI: 10.4324/9781003167921-5

and girls can be put down to simple biology. Men were the hunters and needed to be active, aggressive and competitive. Girls and women were the home-makers, so they have evolved with the kinds of skills needed to be successful in the home – empathy, nurture, passivity, creativity. Right?

There is a wealth of research out there showing that these ideas are outdated and not based on good science, but there are also studies that claim to show the opposite: that men (and boys) are from Mars, and women (and girls) are from Venus. It can be hard to know where the truth lies and it can take time to sift through all the arguments and counter-arguments. So here we will summarise some of what we have found over the years that we have been doing this work, and point you in the direction of some of the experts from whom we have learned, in case you have the time to delve into this more deeply.[1]

A Bit of Brain Science and a Bit About Hormones ... Is It All Down to Biology?

A good place to start if you want to understand what the real deal is with so-called innate, hardwired or biological differences between the minds and brains of boys and girls, and why there are still so many "experts" claiming it's all down to nature, is with the work of two scientists, British neuroscientist Gina Rippon and Canadian psychologist Cordelia Fine. When we started on this journey, Susie and I could clearly see that nurture had a pretty big role to play in the gendered differences we see, and that our approach could play a part in reducing the harms associated with them. But the scientific evidence seemed to be conflicting and there were still plenty of studies, and newspaper headlines, claiming it was just "nature". So when we came across the work of these scientists and found out more about what they were saying, we were excited about being able to point to really robust research supporting our view.

In her book *Delusions of Gender*,[2] Fine looks at modern-day gender inequality, particularly in the workplace, and asks whether these ongoing inequalities are really down to our very different brains, or to the structures in society that govern how we think and act. She looks at issues like stereotype threat, the glass ceiling and the motherhood penalty (all of which we'll discuss later in this book). She explains some of the gaping holes in well-publicised research that appears to show that there are important "hard-wired" differences.[3] She ends by showing how the highly gendered environment in which we live influences children's awareness and understanding of gender and themselves.[4]

Neuroscience is a relatively new scientific discipline (before neuroscience, you could study a brain only after its owner had died – which clearly has its drawbacks in terms of studying brain *activity*; or you could study the effects of brain damage or disease, linking the area of damage to an associated skill deficit or behaviour change). Those now-familiar colourful images of different areas of the brain lighting up when we are exercising, eating chocolate or cuddling our newborn baby are the products of neuroscience. They are fascinating, and can be useful when used with care. But they have also been seized upon by scientists and popular writers alike to present conclusions about how the different lighting up of male and female brains means we are hardwired differently. As Cordelia Fine states in *Delusions of Gender*, there is a huge responsibility on scientists presenting their research to exercise caution here because of the huge impact that information about sex and gender has on our perceptions of what we can and can't do.

Gina Rippon's 2019 book *The Gendered Brain*[5] takes this responsibility seriously, first by dealing with the history of brain research, from very early psychiatry and psychology up to the present day.

If you're anything like me, you might tend to think of science as being rational, objective and unbiased, but as Rippon points out, we need to remember that, like everything else, science happens within a cultural context. In the early days, the sciences were dominated by men, at a time when society believed that women were irrational, hysterical and incapable of dealing with complex matters like education and politics. Here is an example from 1879 quoted in *The Gendered Brain*, showing exactly what kind of views were held by the scientist Gustav Le Bon:

> Without a doubt there exist some distinguished women, very superior to the average man but they are as exceptional as the birth of any monstrosity, as, for example, of a gorilla with two heads; consequently, we may neglect them entirely.[6]

It is difficult to see how someone who views an intelligent woman as a monstrosity can really be objective in investigating whether women are as intelligent as men! Taking that as their starting point, it's not surprising to see that these scientists usually found exactly what they were looking for: that men and women have very different brains, and that this "fact" explains the differences they observed between men and women and justifies men's superior status in society. Techniques to prove this began with measuring skull size and capacity by filling human skulls with lead shot. Men's brains were found on average to be bigger (not surprisingly since they have bigger bodies and heads); therefore, men were deemed more capable of learning and greatness.[7] Of course, we now know just how complex our brains are and that intelligence has much more to do with the interconnections between different parts of the brain than its size. But at the time, their conclusions were taken at face value.

Gina Rippon told me that in the early part of her career she was interested in how mental health related to the differences between male and female brains. But the further she looked, the clearer it became that these differences were exaggerated:

> When you start looking into the data in more detail you realise that actually the differences are really very tiny, there's a huge amount of overlap between the groups ... and so I started being a bit suspicious about this whole area of male/female brains.

Later in her career, she returned to this subject:

> I focused on a lot of the misrepresentation which was becoming evident in popular press ... the Mars/Venus areas and all sorts of "why men can't iron or why women can't read maps" type of stuff, and I saw that there was again this huge misunderstanding, no acknowledgement of the amount of overlap there was, no acknowledgement of the fact that most studies involved lots and lots of comparisons, and the majority, maybe up to 90% actually showed no difference. But all that people were reporting was the differences.

You may have heard of phrenology (the measurement of bumps on the skull to predict mental traits). It was popular mainly in the nineteenth century and was used to justify the racist belief that the brains of non-Caucasians were inferior because they supposedly lacked the capacity for great artistry among other things. Craniology, the measurement of different components of the skull and the angles between them, was similarly popular in the late nineteenth and early twentieth centuries. Both of these disciplines, although now discredited, were considered by some at the time to be promising scientific fields. Both were used to support the idea that the human race could be sorted into categories that were said to have differing levels of intelligence. Not surprisingly, given who was funding and carrying out the research, Caucasians were deemed most intelligent, and these conclusions were used to justify slavery and other racial injustices.[8] These claims are now completely discredited (and acknowledged for their racist motivation), but ideas about male and female brains keep on resurfacing, and keep on influencing scientific research and popular discourse. Rippon refers to them as "Whack-a-Mole" myths and says that "although we've moved on a bit from there, they still inform what I call the hunt-the-difference agenda". Eminent scientists have, as recently as 2018, been getting into trouble for claiming that the small numbers of women in science is down to their less science-y brains.[9] In the world of education and on the self-help bookshelves, advice abounds on how to get through to boys whose brains are supposedly hardwired to need more competition, stimulus and variety in their lessons than girls (I came across an example of this a few years ago on a government-funded education website, which has since changed its approach and will therefore remain anonymous). Or on how to parent four-year-old boys whose testosterone supposedly makes them unable to sit still for five minutes.

Rippon and Fine also deal with the idea that hormones play an important role in all this. We know that prenatal hormones contribute to the development of physical characteristics, and in particular the reproductive system, and that later in life they are responsible for other physical developments. In *Testosterone Rex*,[10] Fine unpicks the popular idea that we are all at the mercy of these hormones – that men are just the hapless victims of "all that testosterone", making them into competitive risk-takers. A better look at the evidence here tells us that, rather than hormones being totally in charge of what we do, they are actually responsive to our environment. Animal testosterone levels can vary according to social ranking or geography; human male testosterone levels can be reduced simply by becoming a father.[11] Rippon looks at how the discovery of hormones and "premenstrual syndrome (PMS)" have led to an undue importance being placed on mood changes that could easily be attributed to other factors in a woman's life – so the idea of PMS producing unstable and slightly crazy women on a regular basis is really a bit of a handy excuse for marginalising and discriminating against women.[12]

So do we still see women as emotionally unstable creatures at the mercy of raging hormones who shouldn't be trusted with important decisions? And men as needing to satisfy sexual needs any way they can because they can't control all that testosterone? Hopefully we are moving towards a place where these outdated ideas are recognised as just that. But you may still encounter them.

As early years practitioners, you will be very aware that the brains of babies and young children are often described as being "like sponges", soaking up all the information and learning they can from every experience. Children are busy trying to find out who they are, how they fit into their family and society, how to do things and how to behave. What they experience as babies, toddlers, preschoolers and beyond plays a crucial role in forming the connections in their brains that help them become the little people they need to be in order to get on in life.

Rippon says that rather than this being a "nature versus nurture" argument, both play a part in an entangled "nature-nurture-nature" sequence. So yes, there are some small biological differences between male and female baby brains (although there are actually more interesting and important differences among the brains of a group of boys, or a group of girls). Because of our great neuroplasticity, if girls and boys are exposed to the same training and educational experiences, then these tiny differences won't matter. But as children experience the gendered world around them, for most of them these differences, rather than being overcome, are reinforced and exacerbated so that, in a kind of self-fulfilling prophecy, we see boys being given chemistry sets and sports equipment and girls being bombarded with messages about their appearance and instructions to "be kind" – and, hey presto, we do find more boys being adventurous and more girls displaying caring attributes. In later chapters, we will take a closer look at what some of these different experiences might be, what messages they give to children and what this means for their development. A gender-equitable approach is about supporting children to overcome the impact of those different beginnings and different experiences.

Developmental Stages

When we were in the early stages of thinking about the Gender Friendly Nursery, the Disney film *Frozen* came out. My daughter, then aged six, and son, then aged four, both went crazy for it. Both would happily watch the DVD and both would sing along to the songs. But within a few months, all this had changed. At some point I noticed my son saying he didn't like *Frozen* and didn't want to watch it. When I asked him why, he said simply, "because I found it in the girls' section of the toy shop".

So that one moment of discovering that a film and the merchandise associated with it were "for girls" was enough to impose a limit on him: he no longer felt permitted to follow that interest. He knew that he was a boy and that *Frozen* was not "for boys". In the course of developing and delivering the gender-equitable approach, I had many conversations about this topic with a variety of people, and versions of my *Frozen* story and others like it kept popping up. Countless sad and angry parents and carers had seen their sons or daughters being "told" by society what they should and shouldn't be doing.

What I now know is that this kind of realisation that your gender seemingly defines what you can and can't do is part of a series of developmental phases that children go through in their socialisation process in relation to gender, influenced by the messages they get from their world. Broadly speaking, these can be broken down into three phases, which we will now examine. Some of what follows is based on Lawrence Kohlberg's theory, which was developed in 1966, but we also take into account perspectives and theories that have developed since then, which sometimes contradict Kohlberg. As society's attitudes and values change and as research develops, so do theories. So this is intended as a rough guide to what research tells us, and not the definitive answer to everything.[13]

Birth to 24 Months: Gender Labelling

We know that, far from being passive recipients of the world around them, baby brains are busy from the moment they are born, finding out about that world and how they fit into it. Babies are developing a sense of themselves, and part of this is a knowledge of what groups or categories of people they belong to. Their world is telling them that one of the most important categories is the one that has two types of people (male and female), and that there are pretty big differences between those groups. So babies set about looking for clues about which of these groups they belong to and what is expected of people in this group. Studies reviewed by Martin et al. in 2002 revealed that six-month-old infants can distinguish between male and female voices; that most nine-month-old babies are able to discriminate between photographs of men and women and that around 11–14 months, infants can recognise the associations between women's and men's photographs and their voices (women's faces "go with" higher voices).[14]

By the age of about two years, most children can tell you that they are either a girl or a boy and can refer to themselves as "he" or "she".[15] And, as we will show in later chapters, there is no end of subtle and not-so-subtle clues to lead them to the conclusion that:

girls = pink = princesses and fairies = gentle, caring, chatty and pretty
boys = blue = pirates and trucks = boisterous, adventurous and scientific

What's also interesting is how infants use this knowledge. In order to survive, babies also need to know what to do to be successful at life: how to get the care and attention they need. So they need to pay attention to the responses of those around them to different behaviours. Crying, laughing, first steps, throwing the teddy out of the pram – babies learn very quickly how other people will react, and use that knowledge to determine whether it's a behaviour they want to repeat. A 2018 study[16] tells us that at around 18–24 months, children adjust their behaviour according to whether they think they are being observed, and how they think the observer values their behaviour. This means that they will normally behave in the way they think the adults around them approve of (which the grown-ups show them by smiling, clapping and praising), and will avoid behaviours that bring disapproval (frowns, raised voices, physical violence). This is really significant because, if gender is such an important characteristic for children to learn about, then once they are aware of their gender category, the natural next step for a child is to seek approval by behaving in the approved way for that group. It follows that if grown-ups are more tolerant of boys being angry, noisy and "naughty", then boys will be more likely to repeat these behaviours. If caregivers encourage girls to play with soft toys and talk more to them in the belief that they have, and need to have, better linguistic skills, then girls will respond to this and do more playing with fluffy toys and trying out new words.

And grown-ups *do* do these things – even grown-ups who think they are open-minded and don't treat boys and girls differently, as the research shows again and again – read on for more on this! This starts before they are born with baby showers and gender reveal parties, the buying of clothes, the decorating of nurseries and the daydreams of what that tiny bump will become. In an online group I was in while I was pregnant, mums-to-be talked about their "pink" or "blue" bumps (or "yellow" bumps if they didn't know or didn't want to reveal the sex). The activities that parents imagine undertaking with their child often fall along gender-stereotypical lines.

After these pink, blue and yellow babies are born (with the yellow ones turning pink or blue at birth), the differences continue. The *Eye of the Beholder* study[17] asked parents to rate newborns on various attributes. Parents of girls tended to describe them as prettier, softer, more delicate, weaker, finer featured and less attentive than parents of boys described their infants, and fathers tended to more extreme characterisations than mothers.[18] Mondschein, Adolph and Tamis-LeMonda showed that mothers over-estimated their sons' crawling abilities and under-estimated those of their daughters, and that their estimations were not based in fact.[19] And a 2016 University of Sussex experiment showed that, despite no actual difference in pitch between the voices of girls and boys before puberty, participants would attribute a sex to a baby based on the pitch of the cry (higher pitch = female).[20] The 2017 BBC documentary *No More Boys and Girls* showed an experiment where participants were falsely told the sex of a baby (with a baby boy in a dress given the name "Sophie", and a baby girl in a shirt called "Oliver"). They were then asked to interact with the baby using a range of toys that were provided. The participants consistently encouraged "Oliver" to play with vehicles, dinosaurs and technical or spatial toys, and offered "Sophie" soft toys and dolls. When confronted with the truth, the participants were horrified: they had all previously thought of themselves as quite open-minded.[21]

Three to Five Years: Gender Stability and Gender Constancy

By three to four years of age, children can take these connections that they have made between the categories "boy" and "girl" and specific attributes, and begin to form rigid rules and expectations about how each gender behaves and looks.[22] For example, we already saw babies making connections between men and deep voices/women and higher voices (a biological difference); now they can extend this to understanding that men "don't" wear dresses and girls "don't" play with trucks (a social/cultural difference).

Children now understand that gender is fixed or stable: boys grow up to be men; mum used to be a little girl. However, they don't yet understand that gender remains consistent across time, context and physical changes. So children may say that if we put a dress on a male doll, he becomes a woman, and if my sister cuts off her long hair she becomes a boy, because women wear dresses and boys have short hair.

Activity: Gender Constancy

To see this in action, try a quick online search for videos of Kohlberg theory demonstrations, or try it with the children with whom you spend time by changing the clothing on a doll and observing their reactions.

Gender constancy comes a little later at around five or six years of age, and at this point children know that a boy with long hair is still a boy, and girls in trousers are still girls. Research shows these developmental stages to be the same across children of different ethnic groups.[23] Children understand that there is something unusual, or funny, about a man in a pink dress, because they are acutely aware of society's rules and of the pressure to comply with them.

Back to those sponge-like brains that children have, which are absorbing every little piece of information they might need to be accepted, and get on, in their world. Now that they have worked out some of the rules about how to behave, they start to develop firm beliefs about this, and will say that certain things are "for girls" or "not for boys". My son (along with many other boys) had his fallout with *Frozen* because he learned from the layout of a toy shop that it wasn't "for him".

Nancy Freeman found in 2007 that, even with parents who claim to reject gender stereo-types (saying they don't mind their sons playing with dolls or their girls playing with trucks, or even encourage them to do so), the sons of these same parents believed their parents would prefer them to play with stereotypically boys' toys.[24] This is quite a powerful argument against those who say that, despite their best efforts, boys "just naturally gravitate" towards toy vehicles, and girls towards dolls and prams. Our beliefs and values can be at odds with what we actually do based on the stereotypes we have grown up with, and children can often see right through us. As we have already seen, our approval is very important to their growing sense of belonging to their world.

In 2019, NHS Greater Glasgow & Clyde produced a short film to support the delivery of the Gender Friendly Nursery training course. Four- and five-year old children are asked various questions about gender, with some very funny responses. Two boys are asked what would happen if a boy played princesses and a girl played with trucks. "That would be crazy!" comes the laughing response. Another boy states very seriously that "that would make their brains all mixed up".[25] Clear examples of how entrenched these ideas are by this stage.

Five and Over: Gender Compliance

By five years of age and beyond, children are readily complying with what the world has told them about who they are and what they can and can't do. In the early stages of primary school, we can already see the influence this has on their beliefs about, and confidence in, themselves and their abilities. Girls choose not to play with toys that they are told are for "really, really smart" people because they don't believe they fit into that category.[26] Boys are already behind in literacy and some approaches to tackling this play into gender stereotypes: my son's teacher once gave him (and, I presume, the other boys) a car magazine at the end of summer term to encourage him to read over the holidays. I never found out what the girls were given but I can imagine pink school bags filled with magazines about arts and crafts or horses and kittens. (He did flick through a few pages but guess what? He didn't read it.)

The good news is that at this stage children have an increased capacity for understanding and discussing morals and values, so it is possible to debate with them about whether these rigid classifications and rules are right or fair. The bad news is that so much of the world around them continues to give them stereotyped messages that very often their already gendered views are reinforced.

One example of where this can lead can be seen in a study we will examine in Chapter 6. It showed that by the end of primary school, children's understanding of gender influenced their thinking on violence in relationships. They expressed strong views about women's role in pleasing their male partners, keeping them happy and keeping the peace. They absolved men of any responsibility for negative behaviours and found fault with the female partner.[27]

So next time you hear someone say that girls and boys just seem to gravitate naturally towards certain kinds of toys, or seem to be hardwired for certain behaviours from the moment they are born, please remember what this research is telling us. Even people who reject gender stereotypes and believe in gender equality do these things without realising it, and every time they do so it sends a message to a child's developing brain. If spatial awareness, scientific inquiry and ball skills are being encouraged in boys from the word "go", is it any wonder that they practise them, enjoying the praise they get, and within a few years are generally better at or show more enthusiasm for tangram puzzles, experiments and playing football than girls?

I should say at this point that I don't claim to be an angel in this respect. Looking back at when my children were that age, I can think of times when, despite believing in gender equality, I inadvertently sent them gendered messages through toys, books, clothes and behaviour management, and I probably still do it now that they are a bit older (although I try really hard not to). We aren't setting out to blame parents, or early years practitioners, or any other caregivers, who are so busy trying to do the best they possibly can for their children in a very complex world. But it's important to acknowledge that this is happening, because from there we can start to do something about it.

What Does This Mean for Early Years Practitioners?

It is important to restate here that there is good news in all this. Our neuroplastic brains continue developing and adapting to the requirements of our world throughout our lives. So despite all the limitations being imposed on girls' and boys' aspirations before they arrive at nursery, and when they go home at night and over the weekend, there is much that you can do to redress the balance.

A couple of pleas from Gina Rippon for those of us who want to reduce gender stereotyping: "Just call it out! People might feel it's trivial but if you can actually say, no it's not...

I think you're pushing against an opening door which is helpful." And, "Educate yourself, so when you see this headline, just wonder what's behind it."[28]

We'll go into what actions you can take, what you can do to educate yourself and how you can start calling it out later in the book, but for now it's worth remembering the vital role of the early years in preparing children for life in our world. If you can influence them so that they protect their health by washing their hands, make a better world by treating each other with kindness, or know who to go to if they are worried, then you can also help them to see an alternative view of the world as a place where people can participate as equals regardless of gender. This will take practice and effort, but the importance of getting the message right can't be under-estimated.

Notes

1 A note of caution: we will refer to "typical" patterns of development here, but with an awareness that some children's early development can be affected by trauma, lack of attachment or atypical brain development like autism. We don't claim to be experts on these topics, but we want to acknowledge at the start that there may be differences in the ways that children's brains develop in relation to gender. There is probably a whole world of research waiting to be done on this.

2 C. Fine, *Delusions of Gender* (London: Icon Books, 2010).

3 To summarise some of the problems with these very briefly, some conclusions are extrapolated from studies of animals and assumed to work in the same way for humans; others have flaws in methodology; yet others work with small sample sizes but are taken to be representative of the whole human race.

4 For balance, I should say there are those who disagree. Simon Baren-Cohen is another neuroscientist whose research appears to point to evidence of more significant biological brain differences.

5 G. Rippon, *The Gendered Brain* (London: Bodley Head, 2019).

6 G. Le Bon, cited in Rippon, *The Gendered Brain*, p. 6.

7 This is a very simplified and truncated version of a long and really interesting tale of historical attempts to prove men's apparent superiority and justify their superior status to women, by studying the brain. Chapter 1 of Rippon, *The Gendered Brain* gives a much fuller picture, and is also a really entertaining read.

8 For an interesting discussion on scientists' attempts to classify humans into races and to measure their skulls to "justify" notions of superiority, Episode 8 of the *Seeing White* podcast is a good start. Available at www.sceneonradio.org/wp-content/uploads/2017/12/SeeingWhite_Part8Transcript.pdf (accessed 7 January 2022).

9 P. Ghosh, "Cern scientist: 'Physics built by men - not by invitation'" (1 October 2018). Available at www.bbc.co.uk/news/world-europe-45703700 (accessed 7 January 2022).

10 C. Fine, *Testosterone Rex* (London: Icon Books, 2017).

11 Fine, *Testosterone Rex*, p. 144.

12 Rippon, *The Gendered Brain*, pp. 28-31.

13 For a much more thorough examination of the research and changing theories on this topic, see C.L. Martin and D. Ruble, "Children's Search for Gender Cues: Cognitive Perspectives on Gender Development". *Current Directions in Psychological Science*, 13(2), 67-70 (2004); and D.N. Ruble, C. Martin and S. Berenbaum, *Handbook of Child Psychology* (London: Routledge, 2007).

14 C.L. Martin, D.N. Ruble and J. Szkrybalo, "Cognitive Theories of Early Gender Development". *Psychological Bulletin*, 128 (2002), 903-33.

15 Martin and Ruble, "Children's Search for Gender Cues".

16 S.V. Botto and P. Rochat, "Sensitivity to the Evaluation of Others Emerges by 24 Months". *Developmental Psychology*, 54(9) (2018), 1723-34.

17 J.Z. Rubin, F. Provenzano and Z. Luria, "The Eye of the Beholder: Parents' View on Sex of Newborns". *American Journal of Orthopsychiatry*, 44(4) (1974), 512-19.

18 More recent recreations of this study have shown that, despite changes over time, some of these stereotypes still prevail.

19 E. Mondschein, K.E. Adolph and C.S. Tamis-LeMonda, "Gender Bias in Mothers' Expectations About Infant Crawling". *Journal of Experimental Child Psychology*, 77(4) (2000), 304-16.

20 D. Reby, F. Levréro, E. Gustafsson, E. et al., "Sex Stereotypes Influence Adults' Perception of Babies' Cries". *BMC Psychology* 4(19) (2016), https://doi.org/10.1186/s40359-016-0123-6.

21 *Girl Toys vs Boy Toys: The Experiment*. BBC Stories (16 August 2017). Available at www.youtube.com/watch?v=nWu44AqFOiI (accessed 7 January 2022).

22 M.L. Halim and D. Ruble, *Gender Identity and Stereotyping in Early and Middle Childhood*. In J.C. Chrisler and D.R. McCreary (eds), *Handbook of Gender Research in Psychology* (New York: Springer, 2010), 495-525.

23 M.L. Halim, D. Ruble, C. Tamis-LeMonda and P.E. Shrout, "Rigidity in Gender-typed Behaviours in Early Childhood: A Longitudinal Study of Ethnic Minority Children". *Child Development*, 84(4) (2013), 1269-84.

24 N. Freeman, "Preschoolers' Perceptions of Gender Appropriate Toys and their Parents' Beliefs About Genderised Behaviours: Miscommunication, Mixed Messages, or Hidden Truths?" *Early Childhood Education Journal*, 34(5) (2007), 357-66.

25 *NHSGGC – Early Years & Gender* (3 July 2020). NHS Greater Glasgow and Clyde. Available at www.youtube.com/watch?v=Ak4p8y2CxDU (Accessed 7 January 2022).

26 L. Bian, S.J. Leslie and A. Cimpian, "Gender Stereotypes About Intellectual Ability Emerge Early and Influence Children's Interests", *Science,* 355 (2017), 6323.

27 N. Lombard, "'Because They're a Couple She Should Do What He Says': Young People's Justifications of Violence: Heterosexuality, Gender and Adulthood". *Journal of Gender Studies*, 25(3) (2016), 241-53.

28 This paper may help you with this: C. Fine, D. Joel and G. Rippon, "Eight Things You Need to Know About Sex, Gender, Brains, and Behaviour: A Guide for Academics, Journalists, Parents, Gender Diversity Advocates, Social Justice Warriors, Tweeters, Facebookers, and Everyone Else". Available at https://sfonline.barnard.edu/neurogenderings/eight-things-you-need-to-know-about-sex-gender-brains-and-behavior-a-guide-for-academics-journalists-parents-gender-diversity-advocates-social-justice-warriors-tweeters-facebookers-and-ever (Accessed 7 January 2022).

4 How Gender Stereotypes are Reinforced

Susie Heywood

The idea that gendered preferences around things like toy choice, colour preference and career aspirations are something with which children are born has largely been debunked. Instead, we have learned the undeniable influence of prevailing societal gender norms in shaping how children learn about what is expected of them in relation to their biological sex. These gender stereotypes, which are often unnoticed or small in nature, are reinforced in a "drip-drip" effect across the lifespan. Sociologists Cecilia Ridgeway and Shelley Correll explained this lifetime accumulation of messages well when they wrote:

> Individual lives are lived through multiple repeating, social relational contexts ... the small biasing effects accumulate over careers and lifetimes to result in substantially different behavioural paths and social outcomes ...[1]

The previous chapter showed how this gender messaging begins early, so now let's look at how it continues across the life-course using some specific examples, demonstrating this drip-drip effect.

Children's Television

Any of us who have spent any time around children will recognise the dominance of children's media in family homes and childcare settings, and cannot fail to have noticed some of the less-than-subtle messages about gender that they send. Starting with children's television, it will come as no surprise that the pink/blue colour divide is a common feature, but of greater concern is what male and female characters get to be or get to do, and how they act or are represented. Let's start with a simple exercise.

 Exercise: Kids Television

I am assuming that if you are reading this book, you spend some time around children, and will have some familiarity with children's television programming. Take a couple of minutes to list some of the characters you can think of, male in one column and female in another (though they may not always be human, their sex will be clear). Now write

DOI: 10.4324/9781003167921-6

next to each a few words about their role, persona or traits. Think about what they do as a job. How do they act? What role do they play in the programme?

Have a look at your lists and ask yourself the following questions:

*   Are there any clear differences between the male characters and female characters?
*   What types of things do male characters get to be or do? What about females?
*   Are there clear differences between how male and female characters act?
*   Is there anything else you notice about your list?

When we have done this sort of exercise during training, it has always provoked a rich discussion. Male characters play a leading role across programming generally, both in terms of numbers, and the prominence or importance of their characters. Female characters are often the sidekicks to a more adventurous leading male (think Lily in Peter Rabbit) or are simply outnumbered by their male counterparts – perhaps the token female of the group (think *Octonauts*, *Thomas the Tank Engine*, *Blaze and the Monster Machines* or *Lego Ninjago*). This might seem relatively harmless but there are potential consequences.

I have two young children: a smart and conservative little boy who is four years older than his wild and inquisitive sister. My daughter loves *Paw Patrol*. For the lucky ones among you who aren't familiar, *Paw Patrol* follows the exploits of Ryder and his troop of six rescue dog pups. Each of the pups has a particular role – for example, Chase is a police dog, Marshall is a firefighter, Rubble is a builder and Skye, the token female, pilots a rescue helicopter. One day my daughter and I were playing *Paw Patrol* and I asked her who she wanted to "be". She immediately answered "Rubble", her favourite. On hearing this, her older brother immediately jumped in to say, "You can't be Rubble because he is a ..."

You can guess what he was intent on saying, but I interrupted and made sure my daughter knew she could be any dog she wanted. My son continued to insist that his sister had to play a female character. (You won't be surprised to know that I used this as a "teachable moment" for discussion.) We know that young children can police gender roles among their peers, particularly from around the age of five, so it is quite likely that similar situations are happening in play situations everywhere.

 Reflection: Gender Policing

Do you notice children policing each other's gender either in your home or your setting? What kinds of things do they say? How do the children react?

Sticking with the Paw Patrol example, what impact might this have? If continually policed in this way, girls would only have the choice of one character and one very specific role, while boys have a variety of roles to choose from. We all know the important role of play in how children learn and develop both their understanding of the world and of themselves. Things like this are literally limiting children's capacity to learn and grow!

The 2019 Hopster report into representation in mainstream children's television programming came along after we had been delivering training around this topic for a number of years.[2] The report looked at representation across mainstream kids' television programming in the United Kingdom, and found an alarming level of gender stereotyping still prevalent among the most popular shows. This included a dominance of male protagonists who were more powerful or important than their female counterparts and a reinforcing of old stereotypes such as boys who fight, girls who are concerned with their appearance, male knowledge-bearers or protectors, and women who clean. On occasion, female characters were shown being undermined by males, or objectified using female body ideals and stereotypes of femininity. Villains and naughty characters were more typically male, and male characters often had overly muscular physiques.

Animated Movies

Similar issues can be found in children's films. When we look at Disney heroines, for example – or Princesses as they are more commonly known – it's clear that their characters often reflect culturally dominant ideals of femininity at the time.[3] The early princesses, like Cinderella and Snow White, typified a delicate femininity centred around domesticity, modesty and care for animals and others. As we move into the 1980s and 1990s, we see characters like Jasmine, Tinkerbell and Ariel, who occupy more active, rebellious or seemingly empowered roles, but still with the ultimate goal of marrying the prince and still needing said prince to complete their rescue. We also see them being given a dramatically sexualised appearance: huge eyes, tiny waists and skimpier clothing … Our more recent Princesses are often lauded as more positive role models for young girls – feisty, independent, clever women who very often reject society's (often patriarchal) expectations of them. We see in *Frozen* a different take on the "saved by true love" storyline, with the female protagonist being saved by the love and bravery of her sister. However, even today the characters still tend to be slim and pretty, with exaggerated facial features.[4] Disney is a business, after all, and so will develop characters based on what their target market wants – for example, it is no coincidence that *Encanto* (which features a Colombian family and contains themes around displacement and intergenerational trauma) was one of the first big Disney releases following the Black Lives Matter movement and protests, and the increasing discussion around Black and ethnic minority representation. Media shapes society, but society also shapes media.

It is notable that, despite the cultural dominance of the "Disney Princess" phenomenon, only 19 per cent of films produced by the top animation studios over the last 30 years featured a female lead or co-lead.[5] This under-representation of female characters is not limited to children's movies – we see similar issues in adult movies. The Gina Davis Institute on Gender in Media has been a leading voice in calling for better representation and a reduction in negative stereotyping across media, and has funded a wealth of research highlighting the issues. Its work is rooted in the belief (which we share) that the stories we tell through our entertainment media send a strong message about what we value and where we place importance. While things have improved, there is still a two-to-one ratio of male characters to female characters across advertising, film and television.[6] Representation clearly remains an issue. We really don't know exactly how all this affects the children, particularly the young girls who consume this media; however we do know that audiences are not passive and even young children will be making meaning from what they are consuming.

During our training course, we talk about the physical transformation of some of our other much-loved children's characters over time. Search online for "Applejack then and now" to see the changing look of My Little Pony, who has gone from looking like an actual horse to something very different. The ponies now have an elongated neck, are slimmer but have a very curvy appearance, enlarged eyes and over-the-top hair. We have seen the same transformation take place with other characters: see whether you can find the Tween version of Dora the Explorer, for example.[7] This one always shocks people – it's definitely worth taking a look! Yes she's gotten older, but does she still look equipped for her usual jungle adventures with her ballet pumps, flowing locks and jewellery? The messages these transformations, and the appearance of countless other female characters, are sending to children about the ideals of female beauty and appearance cannot be ignored.

And male characters are impacted too! How has superhero favourite Batman fared, for example? There has been quite a shift from the Wham! Kapow! "could be anybody's dad in a costume" Batman of the 1960s to the muscly ultra-menacing violent *Dark Knight* batman of recent years who very much embodies the idea of "toxic masculinity" that we will discuss in later chapters. There is no doubt that this will be influencing the play of young children pretending to be this hero figure. We have seen similar transformations across the range of superhero characters. We will all have seen young boys in particular coming dressed as superheroes in costumes complete with built-in muscles and six-packs! The body image pressures start early. And of course, where are the nurturing and caring male characters?

The impact of all this subtle messaging can't be ignored. We know that children are consuming increasing amounts of media from a very young age and in a variety of ways. Recent research shows that 48 per cent of three- and four-year-olds own their own tablet computer, for example, with around 86 per cent watching online video content on platforms such as YouTube.[8] There's no judgement from us about this (as I write this, both my children are glued to their screens), but it's an illustration of just how strong an influence media is in the lives of many children.

Stories and Books

 Exercise: Rapid Storybook Audit

Pick a random selection of 10 story books from the shelf in your setting and have a look to see what proportion of the characters are male and female.

How closely do the characters align to the gender stereotypes we hold in society?

We see similar messages in children's books. As a child, I inhaled books – I learned so much about the world from the characters and stories I found in them. While there are many brilliant stories that show male and female characters occupying non-stereotypical roles, many stories – particularly some of the more traditional fairy tales, can be problematic, reinforcing stereotypes and gender norms. Research by *The Observer* newspaper in 2018 showed that male characters in popular picture books were twice as likely to have leading and speaking roles, and villains were more likely to be male.[9]

The same issues of over-representation of male characters are present with the addition of a strong "male default" when it comes to non-human characters. The research also found that non-human characters were 73 per cent more likely to be male than female, and those that were identified as female were more likely to be smaller, more vulnerable and domesticated animals such as cats, squirrels or mice. As a parent, I usually change most characters to female when reading out loud (which requires a level of concentration that I am often lacking at bedtime); however, even with this deliberate effort, I have noticed that in play my children continue to assign male gender to most animal figures and toys. I once read that even changing every character in every book read to a child to female would not be enough to stem the impact of the wider societal male default!

A study published in the *Psychological Science* journal looked at the words used in children's story books and asked participants to rate them according to their association with masculinity and femininity, arguing that gender bias and gendered messages were being delivered in more subtle ways beyond the content and characterisation of the stories. They also found that the books clearly written with girls in mind were more likely to be reinforcing stereotypes about girls, and vice versa for boys.[10]

The Toy Industry

The toy industry also has a lot to answer for. Despite the brilliant work and successes of campaigning organisation Let Toys Be Toys, toys are still produced and marketed along gendered lines. Not only does this feel like a cunning ploy to sell double the amount of toys – I am sure we all know someone who has bought a pink one of everything only to have to replace it later with the blue version – but it's also sending clear messages that reinforce traditional gender roles. It may be no coincidence that we have seen massive rises in gendered marketing over the time that the women's movement have made great advances.[11]

In 2015, volunteers for the Let Toys Be Toys campaign watched nine UK channels over 30 hours of programming to see how boys and girls were represented in TV advertisements for toys in the United Kingdom. Before we tell you what they found, have a look at the two word clouds in Figures 4.1 and 4.2, and take a guess at which one relates to the language used in advertisements targeted to boys and which one relates to those targeted to girls.

Let Toys Be Toys found that most TV adverts show boys and girls playing separately, in very stereotypical ways. Boys were shown as active and aggressive, and the language used in adverts which were clearly targeted at them emphasised control, power and conflict. Not one advert for baby or fashion dolls included a boy. Girls, on the other hand,

Image 4.1

Image 4.2

Words used in TV ads featuring girls
lettoysbetoys.org.uk/tvads2021

Image 4.3

Words used in TV ads featuring boys
lettoysbetoys.org.uk/tvads2021

Image 4.4

were generally shown as passive, unless they were dancing. The language used focused on fantasy, beauty and relationships. Out of 25 ads for toy vehicles, only one included a girl. Most toys were clearly marketed towards a specific gender along stereotypical lines. For example, those targeted at boys were mainly for toys such as vehicles, action figures, construction sets and toy weapons, while those targeted at girls were predominantly for dolls, glamour and grooming, with an overwhelming emphasis on appearance, performing, nurturing and relationships. It is the "girl toys" that tend to encourage caring, social skills and empathy-building, with boys losing out on the opportunity to develop these vital softer skills, locked out due to the need for them to stay inside the boundaries of their gender box.

The experiment was repeated in 2021,[12] and while things have improved slightly in terms of the themes, adverts "for girls" continued to push beauty, appearance, magic, relationships and consumerism, and in those "for boys", action and conflict still dominated. While there was an increase in adverts that featured boys and girls together, these tended to be for traditionally masculine activities – there was still very little in the way of boys participating in traditionally feminine play activities. So despite all the brilliant campaigning, there's still a long way to go.

Clothing

Clothing too plays a role. When we step into a high street store or supermarket children's clothing department, it's pretty clear which clothes are for whom. This goes beyond the "skirts and dresses for girls and trousers and shorts for boys" rule. Gender coding through colour, slogans and pictures is overt and falls along stereotypical lines. Think pink, glitter, domesticated animals, princesses, unicorns, kindness and love for girls and every other colour but pink and purple, wild predatory animals, astronauts, superheroes, gaming, technology, action and adventure for boys.

Gendered school uniform policies are also problematic, not only because they send clear messages about difference, but also because often the female options are often impractical and uncomfortable. Why does it seem more important that a little girl looks a certain way than able to participate in school life in comfort?[13]

As We Get Older

These gendered messages continue as we grow. We will pick up on some of the themes included in this section in later chapters, but it's useful to summarise some of the sources and prevalent themes.

Before the advent of gaming consoles and handheld devices, television was the primary source of screen-based entertainment for all the family. The days of gathering the family together to watch the latest Saturday night family show now seems like a thing of the past, replaced by subscription-based on-demand TV, streaming services and viewing platforms such as YouTube, which offer pretty much anything you could ever think of. This means we can access a wide range of content at any time of the day. Gone is the old watershed before which we could be assured that anything being screened was family friendly. Increasingly violent and sexualised imagery is commonplace across programming. Soap operas, which are often watched by children and young people, now tackle very serious adult themes. While the awareness-raising around serious societal issues such as domestic abuse, rape, suicide and mental illness is to be welcomed, there is some concern about the messages that children may be picking up, particularly children of an age where they may not fully understand what they are viewing.

The Music Industry

The music industry is another arena where we see very defined and often unhealthy ideas of masculinity and femininity. It is unsurprising that in a male-driven and deeply misogynistic industry we see a real disparity in how men and women are represented. Female artists are often presented in a highly sexualised way, while men are usually fully clothed and positioned in a position of power or authority. Think of a fully dressed Harry Styles surrounded by scantily clad women in the 2019 "Watermelon Sugar" video or the way in which Ariana Grande has been presented in an infantilised yet sexual way in many of her videos (look up 2019's "7 Rings" video, for example). Of course, there will always be artists who will buck the trend, but there is no doubt that the industry pushes harmful stereotypes about men and women and their roles in society.

It is important to say here that we should try to avoid placing the blame for any of this on individual artists – particularly female artists, who are often scrutinised for the messages that they are sending to young girls. While there may be a few highly successful female artists who feel they have full control over the image they choose to portray, on the whole we know that there is massive pressure from within the industry for female artists, and even more so Black female artists, to present themselves in a certain way if they want to be successful.[14] Railton and Watson (2005) argue that the sexualisation of Black female music artists is a continuation of the way Black women were sexualised and fetishised in Victorian times, and compared with "unavailable" white women and their repressed sexuality.

Pop song lyrics can also be problematic, a classic example being Robin Thicke's 2013 "Blurred Lines", which presents Thicke as unable to prevent himself from groping women who, according to him, "want it", and also talks of sexual violence and sex that hurts and is "work" … and was played on radio stations and sung along to by people of all ages, with only a few of the worst words blanked out. There are many other examples of songs about toxic and abusive relationships, which is problematic. On the one hand, they can be seen as expressing the pain and dilemmas faced by people in this situation, and perhaps helping others to recognise or come to terms with what they have experienced, but on the other can also glamourise relationship abuse for impressionable children and young people who don't understand the nuances.

Consider for a moment how much some children and young people are exposed to these images and lyrics, with music video television channels playing in the background in homes and takeaway shops, and many of these songs being used in dance classes and at parties and gatherings.

Social Media

Social media has become an extension of our real life-worlds, bringing us together with family, friends and people from all over the world to interact and share content in a variety of ways. We will all be familiar with the move to ban photoshopping technology from the advertising industry. A number of high-profile celebrities have called out the photoshopping of their images and how their true appearance has been misrepresented. Through social media, we now all have the same kind of technology at our fingertips, and the ability to alter our image before we post it online. This has led to a situation where we can never be sure whether what we are seeing is real, where we may be comparing how we look to false images, increasing our unhappiness with our bodies. We will pick up on this later when we examine the impact of gender stereotypes on how we feel about our bodies.

Pornography

Another source of problematic and sexist messaging is the pornography industry, which has grown exponentially and adapted to new technology that allows easier access. Gone are the days of top-shelf magazines (although they do still exist); anyone can now access graphic pornography free of charge via a range of online pornography sites. Yes, they may have an age filter, but it doesn't take a genius to find a way around these, meaning that access to pornography is at the fingertips of children who we know are often able to access the internet unsupervised. Children as young as seven or eight are being unintentionally exposed to pornography when they accidently stumble across it according to research by the British Board of Film Classification.[15]

The vast majority of pornography is full of images that are violent, abusive and unrealistic, and that have been created for the male gaze. They promote stereotyped roles where men are in charge and women are there for men's pleasure. Pornography promotes the idea of male entitlement to sex whenever they want it, and undermines messages about healthy relationships and consent. Even for adults accessing pornography, this can be harmful and can lead to addiction. When these images are seen by young people (and we know that, in the absence of really good sex education, many young people will use porn as a source of information about what to do and how to do it), they can have a huge influence on their expectations of relationships in terms of how much sex they should be having, what sexual acts they should be engaged in, who should initiate it and who has the power and control.

These expectations then feed into young people's interactions and relationships, and there is evidence that people who consume a lot of porn become dissatisfied with the more ordinary, realistic aspects of relationships and come to expect the more extreme and violent acts they have seen.[16]

Gaming

We see these same themes when we look at the gaming industry. As well as being increasingly realistic and violent, with amazing graphics and first-person play meaning that players feel much more like they are experiencing the action themselves, individual games have some deeply alarming content. Take the *Grand Theft Auto* (GTA) series, for example, which sees players rewarded for bad behaviour, like beating people up and stealing cars. One way in which players can progress in the game is to pick up and have sex with prostitutes (again, in realistic first-person), which gives them extra "health" points. This costs money, but they can get their money back by murdering the woman in a variety of ways (once again, in case you'd forgotten, in first-person). For those of you not familiar with GTA, a quick online image search will also show you a variety of male characters all dressed and ready for action, with the small number of female characters depicted in ways that make it clear their role is either irritating obstacle (angry girlfriend) or sex object.

Like the porn industry, there are age ratings on GTA and other games, but we know that very young children play them, or sit watching while older relatives play. And even the more age-appropriate games tend to encourage (usually male) violence, whether it be cartoon violence against proper "baddies" or the kind of graphic violence against bystanders that we saw above.

The Fashion and Beauty Industry

Where to start with this one? There, is of course, the long-running debate about the impact of the fashion and beauty industry on women's and girls' self-esteem, with very young girls being influenced by images they see to look a certain way (often reflected in those modernised or grown-up versions of the cartoon characters we talked about earlier). There are concerns about the exploitation of young women in modelling. There is also a darker theme that can be observed in the advertising of high-end fashion (and sometimes other products, like alcohol, targeted at men) where images depicting highly glamourised and sexualised violence against women, including domestic abuse, gang rape and murder, are used to sell aspirational products.[17] How have we reached this place?

It's Not Just Media ...

There is no doubting the role that capitalism and economics play in some of the decisions these big companies and marketers are making about which products to produce and how to sell them. For example, why make a toy in just one gender-neutral colour when you can make a pink version and a blue version, meaning many parents will feel the pressure to buy one of each. However, we also see negative gender stereotypes across a range of public sector documents and reports.

Campaigning organisation Fathers Network Scotland was instrumental in highlighting this issue in relation to dads in particular. Its 2013 report, *Where's Dad?*, examined the imagery in a range of family or child-focused policy or information publications and found that dads were either missing entirely or worryingly presented in a negative light.[18] Thanks to this campaign, things have improved; however, we still continue to see other examples of where gender stereotypes are reinforced. For example, you may have seen one of the many public safety messaging campaigns which ran during the COVID-19 pandemic urging us to stay home to save lives. This particular example featured an image of four houses. Three of them included women undertaking various domestic chores (mopping a floor with a female child, crouched on the floor doing home-schooling, and in the third holding a baby next to what looks like an ironing board), while the fourth – the only one featuring a man – showed the family sitting down to watch TV. Hopefully you can see the issue with this image, which was asking all of us to stay at home during the height of the lockdown period. I might be making assumptions about how things are done, but I would expect that before being signed off as suitable, this would have had to cross a few desks. Yet nobody seemed to have picked up on the fact that the only man in the image was sitting back, presumably watching television, while the women in the other homes were busy keeping the home running. Funnily enough, when this hit the headlines, it was quickly withdrawn.[19]

Don't Be Disheartened!

We are absolutely not here to bash children's TV characters, to ban Disney movies from child-care settings, to ask you to remove every trace of a traditional fairy tale from your reading corner or ensure every item of clothing you have is gender-neutral. But if children are being subjected to idealised and unrealistic images of beauty or personality in many areas of their lives, then we need to consider the impacts of this in what they believe others expect of them or what they expect of each other in terms of their looks and behaviour. We hope we are beginning to demonstrate the cumulative effect of these messages even on young children, and provoking you to consider what you could possibly do to counteract some of these harmful stereotypes in your day-to-day interactions. More on that later!

I think sometimes when we see this stuff in isolation, it's easy to dismiss it as a one-off, and not as part of a pattern or bigger problem. However, it has been our experience, and the experience of people who have heard us talk about this stuff, that once you are alerted to the problem and see a few examples, you start to see it everywhere. It becomes clear that these stereotypes form a huge part of the tapestry of our lives – that "drip-drip" effect we may barely notice but that gradually seeps in.

There is a growing recognition of the problems with this stuff. For example, in 2019 new Advertising Standards Authority rules came into force, which banned advertisements of any kind that perpetuated harmful gender stereotypes.[20] As a result, we have seen advertisements featuring hapless and hopeless dads, and women in passive domesticated roles among more active males, being blocked from our screens. This is a step in the right direction, but there's so much still to be done to convince people that these things are not harmless jokes.

We will pick up on many of these themes as we move through the book, but hopefully we might just have convinced you of the scale of the problem we are facing. It could be easy at this point to be disheartened – to feel that the issues are just too widespread for anything we can do to make much difference. It's true that we are up against it, but we firmly believe that culture change is possible. We have seen massive culture change before – it *can* be done if enough people get on board.

Notes

1 C.L. Ridegway and S. Correll, "Unpacking the Gender System: A Theoretical Perspective on Gender Beliefs and Social Relations". *Gender & Society,* 18(4) (2004), 510–31.
2 Hopster, *Is TV Making Your Child Prejudiced? A report into pre-school programming* (2019). Available at: https://hopster_wordpress_v2.storage.googleapis.com/Hopster-Predjudice-Report-DIGITAL.pdf (accessed 7 January 2022).
3 D.E. England, L. Descartes and M. Collier Meek, "Gender Role Portrayal and the Disney Princesses". *Sex Roles,* 64 (2011), 555–67.
4 There is so much we could say about Disney Princesses: we have only touched on it here, and haven't even begun to look at what we might find on platforms such as Disney+ or Disney TV channels, so we are excited that there will soon be a book that covers it all in depth. Keep a look out for a new book by Robyn Muir, *The Princess as the Political: A Feminist Analysis of the Disney Princess Phenomenon* (Bristol: Bristol University Press), which will provide a comprehensive overview of the research, theory and discussion around this topic.
5 K. Schiele and S. Chen, "Feminism in Youth Media: A Study of Disney-Pixar Animation". *Business Horizons,* 63(5) (2020), 659–69.
6 The Gina Davis Institute website is a mine of useful information and research around gender and diversity of all kinds in media. Available at https://seejane.org (accessed 7 January 2022).
7 It's good to see that there was some reaction among parents to these changes – check out this short clip: CBS News, *Dora's Tween Makeover* (2009). Available at www.youtube.com/watch?v=uyV6DGD4fls (accessed 7 January 2022).
8 For more discussion on children's media use, see Ofcom's useful report *Children and Parents: Media Use and Attitudes 2020/21* (London: Ofcom, 2021). Available at www.ofcom.org.uk/__data/assets/pdf_file/0025/217825/children-and-parents-media-use-and-attitudes-report-2020-21.pdf (accessed 7 January 2022).
9 D. Ferguson, "Must Monsters Always Be Male? Huge Gender Bias Revealed in Children's Books". *The Observer.* Available at www.theguardian.com/books/2018/jan/21/childrens-books-sexism-monster-in-your-kids-book-is-male (accessed 7 January 2022).
10 M. Lewis, M.C. Borkenhagen, E. Converse, G. Lupyan and M.S. Seidenberg, "What Might Books Be Teaching Young Children About Gender?" *Psychological Science*, 33(1) (2021), 33–47.
11 For more on this, read this fascinating article: E. Sweet, "Toys are More Divided by Gender Now Than They Were 50 Years Ago". *The Atlantic* (December 2014). Available at www.theatlantic.com/business/archive/2014/12/toys-are-more-divided-by-gender-now-than-they-were-50-years-ago/383556 (accessed 7 January 2022).
12 Let Toys Be Toys, "Who Gets to Play Now? What Do UK TV Toy Ads Tell Children About Boys and Girls' Play in 2021?" Available at: www.lettoysbetoys.org.uk/tvads2021 (accessed 7 January 2022).
13 For more discussion on gendered clothing and school uniforms, check out the work of Let Clothes Be Clothes. Available at www.letclothesbeclothes.co.uk (accessed 7 January 2022).
14 See this article on the exploitation of women of colour in music videos: F. Solomon, "The Exploitation of Women of Color in Music Videos Needs to End" (Women's Media Centre, 2016). Available at https://womensmediacenter.com/fbomb/the-exploitation-of-women-in-color-in-music-videos-needs-to-end (accessed 7 January 2022).
15 British Board of Film Classification, "Children See Pornography as Young as 7 New Report Finds" (2018). Available at www.bbfc.co.uk/about-us/news/children-see-pornography-as-young-as-seven-new-report-finds (accessed 7 January 2022).
16 The Fight the New Drug website is a great guide to the facts about pornography and includes peer-researched articles on the impact on our brains, bodies, relationships and the world. Available at https://fightthenewdrug.org (accessed 7 January 2022).
17 For some examples, see this article, or do an internet search for fashion ads and violence against women: TFL, "Why Do Ads and Editorials Depicting Violence Happen in Fashion?" (October 4, 2017). Available at www.thefashionlaw.com/why-ads-editorials-depicting-violence-keep-happening (accessed 7 January 2022).

18 G. Clapton, (*Where's Dad? Father Proofing Your Work* (Edinburgh: Fathers Network Scotland, 2013).
19 You can see some of the commentary and the image at www.bbc.co.uk/news/uk-politics-55844367 (accessed 7 January 2022).
20 Advertising Standards Authority, "Regulatory Statement on Gender Stereotypes in Ads" (2018). Available at www.asa.org.uk/resource/regulatory-statement-on-gender-stereotypes-in-ads.html (accessed 7 January 2022).

PART 2

5 What's the Harm?

Barbara Adzajlic

As we go through this book, we will establish that gender stereotypes are everywhere: they form a background to every child's life, no matter how progressive their parents or carers might be; they intersect with other stereotypes about race, (dis)ability, class and other characteristics; and they influence the ways in which children think about themselves and others.

But – and this is the question that people may well ask you – what does it matter if our boys are geared towards dinosaurs and trucks? So what if we compliment our girls on their looks? That's nice, right? What's the harm in strong, blue boys who get stuff done, and gentle, pink girls who organise and tidy up after them?

Now you have started thinking more about gender stereotypes, it might be tempting to skip to the "how" section so you can start doing something about it. But please take the time to read the chapters in this "why" section first because it will provide you with the ammunition you need when someone asks you "What's the harm?" In these chapters, we explain exactly what the harm is – or rather, what the *harms* are, because there are many aspects of our lives that are affected by the expectations and limitations imposed on us by gender stereotypes. In our work as public health practitioners, we and our colleagues work hard to prevent some of these harms and to mitigate their impact. But like all public health matters, this is something we all need to work on together, and the part you can play as an early years practitioner, or manager, or the parent of small children is really important.

Upstream Approach

As already mentioned, public health is about preventing, or mitigating, the factors that can lead to poor health outcomes. It is also about reducing health inequalities, where we see unfair differences in the health outcomes of different people. By unfair we mean that they are caused by circumstances over which most people don't have a lot of control, and are a result of an unequal distribution of power, wealth and income across society. So, for example, a child growing up in a disadvantaged community might live in poor-quality housing that affects their physical health. They might not have the same access to safe green spaces where they can enjoy fresh air and physical activity and they might not have the money to take part in after-school clubs and activities. They might not have a quiet space where they can do homework, or they might arrive at school hungry and unable to concentrate. While

DOI: 10.4324/9781003167921-8

nothing is inevitable, and many people who start out living in poverty go on to be healthy and successful in life, we can still see how this child will face greater challenges than a similar child growing up with more resources and privileges.

Class, race, disability, sex and gender are all characteristics that can lead to inequalities in the physical, emotional and social health outcomes of different groups of people. In the rest of this chapter, we'll be explaining how this works for gender in particular while also giving some thought to how gender intersects with those other characteristics.

Preventative approaches are also sometimes described as "upstream approaches". To explain this, let me tell you a story.

There was once a village of fisherfolk, set beside a deep, wide river. The fisherfolk went out in their boats every day and caught fish. One day the people in one of the boats noticed a person in the water, floating towards them and calling for help. Quickly they moved their boat towards the person, threw out a lifebelt and managed to pull the person to safety. The next day, two other boats rescued people from the water, and the next day there were more people in the water again. As time went on, more and more people were pulled out of the water. Sometimes there just weren't enough boats, or lifebelts, to save them all. The fisherfolk were sometimes so busy rescuing people that they didn't have the time to fish, and their families sometimes went hungry.

The fisherfolk started to ask themselves what was going on upstream from their part of the river to cause all these people to end up in the water. Eventually they held a village meeting where it was decided to send a delegation to investigate. A group of fisherfolk travelled upstream and came to a bend in the river where the scenery was really beautiful, but where there was a steep cliff with no safety barrier. They realised that people were stopping at this beauty spot to admire the view, but that the cliff was dangerous and some people were falling in.

The fisherfolk spoke to the locals, who were also concerned that tourists, and some of their own people, were falling into the river. Together they decided to erect a "DANGER" sign, as well as a strong barrier, at the top of the cliff. They also built a path down to the river so that anyone who wanted to reach the water had a safer way to do so.

After that, things got better. People still occasionally fell into the river because they couldn't read the sign, or because they strayed over the fence, or because the path was slippery after rain, but the fisherfolk kept an eye out for this and made sure they had plenty of lifebelts.[1]

The story shows how problems can have a variety of causes that need to be dealt with at their source, as well as further downstream. This is what we mean by prevention. Examples of prevention activities might include road safety education to prevent accidents; early tobacco, alcohol and nutrition education to support people to make healthier lifestyle choices; and mental health interventions like the PATHS resource, which is used widely across Scottish schools and nurseries,[2] or funded counselling services in schools or through workplace initiatives, or Mental Health First Aid training for professionals and community members.[3] As you can see, these are activities that aren't limited to public health practitioners: they might involve the police, schools, businesses, the third sector or others. As people involved in the lives of children, we will all be doing upstream prevention work without even realising it – for example, if you are a parent, you will be teaching your child to brush their teeth and cross the road safely.

In terms of gender stereotypes, we will spend the next few chapters talking about specific areas of public health that are of concern, and where gendered differences can clearly be seen. You will see what those gendered differences are, and why gender, gender stereotypes and gender inequality play a role. You will also see why, just like the types of activities I have described above, intervening in the early years is one important part of preventing these gendered public health issues and improving outcomes for all children.

Gender Boxes

I would also like to introduce you to gender boxes, because they will keep coming up over the next few chapters. These were first used in training activities by Paul Kivel[4] and the Oakland Men's Project back in the 1980s, and recently became more widely known by Tony Porter, who does a great TED Talk explaining exactly what we mean by the harms caused by gender stereotypes.[5] The gender boxes help us to understand what happens to people when we impose gender stereotypes on them: how it influences the way they think and act, and what happens when we step outside these boxes.

Think of the phrase, "Behave like a lady!" Hopefully this isn't a phrase you use very often (or at all!), but you may hear it – or versions of it – from family members, people in the community, the media and elsewhere. How about "That's not very ladylike!" or "Daddy's little princess"? Now think about the phrase "Act like a man" or similar phrases like "Come on, son, be a man", "Don't cry like a girl" or those all-time favourites, "Man-up!" and "Grow a pair!" Now imagine a child growing up hearing those phrases directed at themselves or others, and imagine them constructing a box of all the instructions they are given about how they as a boy, or girl, should be. Add into it everything we've discussed already from the media about how we should look, what clothes we should wear, what activities we should do, what personalities we should have, what friendships and relationships we should develop, what school subjects we should enjoy or be good at, and what careers we should follow. Don't forget the roles we should play in our romantic relationships when we grow up. You could end up with a couple of gender boxes that look something like those in Figure 5.1.

These are the boxes we are given at birth – or, as we've already seen, even before we are born. As Gina Rippon and others showed us in Chapter 3, children, or "junior gender detectives", start filling them in with ideas based on what society tells them, and add to them as they get older. By the time we are adults, they might begin to look something like Figure 5.2.

As I'm sure you will agree, none of us fits inside our given box – that is, the one assigned to us at birth depending on whether we have a male or female body – all the time. Even while they are picking up on the gender clues society gives them, children will sometimes try out something different (maybe because they are bold enough to venture outside gender

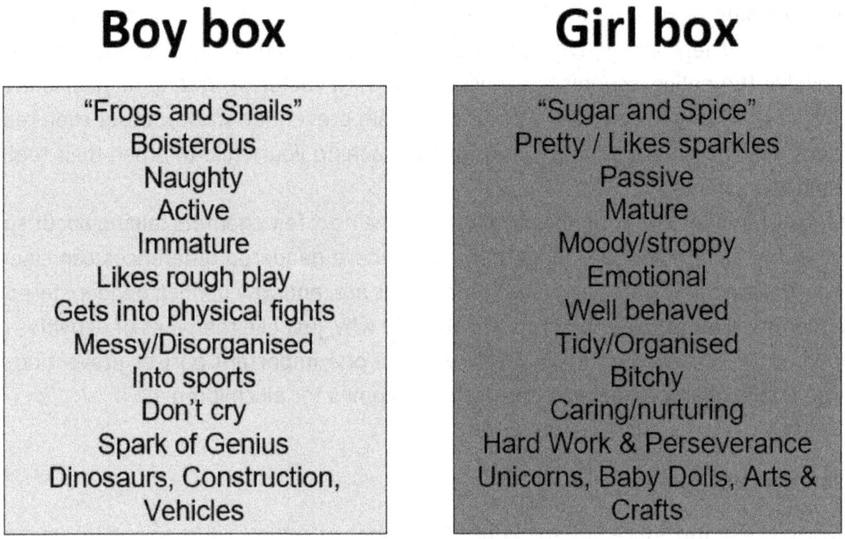

Boy box

"Frogs and Snails"
Boisterous
Naughty
Active
Immature
Likes rough play
Gets into physical fights
Messy/Disorganised
Into sports
Don't cry
Spark of Genius
Dinosaurs, Construction, Vehicles

Girl box

"Sugar and Spice"
Pretty / Likes sparkles
Passive
Mature
Moody/stroppy
Emotional
Well behaved
Tidy/Organised
Bitchy
Caring/nurturing
Hard Work & Perseverance
Unicorns, Baby Dolls, Arts & Crafts

Figure 5.1

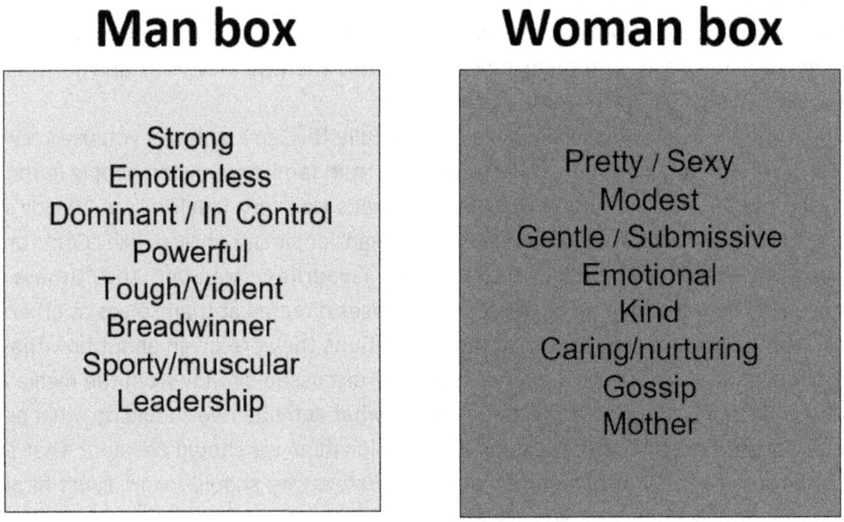

Man box

Strong
Emotionless
Dominant / In Control
Powerful
Tough/Violent
Breadwinner
Sporty/muscular
Leadership

Woman box

Pretty / Sexy
Modest
Gentle / Submissive
Emotional
Kind
Caring/nurturing
Gossip
Mother

Figure 5.2

norms, or because they forget the "rules" they have learned, or maybe because it's an area where no one has yet told them the gender "rule" – like my own example in Chapter 3 of a little boy singing along happily to "Let It Go"). As they get older, we might see boys who want to join dance classes, wear a sparkly t-shirt or enjoy sewing or baking. We see girls who take an interest in science, are good leaders or are assertive and clever enough to question something or contradict someone in class. Later we see young people in relationships that might not fit this heterosexual, gendered norm, or who don't dress in a way that neatly fits their given category. Increasingly, we see dads choosing to stay at home with their children and mums who want to return to work and climb the career ladder, or women choosing not to have children at all. We have female public figures who speak out against gender stereotypes, racism, the climate crisis and other forms of injustice.

All this means that it is possible to step outside of your gender box. But what happens to those who do? Think about what society says about children, young people or adults who do these things. What words and phrases are used about them? How do others react?

Unfortunately, for many people in these situations, the reaction is quite negative. We have thankfully moved on from the "sticks and stones may break my bones but names will never hurt me" mentality, and realise the power of words. People who step outside these boxes may hear many negative, offensive and hurtful things said about them over and over again. Often these words and phrases involve questioning a person's sexuality - something we will pick up on later. Some involve threats - think of the rape and death threats and other abuse that female politicians face, particularly online, on a daily basis (particularly, and disproportionately, Black and minority ethnic women members of parliament).[6] Sometimes things go beyond threats to actual physical or sexual violence.

All this "gender policing" is a demonstration of the enormous pressure that society exerts upon people to stay in their boxes. Over the following chapters, we will dive into some examples of these to look at why exactly this pressure exists (What exactly is the gender "crime" that has been committed?), as well as at the impact of experiencing this pressure and the punishments for not conforming.

So why do we have these boxes if all they do is harm people? Most societies today and through history are organised along patriarchal lines. This means men have control over property, moral authority, political leadership and social privilege. Until relatively recently in our history, all this has been upheld by law - for example, divorce, property and inheritance laws, voting rights and political representation, who was allowed to govern, preach, educate or be educated all favoured men over women.

> Did you know that until as recently as 1989, it was legal for a man in Scotland to rape his wife - and that in England it took until 1994 for marital rape to become illegal?

Today we are still struggling with issues like the gender pay gap, and allowing and encouraging men to take paternity leave. Although our laws have recently changed (and are continuing to change), and new generations are demonstrating changes in attitudes, there is still a long way to go, as we will show over the next few chapters. The people who stand to gain from the gender boxes are those who currently have (and historically have had) the most privilege: affluent, able-bodied, heterosexual, White men. An affluent, able-bodied, heterosexual, White man can also be harmed by the gender boxes, as we will also show, but in general he stands to gain more in the way of power and privilege from them than anyone else in the system. Whenever there is a power structure, those with the most power need tools to keep that structure in place, and the gender boxes are one of those tools.

What about everyone else? Why do we all keep going with these gender boxes? There are two reasons. Even those who aren't at the top exist within a hierarchy where we get to exert little bits of power over other people. For example, those of us who earn might be judgemental towards people on benefits because it makes us feel superior; or White feminists have been accused of excluding and silencing Black feminists because issues of racism are seen as a distraction from the mainstream feminist agenda; or an able-bodied person might ignore the needs of a disabled person because it's just easier. It is also easier to hang on to the small amount of power, or privilege, that you have than to recognise it and risk losing it. Second, this system has been going for thousands of years – and certainly for all of our lifetimes – so, like the gender stereotypes that confront us before we are even born, we have internalised it. It governs how we see ourselves, and others, in the world, so of course we carry on acting it out – until we recognise it and stop to think, and hopefully then work out how we can do things differently.

It's All Connected ... the Allport Scale

A final thought on the "What's the harm?" question comes courtesy of a 1950s psychologist, Gordon Allport. It might seem a little off-topic at first, but this is important for those moments when someone says, "Lighten up, it's only a joke!", so please bear with me and all will become clear.

Allport was interested in explaining the fairly recent (at that time) Holocaust and the fact that millions of people had gone from being neighbours and friends and even family with Jewish people to standing by while they were murdered on the streets in front of them, or in concentration camps. He realised that this change in attitude and behaviour didn't happen overnight: there was a process that began with tolerating (and even encouraging) negative language towards Jewish people –for example, spreading rumours and lies about their supposed role in the bad state of the German economy. Later, laws were introduced that restricted the movements of Jewish people, and limited their ability to trade and to socialise with non-Jews. Kristallnacht, when Jewish-owned shop windows were smashed and properties looted and vandalised, followed and Jews began to be attacked on the streets and arrested and removed from their homes by representatives of the state, with ordinary citizens joining in or standing by. Finally things reached the almost-unbelievable situation where a lot of thought and organisation went into the state-approved methods of mass extermination of Jews, and others seen as 'undesirable' (including communists, gypsies, disabled and LGBT+ people) in concentration camps.

Allport came up with a model, the Allport scale of prejudice, which has been used and adapted many times, and which shows this progression from words at the bottom to murder at the top. Figure 5.3 shows a version of the scale that we have created.

We can adapt Allport's scale to understand prejudice and discrimination against any group of people. To explain where we come in with gender, the examples across the bottom show those words, phrases, "jokes" and "banter" that take place in many playgrounds, workplaces and pubs across our society. Some of these we saw when we looked at the media; others we will discuss as we go on. Further up the scale we can see stereotypes and examples of

Figure 5.3

outright discrimination, and towards the top of the scale are some of the harms we'll be talking about in this section of the book.

Movement up the scale isn't inevitable: people who make jokes in pubs don't have to go on to commit crimes like sexual assault and murder – and the vast majority don't. That's why the scale is a pyramid: the stuff that happens at the bottom is much more widespread, and it supports a smaller number of people doing the stuff at the top. Tolerating the behaviours at the bottom of the scale (for example, laughing at sexist jokes and not calling out stereotypes) allows some people to think these things are okay (and to believe that other people think they are okay), and to progress to more harmful behaviours. (In Chapter 12, we will also look at the impact of being on the receiving end of these seemingly less-harmful behaviours, also known as micro aggressions.) When states support some of the lower-level activities – for example, a ban on women drivers and restrictions on women's movements without a male 'protector' – the consequences at the top can also be seen at a state level (for example, a lack of legislation against domestic abuse and capital punishment for adultery. But even on an individual level in a country where we don't have such draconian laws, if we tolerate the behaviours at the bottom, we clear a path for some people to form attitudes and practise behaviours that may incrementally lead them and others towards the top where they are actually hurting and killing people because of their stereotyped views about them, along with other factors.

Speaking out against things can be uncomfortable, difficult, even risky – to our personal safety, our personal relationships, our careers. In Chapter 18, we will look at ways of building confidence and abilities in this area – both our own and those of the children in our lives.

The overall message here is that you, as early years practitioners and just as people, have an important role to play in tackling the stuff that happens at the bottom of the Allport Scale. So if anyone ever challenges what you are doing or asks whether it really is such a big deal, or if you yourself begin to have doubts that this matters, just remember that it's all part of a sliding scale. What you do now for the children in your care will have consequences for them throughout their lives.

Notes

1 This is an adapted version of a well-used story that is often used to illustrate the idea of upstream approaches. There isn't a definitive, original source but there are animated versions on YouTube.
2 www.pathseducation.co.uk
3 https://mhfainternational.org
4 https://paulkivel.com
5 *Tony Porter –A Call to Men*, 10 December 2010. TED Talk. Available at www.youtube.com/watch?v=td1P bsV6B80 (accessed 2 January 2022). See also www.acalltomen.org (accessed 2 January 2022).
6 Amnesty International, "UK Black and Asian Women MPs Abused More". Available at: www.amnesty. org.uk/online-violence-women-mps (accessed 2 January 2022).

6 Violence Against Women and Girls

Barbara Adzajlic

Why You Should Read This Chapter

Working with children and families, it's important to know the extent of violence against women and the impact it can have on children. Around one in three women will experience domestic abuse or another form of violence against women in their lives. That means many of the children with whom you work will have family members who are affected, some will have direct experience of it themselves and others will experience it when they grow up. Gender inequality is a root cause of violence against women. We will look at how gender stereotypes influence the way we view relationships, power dynamics and the values we place on women and men, girls and boys. We will finish off with suggestions for things you can start doing right now to disrupt the damaging narrative that underpins violence against women.

Over the course of this chapter and the next, we will look at male violence. It is a complex issue in terms of where it comes from, how it manifests and what can be done about it. As always, we'll direct you towards further reading if you want to delve further. In the next chapter we look at men as perpetrators *and* victims of violence, but in this one we look at a specific form of male violence: violence against women and girls (VAWG).[1] We cover what it is, why it's a gendered issue, how gender stereotypes, from the early years onwards, influence the violence that women and girls experience from men and boys, and how they impact the way society responds.

For me, this topic is what convinced me that we need to do something about gender stereotypes. Working for several years on the prevention of VAWG, coming into contact with some of the brilliant organisations operating in Glasgow, Scotland and around the world to prevent and respond to it, I became more aware of the underlying issues that allow VAWG to continue to be such a huge issue in every society. I was involved in developing what we were calling "prevention work" for schools, including drama education programmes helping children and young people to identify unhealthy relationships and encouraging them to seek support. While these programmes were great, I still felt we weren't really *preventing* the problem – more trying to intervene early. It was while I was puzzling over this that I attended

DOI: 10.4324/9781003167921-9

that conference with Susie where the ideas behind our approach were born, and things started to fall into place.

What is Violence Against Women and Girls?

VAWG is an umbrella term that covers a range of behaviours committed, overwhelmingly by men, against women and girls. The Scottish Government, many campaigning bodies across the United Kingdom and abroad, and international bodies like the United Nations and the World Health Organisation (WHO), recognise that VAWG is both a symptom and a cause of gender inequality.[2]

VAWG includes domestic abuse (also known as domestic violence); rape and sexual assault; stalking and harassment; commercial sexual exploitation; forced and child marriage; and female genital mutilation (FGM). At the time of writing, increasing attention is being paid to the worrying levels of misogyny that girls are experiencing at school and in the community, in the United Kingdom and across the world.[3] While we know that many of these issues also affect men and boys, the statistics show us that the vast majority of perpetrators are men and the vast majority of victims/survivors are women or girls.[4] And while we know that it can be very difficult for men to report things like domestic abuse and sexual assault when it happens to them (for reasons related, as always, to gender stereotypes and the cultural pressure to not be seen as a victim), we also know that women and girls under-report.[5] The #MeToo movement and the many revelations that followed point to how many women felt unable to speak up about rape and sexual assault because the men involved were too powerful; because they felt they wouldn't be believed; because of the potential impact on their careers and reputations; and because it was seen as normal behaviour, to be expected and to be put up with.

Returning to the Allport Scale that we discussed in Chapter 5, there are also layers and layers of sexist and misogynistic behaviours that women do not report for these same reasons - for example, street harassment and sexual harassment at work and in school. These experiences contribute to the climate of fear with which many women live daily, and that impacts their decisions about whether to go out jogging alone, meet up with friends at night or spend money on taxis home. So although men are much more likely *statistically* to experience violence from other men, we must still acknowledge the very real fears that women have to work around, the massive scale of unreported threats and assaults they experience and the fact that women face the most danger in their own homes and from men they know, in the form of domestic abuse.

Another area where VAWG is often different from violence that happens to men within relationships concerns the impact it has. Qualitative analysis of the 2000 Scottish Crime Survey found that "the 'typical' female victim was more severely victimised, more fearful, more unhealthy, and less financially independent than both the 'typical' male victim and other non-victimised women".[6] It also found that the scale of domestic abuse was over-reported by men in the original survey, partly due to misunderstanding the question. These are both important points in understanding the gendered nature of domestic abuse and other forms of VAWG.[7]

The issues here are very much gendered at every level: who commits violence and why; against whom; who gets believed and why; how it gets reported; and what the consequences are. Gender stereotypes are at the heart of it.

The Impact of VAWG

Domestic abuse is recognised as an adverse childhood experience (ACE) and, like other forms of trauma and violence experienced by children, of course there can be a huge impact on those children's lives. Mental, physical and social health consequences for children include the emotional impact of seeing or hearing their parent subjected to physical or verbal abuse, or of being used by the perpetrator as part of the abuse; barriers to socialising with other children due to what is happening at home; loss of relationships, homes, possessions and pets; the physical danger of being caught up in the violence; and the impact all this can have on a child's performance at school and their future education, career and relationship prospects. Some adult victims turn to substance abuse as a way to cope; others lose careers, homes, friends and family; and there is a huge risk of physical injury, mental illness and loss of life. This is far from an exhaustive list, and the other forms of VAWG also have a range of consequences. It takes incredible strength and resilience to survive and escape these situations. But there is also a wider impact on the whole of society: emergency services dealing with the immediate effects of an assault (over 20 per cent of all operational police time in Scotland is spent responding to domestic incidents);[8] third-sector organisations and social workers trying to protect children and vulnerable adults; mental health services dealing with the trauma; court processes dealing with perpetrators; and the impact on the families, friends and communities of victims/survivors and perpetrators. A 2019 estimate put the total economic and social cost of domestic abuse in England and Wales at £66 billion.[9]

All this is to say that VAWG has a huge cost not just to individuals but to society as a whole, and that stamping it out would benefit everyone.

What's the Link with Gender Stereotypes?

So how are gender stereotypes contributing to this problem? VAWG is both a cause and a consequence of gender inequality. This means that being subject to, or under threat of, these forms of violence – often on a daily basis – undermines women's and girls' opportunities to participate equally in society. But it also means that gender inequality at every level of our society affects the way we view, and behave towards, each other, and also contributes to VAWG.

Think back to the gender boxes in Chapter 5 and to the conclusion that, although they are harmful to nearly everyone, the "man" box holds power over the "woman" box. As we discussed, most societies consider man box qualities to be superior and women box qualities to be "less than" – which is why men displaying woman box qualities are often derided or attacked. When we tell one group of people throughout their lives that they are superior to another group, make efforts to back this up with science, protect it with laws or a lack of them, justify it in our media and see it reflected in representations across society, the consequences aren't hard to predict. While there will always be people who rebel against this narrative, it isn't hard to see how, overall, we are teaching boys from a young age that they are superior, should be in control and are entitled to certain things, like access to women's bodies or demanding that they "smile, love". We are also teaching girls that they are inferior, should be protected/controlled and that they should adapt their behaviours according to what others require. How many times have you heard, "He just did it because he doesn't know how else to show he likes you!" or heard about girls' clothing choices being policed by adults?

The consequences of these attitudes manifest differently across different cultures and time, with all sorts of double standards in place. For example, think back to the days of so-called chivalry, when well-off White women were considered delicate and in need of protection from exposure to anything more exciting than the drawing room, but working-class and Black women were expected to work hard and feel no pain, and were raped with impunity by their White masters. Nowadays we have more protection and rights enshrined within law, but also more overt misogyny in the form of men's rights activists, incels and pickup artists – all of which is now being seen in our schools and communities.[10]

For another way to understand these links between gender stereotypes and VAWG, try watching these two very short clips and thinking about some of the themes we have talked about already in this book – from the different language we use and expectations we have of boys and girls to structural inequality and discrimination.

> *Our Watch: Let's Change the Story: Violence Against Women in Australia*. YouTube, 30 March 2017. YouTube video.
> www.youtube.com/watch?v=fLUVWZvVZXw
> *It's Time for Prevention*. YouTube, 7 October 2020. www.youtube.com/watch?v=reOFiNX2Efl

Victim Blaming

The other point to remember about the gender boxes is the fine line women and girls are expected to tread regarding their appearance and behaviour. Girls are expected from a young age to take care of their appearance and, as grown-ups, we reinforce this by acknowledging their appearance and placing a value on it that we don't tend to do for boys: "Don't you look lovely today!" (more on this and what to do about it in the 'how' section of this book). But go too far and they are seen by some as dressing inappropriately and "tempting" men and boys who apparently can't control themselves (back to blaming those "raging hormones", discussed in Chapter 3). This plays into the world of VAWG in a number of ways. A great example is the debate about so-called "modesty shorts" for primary school girls, which retailers have come up with as a solution to girls' underwear being exposed when they do cartwheels and handstands in the playground. On the face of it, it's a good solution for girls who don't feel comfortable that their underwear is on show, allowing them to still participate – but calling them modesty shorts implies that not to wear them would be immodest, and that girls are inviting attention. It is like a sticking plaster that causes a skin reaction – it brings its own problems and it doesn't solve the original issue that we are expecting girls to do gymnastics in totally inappropriate clothing.[11] Once we have planted the idea of "immodesty", we get into all sorts of victim-blaming scenarios: "If you hadn't worn that short skirt he wouldn't have put his hand up it" … "If you'd had his dinner ready on time he wouldn't have lost his temper and hit you." These might seem outdated, but Dr Jessica Taylor has written about women-blaming attitudes using case studies from her research and experience, and shows these attitudes to be very much alive and well today.[12]

To explore this idea further, I spoke with Dr Nancy Lombard, a researcher with Glasgow Caledonian University. In 2014, Nancy conducted research with 11- and 12-year-old children in Glasgow primary schools to explore their attitudes towards violence and how their ideas about gender roles played into victim-blaming attitudes.[13] She made use of short stories about hypothetical characters, like the following example:

> Claire and Lee have been seeing each other for four months. Claire's favourite outfit is her jeans and vest top. Lee has asked Claire not to wear the vest top because he says other boys look at her and he doesn't like this.

Nancy told me that the example "illustrated how the young people justified men's violence against women using gender stereotypes and a rigid understanding of adult relationships framed by heterosexuality". She found "themes of obedience, ownership and possession, entitlement and 'victim' blaming'". The first group of responses demonstrates the way that children believed girls should show obedience, and modify their behaviour:

> *Lily:*   Because they're a couple, she should do what he says.
> *Craig:*   It might upset him if she doesn't do what he's asked.
> *Lucy:*   She could just wear a cardy over it. And then just wear it when she's not with him, so he won't know.
> *Rosie:*   I would wear the top. But I think that if it was really obvious that people were looking at me then I would wear a wee jumper.

Another group of responses show us the children expressing that, as her boyfriend, Lee has some ownership of Claire:

> *Fatima:*   But as long as Claire keeps saying to Lee that she doesn't care. She's going out with him, it doesn't matter what they think, then maybe he would feel a bit more reassured.
> *Craig:*   He's the one who is going to be stood beside her when she's out. And he'll look stupid if he's the one that is going out with her and other boys are looking at her.

And finally, we see a sense of Lee's entitlement to be the boss in the relationship:

> *Samia:* [If you] upset Lee … it might drive him away from you.
> *Daniel:* If she wants to be with him then she shouldn't [wear it].
> *Emmy:* She should do what Lee says if she doesn't want him to leave her. He's told her what she should do.
> *Jake:* It's not fair for her to make Lee feel like that. She shouldn't wear that vest.

Nancy also found evidence of victim-blaming attitudes like those I described earlier in this chapter:

> An example of the process of "blaming the victim" and thereby justifying violence, had to do with the sexualisation of the female body, limiting girls' choices with moral and sexual responsibilities and the restrictive codes attributed to it. These responsibilities included modestly covering her body (with more clothing) and being aware of the reaction that her [clothed] body may incite.

Victim-blaming came up with several of the groups with which Nancy worked, and with both girls and boys. Nancy says that "locating the issue with Claire subscribes to the notion that women are defined by how men view them, with clothing becoming sexualised and encoded with the means of pleasing or displeasing men". In the next set of responses, we can see the children using active "doing words" to describe the scenario, suggesting that Claire was inviting male attention through the sexualisation of her clothing:

> *Stewart:* She is *flaunting* herself in front of other people. She could be enjoying that lots of boys are looking at her.
> *Shaheeda:* She is *revealing* herself to the boys.
> *David:* She wants to wear the pink top to *expose* herself to them.
> *Cheryl:* She's got *slutty* clothes.

I'm sure you'll agree that these are some really shocking attitudes coming from anyone, and particularly when we remember these are 11- and 12-year-old children! Nancy agreed, and because of this decided during her research to flip the question so that it read:

> Lee and Claire have been seeing each other for four months. Lee's favourite outfit is his jeans and vest top. Claire has asked Lee not to wear the vest top because she says other boys look at him and she doesn't like this.

Before reading the responses, please pause for a moment and have a think about what you would expect to hear from the children who made the earlier remarks. Here are some of the responses:

Amy:	She can't tell him what to do.
Robbie:	She's not the boss of him.
Luke:	She can't tell him what to wear. If he likes them, he can wear them.
Jill:	She is just jealous of other girls looking at him.
Nick:	If she felt secure with him she wouldn't ask him not to wear them.
Billy:	It's not on, she can't say that.
Carl:	What gives her the right to say he can't wear his own top?

Surprised? When we have used this in training, we get a mixture of responses – but whether or not people expected to see these double standards, they are always saddened by them. For Nancy, "These contrasting reactions illustrate everything we need to know about how young people understand gender, power and relationships. This is why gender matters in an analysis of violence."

The research also contained interesting findings about the idea of violence:

> [Young people] tended to naturalise violence as an integral part of "male" identity and they justified men's violence using expectations of inequality in gender roles. Violence that occurred among peers and siblings was normalised and therefore not labelled as violent.

Nancy reported that "real" violence was seen as being committed by men; in a public space; serious; resulting in an intervention (like for example two men having a fight in the street, where the police get called and there are consequences like a jail sentence). What does this say about the kind of violence that women might experience in relationships, and how we are setting up girls to experience this? According to Nancy:

> Girls in particular told me about a multitude of experiences of being pushed, shoved, kicked, followed and called sexualised names by their male peers. To them, these examples did not fit the standardised constellation structure of real violence – age (adult); gender (man); space (public); action (physical) and crucially, they were generally without official reaction or consequence. Time and time again when they approached teachers or those in authority, the girls were dismissed for telling tales; ignored because of the so called trivial nature of their complaint or relayed that old adage "he's only doing it because he likes you". So their experiences were minimised and the behaviours normalised. This results in girls being unable to access a framework by which to make sense of their own experiences and it serves to invalidate and minimise many of their experiences of violence and violent behaviour. This is then replicated in their adult lives, where much violent behaviour is seen as the "everyday interactions" between men and women.

#NotAllMen

This hashtag is very prominent at the time of writing because of some high-profile violent male behaviour towards women, and it's incredibly unhelpful. We all know that most men don't rape or abuse their female partners, or pay for sex. But if we think back to the Allport Scale, what would be the behaviours at the bottom of the scale that support, condone or justify these behaviours at the top? Sexist jokes and comments, the normalisation of stalking and controlling behaviour in popular "rom coms" (try rewatching *There's Something About Mary*, *Love Actually* and *The Amazing Spiderman*, which are full of examples of behaviour by the male heroes that, in real life, could land them in jail) and "rating" of women and girls by boys and men on social media, all sit at the lower levels, and all add to the general attitude in society of men being "on the prowl" and women being the prey; of men being entitled to things like access to women's bodies, and women "asking for it". There is a role for all men and boys here to step up and call out VAWG at all levels on this scale, from not laughing at that joke in the pub to challenging their "gropey" friend that his behaviour is out of line.

This is tricky, and calling out bad behaviour can put you in a risky position. But there is some fantastic work going on around the world to involve men in a positive way in ending VAWG. The international White Ribbon Campaign encourages men to sign up to a pledge never to commit, condone or remain silent about VAWG[14]. It brings men into the conversation in ways that challenge the patriarchal structures we all live with and point to how they disadvantage all of us. White Ribbon Scotland Director Davy Thompson has several years' experience working with groups of men and boys in a variety of settings, including schools, youth clubs and other community groups, to help them understand their role in ending VAWG. He describes the "what about the men" bit as the initial stumbling block:

> Because men just feel they're instantly under attack ... in just about every group we talk to, someone will turn around and go, "you do realise we're not the guys that do this?" ... and we go, "yes, that's why we're talking to you" because those are the guys we need to get active!

With the right approach, men and boys can be supported to understand their role in all of this, to acknowledge that it isn't just a "women's issue" and to become allies.

What Can You Do?

Like all our "whys", this is a big and complex issue, and not one that early years practitioners can tackle alone. Change is needed at every level of our society to make sure girls and boys are equally valued, equally respected and, in the words of Scotland's national strategy, Equally Safe. Schools and youth workers, advertisers, the film and music industries, politics, justice and others need to rethink the ways in which they understand and respond to the various forms of violence that men and boys perpetrate against women and girls. It's easy to feel daunted by the scale of the problem. White Ribbon UK and many others were signatories to an open letter to the UK Government calling for early intervention on gender stereotypes, which states that, "This will not be a quick fix, but we have to start right now so that outcomes improve for the next generation."[15]

The good news is that there are many ways that you can make a difference around prevention, early intervention and responding to violent situations you're aware of. Davy Thompson believes that tackling gender stereotypes in the early years is a vital and optimistic part of this effort, and that the link with parents and families is crucial:

From the outset of this I thought [the approach] was fantastic ... it's so important to be in at nursery level. And part of that importance isn't just about getting there in the early years, it's about the fact that nursery teachers get to see parents every day when they drop kids off and pick them up ... it's not that they're having big conversations with everybody every day, but they get that opportunity to clarify what they're doing, regularly. There needs to be the work informing the people who are going to influence the people that you're trying to get on board, and I think that's what approaches like this do, because you've got that opportunity where they can reinforce the thinking, through the parents, and get them on board. There's so much hope built into that.

So take heart from the fact that, as early years practitioners, leaders in the fight to end VAWG recognise your importance!

- Contact your local women's aid and/or rape crisis centre for more information on their work. They may have prevention or partnership workers who can offer training on understanding the warning signs, and how to respond to help the families about which you are concerned. If not, they may be able to point you to online training options, or to further reading that will help you.
- Follow up any concerns you may have according to your normal child protection procedures, or contact your local authority for advice. Be careful about challenging perpetrators as this can sometimes lead to further harm to the victims.
- Be a supportive, listening ear to children or families who are experiencing or have experienced violence or abuse.
- Look out for and support bystander programmes for men, like White Ribbon and others mentioned in this chapter. Encourage the men and boys in your life to get involved. Talk to boys and young men about problematic attitudes in their peer groups, or discuss news items about VAWG and look at the ways victims/survivors and perpetrators are portrayed – help them to develop critical thinking.
- Model healthy, respectful and equal relationships in the ways you normally would through your own language and behaviours, and your resources. Keep an eye out for any early unhealthy behaviours, or attitudes towards roles and relationships, that might be showing up through play or conversation, and use teachable moments to address and gently challenge them.
- Support campaigns for better legislation around VAWG, at home and abroad. There is still much work to be done to tackle institutional misogyny in areas like education, the police force, the criminal justice system. We need to change this and create a culture where women feel confident reporting crimes against them, where they will be believed and supported.
- Tackle gender stereotypes! If children are hearing negative, gender-stereotyped messages at home, in their community or from the media, do everything you can to provide an alternative narrative showing that women are equal to men, girls are equal to boys and no one should have power and control over another person, in any situation. For example:
    - Think about your use of language. Do you inadvertently compliment girls on their appearance? For sitting nicely and being quiet? Boys for being tough?

- Practise early consent messages (NHS Greater Glasgow and Clyde's Early Protective Messages[16] programme is a good example).
- Make sure your expectations of boys' and girls' behaviour are consistent – don't tolerate boys "being boys", or show disapproval of girls' assertiveness.
- Intervene if play situations start to replicate unhealthy or unequal power relations.
- Actively encourage all children, and girls in particular, to speak out if they feel uncomfortable in a situation, and show them that you will take their concerns seriously.

Notes

1 We could also use the term "gender-based violence" because it is helpful in reminding us that this type of violence happens within the context of unequal gender relations, and because it includes more than women and girls. Limiting it to women and girls can allow us to ignore the perpetrators, and also to ignore other issues that come up in this context, around same-sex relationships and power relations between older and younger people. But for the purposes of this chapter and to distinguish between male violence against men in the chapter that follows, we'll use VAWG as a definition.

2 Scotland's Equally Safe strategy was ground-breaking in making this link explicit: See www.gov. scot/publications/equally-safe-scotlands-strategy-prevent-eradicate-violence-against-women-girls (accessed 2 February 2022).

3 L. Clark, "The Trouble with Boys: What Lies Behind the Flood of Teenage Sexual Assault Stories?", *The Guardian*, 26 February 2021. Available at www.theguardian.com/society/2021/feb/27/the-trouble-with-boys-what-lies-behind-the-flood-of-teenage-sexual-assault-stories (accessed 20 January 2022).

4 For example, in 2019–20, 82 per cent of domestic abuse incidents recorded by Police Scotland had a female victim and a male perpetrator: see www.gov.scot/publications/domestic-abuse-statistics-recorded-police-scotland-2019-20/pages/2 (accessed 2 February 2022). By legal definition, (penetration with a penis), 100 per cent of rapists in the United Kingdom are men.

5 For example, the Crime Survey for England and Wales (CSEW) for the years ending March 2017 and March 2020 combined showed that fewer than one in six victims (16 per cent) had reported the assault to the police. See www.ons.gov.uk/peoplepopulationandcommunity/crimeandjustice (accessed 2 February 2022).

6 D. Gadd, D. Dallimore and N. Lombard, "Male Victims of Domestic Violence", *Criminal Justice Matters*, 53(1) (2003), 16–17.

7 This isn't to deny that some men do experience abuse that affects their physical and mental health. Some do (sometimes at the hands of other men, sometimes women), and they deserve support and to have their voices and experiences heard. There are support services for men – see supporting resources for more information.

8 Safe Lives, *Whole Lives: Improving the response to domestic abuse in Scotland* (2017). Available at: https://safelives.org.uk/policy-evidence/whole-lives-improving-response-domestic-abuse-scotl and (accessed 2 February 2022).

9 R. Oliver, B. Alexander, S. Roe and M. Wlasny, *The Economic and Social Costs of Domestic Abuse* (London: Home Office, 2019). Available at https://assets.publishing.service.gov.uk/government/uplo ads/system/uploads/attachment_data/file/918897/horr107.pdf (accessed 2 February 2022).

10 For a better understanding of this fairly recent phenomenon, see L. Bates, *Men Who Hate Women* (London: Simon & Schuster, 2020).

11 Don't get me started on those school shoes that let the rain in and how girls' school clothing (and lots of other girls' clothing) discourages them from being as physically active as boys!

12 J. Taylor, *Why Women are Blamed for Everything: Exploring Victim Blaming of Women Subjected to Violence and Trauma*. London: Victim Focus.

13 N. Lombard, "Because They're a Couple She Should Do What He Says": Young People's Justifications of Violence: Heterosexuality, Gender and Adulthood". *Journal of Gender Studies*, 25(3) (2016), 241–53.

14 www.whiteribbon.org.uk and www.whiteribbonscotland.org.uk. Other examples of men's movements include the UN's He for She campaign and Mentors in Violence Prevention.

15 "Early Intervention Necessary to Prevent Violence Against Women and Girls". Open letter to the UK Government, 31 May 2021. Available at www.fawcettsociety.org.uk/news/joint-letter-calling-for-early-intervention-on-gender-stereotypes

16 www.sandyford.scot/parents-sandyford/pre-5/early-protective-messages

7 Man Up! Gender Stereotypes and Male Violence

Susie Heywood

Why You Should Read This Chapter

As an early years practitioner, it's vitally important to understand the needs of the boys in your care. When it comes to gender expression, boys are heavily policed – deviations from masculine norms are often quickly if subtly corrected. The roots of the health and social problems that disproportionately impact men, such as violence and suicide, can be found in the gender stereotypes and gender roles they are taught from early childhood. This chapter explains this in more detail and provides useful strategies for tackling this in the early years.

We have already explored how the ways in which we define masculinity and femininity can change over place and time, and have introduced the idea of "Gender Boxes" as a way to understand gender stereotypes. This chapter examines the way in which these prevailing narratives about masculinity are fuelling one of the great public health crises we face today – one which harms us all: men, women and children. We are talking about male violence.

Michael Kauffman, co-founder of the White Ribbon campaign that we learned about in the preceding chapter, describes male violence as a triad that includes male violence against women, against each other and against themselves.[1] We know that the majority of men do not commit violence, that men can be the victims of violence and that women can be perpetrators; however, we only need to look at our prison population, or at crime statistics broken down by gender, to understand violence as a gendered issue. While we need to pay attention to what we learned about what society constitutes as real violence, which may be leading to an under reporting of violence against women, our current statistics show that men are both the most likely to perpetrate and to fall victim to violence, so we need to discuss violence as a men's issue.

The Impact of the "Man Box" on Boys and Men

When we talk about the "man box", we are talking about the dominant or hegemonic masculinity in our society – the qualities and characteristics that are held up as the ideal to which

DOI: 10.4324/9781003167921-10

males should aspire should they want to be "a real man". This idea of masculinity is not new, and there is no doubt that what we expect of men has changed – for example, think of how the role of the father has changed from previous generations; however, the narrative of strong, self-sufficient, unemotional men who provide for and protect their families still runs deep. Many people describe this as "toxic masculinity", although this term may be unhelpful. Graham Goulden, a former police officer turned violence prevention trainer explains:

> I don't like the term "toxic masculinity". A lot of the work I do is to try to engage boys and young men to be part of the solution, and I think if you start off with a negative then it induces shame, especially if you are working with young men in prison, for example, who are already shamed anyway. It's not a good place to start. I like starting from the positive. Masculinity in itself isn't toxic for me, but there are a few men out there who really make it difficult for boys and men.

It is good to note that some of the qualities we might associate with "toxic masculinity", such as strength, aggression, stoicism and male solidarity – which are highly problematic when they are used to oppress or exert power over others – can be positive qualities when used at the right time. What is harmful is the pressure to conform to this narrow idea of manhood. The pressure can begin in childhood, and is perpetuated and reinforced in unconscious, subtle and direct ways, causing very real harm to boys and men.

Did you know that:

- In England in 2019–20, boys were permanently excluded from school at three times the rate of girls.[2]
- At the time of writing there were 76,052 men in prison in England and Wales compared with 3232 women.[3] In Scotland, we see a similar pattern: 96 per cent of prisoners are male.[4]
- Over the past decade in England and Wales, there were 4493 male victims of killings and 2075 female victims (31 per cent), and men were far likelier to be the victims of violent assault in England and Wales.[5]
- Men are 2.7 times more likely to suffer a drug related death than women.[6]
- In all Western countries, the suicide rate is significantly higher amongst men. In the United Kingdom, three times as many men take their own lives than women.[7]

The statistics listed above are worrying, and each deserves to be examined in more detail. It is important to note that many of these statistics might tell an additional story about the additional disadvantages faced by certain kinds of men should they be broken down further. For example, when it comes to school exclusions, we know that rates are higher among pupils who are eligible for free school meals, with special educational needs or among Gypsy/Roma pupils. We know that young, working-class, Black men face more punitive policing and harsher sentencing in the criminal justice world, a result of those stereotypes that see Black men as aggressive and threatening. Intersecting inequalities increase disadvantage and it's vital we consider these in any analysis of issues for men. We will touch on these throughout this chapter, which will focus on the relationship between the "man box" and men as victims and perpetrators of violence.

Teaching Boys to Be Men

By far the most common type of interpersonal violence we see in the United Kingdom is physical violence committed by men, most likely against other men. If we look at male violence through a public health lens, we want to identify the root causes – the "why?" Are men naturally more violent and aggressive (perhaps as a result of all that testosterone?) or – thinking again about those "man boxes", does society place an expectation of those sorts of behaviours upon men and boys? Are we unwittingly priming boys for violence?

In Chapter 3, we looked at some evidence suggesting that, far from being a hormonally driven foregone conclusion, our actions and choices (and hormones) are very much informed by the environment and context in which we live. Male violence is not inevitable, but raising boys with expectations around toughness and strength must surely play a part in what we see down the line.

Educator Matt Pinkett certainly thinks socialisation has something to do with it. In the book *Boys Don't Try?*, he describes the mechanisms by which messages about societal expectations of male violence are delivered to children as they grow:

> The toy soldiers and camouflage duvet sets found under the "boys" section of the big department stores, in the plastic guns we give boys from Christmas and the super-hero chocolate eggs we give them at Easter, in the computer game shoot-'em-ups dominated by male "heroes" who shoot and stab and maim and kill, and in the Hollywood movies dominated by muscle-bound action men who solve all the world's problems with knuckles, rather than nous.[8]

We have demonstrated in previous chapters how pervasive messaging around gender roles is – even for children. It is clear that we cannot use biology as an excuse for men's violence, and it's quite insulting to men to suggest that they do not have control over these responses.

Children and Violence

 Reflection

Take a few minutes to reflect on your experiences and observations around violence, aggression and conflict in early years settings. Here are some questions to guide you:

- Do you think there are gender differences in how young children deal with conflict or aggression?
- Do you notice differences in how adults respond to conflict or aggression depending on the gender of the children?

- Do you see gender stereotypes of tough boys playing out in the behaviour of children in your setting? If so, how does it play out or manifest itself?
- Are "violent" interactions common in early years settings?
- How do you define violence?

I recently asked some early years practitioners about their experiences of violence and aggression in young children using similar questions. Their responses were interesting. According to practitioners:

- Children of both sexes, but most often boys, demonstrate feelings of anger and frustration by hitting, pushing, biting and kicking.
- "Violent'" play among boys is linked to TV and film characters such as superheroes, involving "killing baddies", high kicking and telling girls (although other boys are often included) that they can't join in because "it's too dangerous" and "girls can't fight".
- Particular children – mostly boys – lead groups of children – again mostly boys – in play that involves physical fighting, kicking and pretend shooting.
- There are gender differences in how children react to violence, with girls more likely to find an adult to tell and boys attempting to resolve it themselves, often through retaliation or lashing out.
- Children re-enact social cues learned at home or repeat stereotyped messages about what boys and girls should be like.

We know from the work of Cordelia Fine and Gina Rippon discussed in Chapter 3 that aggression is not hard-wired in boys. Gendered socialisation is clearly playing a role – remember that we prime boys from birth around stereotypes of toughness and strength. We know that the stereotypes affect how we interact with children, so it's important to reflect here on whether there are differences in how adults respond to boys and girls when it comes to problematic or aggressive behaviour. I spoke about this with a nursery manager, who explained her own experience:

> The main difference I see is how adults respond to conflict – boys expected to "toughen up" and the "boys will be boys" excuse, and shock and disbelief from adults if a girl responds to conflict in the stereotypically "boy" way. A stereotypical girl response to conflict, if it involves using language, is often viewed as "manipulative" or "nasty" while a stereotypical boy response is often viewed as "physical but more honest". The response of adults to conflicts directly influences how young children behave and perpetuates the stereotypes.

There are so many ways we could view this. Do we police little boys more because we expect them to be naughty? Do we encourage them by giving them more of our attention when they are? Given what we know about the pervasiveness of gender stereotypes and the impact of unconscious bias on our everyday interactions, a situation where boys' aggression is excused on biological grounds ("boys will be boys" – at least while they are young anyway) while aggression in girls (stepping outside the gender box) is seen as more problematic and policed quite differently is also not too hard to imagine – remember girls should be all things nice!

It feels safe to hypothesise that tolerating this behaviour in boys is likely to lead to a continuation of these kinds of aggressive responses through tacit acceptance. It does nothing to alleviate the pressure young boys may feel to maintain the tough guy stereotype. It also feeds the ongoing stereotype of the troublemaking naughty and under-achieving boy which has consequences for our boys. Graham explained his thoughts around this and how an acceptance of stereotypes about boys and their behaviour can negatively impact boys:

> That phrase: "boys will be boys" – we need to reclaim that back from the negative. It's used to excuse behaviour, but we need to claim it back, because boys are really struggling just now, academically, sexually, in relationships, and we expect them just to suck it up. We are playing into the stereotypes that boys are tough and strong, and they're not – they are deeply vulnerable.

We noted the gender difference around school exclusions and suspensions earlier. As a child, I often wondered why adults thought stopping someone from coming to school was a punishment: I mean, some of these kids acted like they really didn't want to be there, so sending them home looked to me to be more of a reward. However, as adults we know the cumulative impact that time out of school can have on children and their ability to achieve and perform, particularly where there are additional issues. The impact of constant tellings-off and punishments on the self-esteem and confidence of children can't be under-estimated either, and we know that boys do get reprimanded and punished more than girls in the classroom. Again, we know some boys may face additional scrutiny due to stereotypes associated with race, ethnicity or class. If our role as adults is to help young children to process difficult emotions, then we need to be aware of the role gender stereotypes can play in our responses and adapt accordingly.

We know too that from an early age, and increasingly as they grow older, boys police each other's behaviour according to masculine norms and expectations. Toughness, dominance, sporting ability and lack of vulnerability become a sort of code to which boys feel they have to adhere. Academic achievement or even being seen to try is often seen as girlish and popularity is often linked to how closely one conforms to masculine norms. Any slights on one's masculinity can be dealt with easily through a display of violence or misbehaviour. There are always exceptions, though, and we must remember that not all boys are like this.

The roots of all this lie in the early years, as already discussed in Chapter 3 where we saw the different ways in which adults interact with and react to the behaviours of infants depending on their sex, and the fact that gender quickly becomes an important identity marker for young children.

American activist and founder of "A Call to Men", Tony Porter, describes in his TED Talk "A Call to Men" the realisation he had about his unintentional responses to crying by his two young children. He describes how when his young daughter was upset he would comfort her as long as she needed, let her cry it out while he soothed and reassured her. However, his son – who was only one year older – received quite a different response. He described how whenever he started crying Tony would only give him a short time before he started asking him why he was crying, what was wrong and telling him to keep his head up, sending him to his room to calm down until he could talk to him *like a man*. Tony recognised that unintentionally he was letting society's expectations of what his boy should become in order to fit the "man box" affect the way he parented his children and the messages he was sending to them about how they should behave. I've had these lightbulb moments myself.[9]

As adults, we need to reflect on our interactions with children and ask ourselves what messages we are sending them about what is acceptable for and expected of them as they grow. If we don't teach boys the language and skills to deal with difficult emotions when they are young, how will they go on to deal with the inevitable emotional difficulties of adolescence and adulthood? We may be leaving them in a position where aggression is the easiest response. And by teaching them that these difficult emotions are somehow not "masculine" and are something to be ashamed of, we are doubling down on these messages. As Michael Kaufman puts it, "It is not simply that men's language of emotions is often muted or that our emotional antennae are somewhat stunted. It is also that a range of natural emotions have been ruled off limits and invalid."[10]

Before we move on, it's also important to note that we are in no way attempting to excuse violent behaviour by boys and men. Violence is always a choice, and those who commit acts of violence should be held personally accountable for their actions. Our interest here lies in how we can prevent such actions, and to do this we need to understand the "whys" around male violence if we are ever going to tackle this issue. We also need to be able to have conversations and responses that are rooted in compassion if we are to include everyone in the solutions.

Examining Male Violence in Adulthood

Those messages that we are teaching male children about what it means to be a boy don't stop as they grow older. They continue to be reinforced by a culture that celebrates aggression and glorifies violence. Graphic depictions of bloody violence – physical and sexual – have become commonplace in film, TV and gaming. Violence is sold as something that, far from being a "last resort" when it comes to disputes, is actually the preferred method – with the added bonus of earning the person inflicting the violence respect, credibility and "real man" status.

Violence is also a method by which a dominant individual or group can establish and maintain power. It can be used as a way of maintaining the dominant masculinity at times when it may be threatened. Jackson Katz sees a correlation between points in history where hegemonic masculinity has in some way been challenged – for example, when there have been gains in civil or women's rights, and the violence we see in film and TV. He argues that when we look at the media during these times, we can see very clear attempts to reclaim traditional masculinity through increased violence, bigger guns or storylines that show the masculine hero using violence to reassert his position. We are encouraged to celebrate these tough guys.[11]

Shows of strength and aggression can intimidate or subjugate, and can bring great benefits to those who wield it. I am sure we will all be familiar with the concept of male privilege, but we also need to recognise that even within a culturally dominant group, there will be a power hierarchy – which means some men will have power over others. Graham Goulden described exactly this when he told me that, "My view is that all violence is gendered. Because me as a man I am often controlled by other men's behaviour and I am at risk of men's violence who are trying to gain power over me."

So, for example, if we created a pyramid of male power, right at the top we are likely to find rich (or upper-class), White, able-bodied men, with working-class men of colour found somewhere near the bottom (note the intersections). This might explain why many men feel unable to identify with or accept the idea of male privilege, as they themselves may feel powerless or oppressed in aspects of their life.

The masculine ideal is one that consolidates male power, yet for most men this ideal is unrealistic and difficult to attain. The failure to achieve this ideal, and perhaps the very presence of traits that fall outside the masculine ideal, can lead some men to use violence as a way to reassert this masculinity, ironically very often against a weaker target. This is the phenomenon we described earlier, whereby men who step outside the "man box" can easily get back inside by picking a fight or using violence against another individual.

Men's Violence Against Themselves

Trigger warning: we are going to talk about suicide now, which can be a difficult topic for some – particularly if they have a personal experience with the issue. Please do look after yourself as you read on, and do find someone to talk to if you feel affected or are having thoughts of suicide yourself.

Some Facts About Suicide

- Every death by suicide is a tragedy that causes a ripple of pain across families and communities.
- For every person who dies by suicide, it is estimated that around 135 people are affected in some way, from the immediate family, friends, colleagues and acquaintances to communities and medical professionals.[12]
- In most Western countries, significantly more men than women die by suicide. In the United Kingdom, the suicide rate among men is three times that of women.
- Suicide is a complex issue, and there are myriad reasons that can lead to someone taking their own life.

The male suicide rate was one of the issues that led to me being involved in gender inequality work. Intuitively, I was making links between the pressures on boys and men to adhere to a certain form of masculinity and the high rates of suicide among men. This was one of the downstream impacts of those "man up" and "boys don't cry" tropes. I wasn't wrong. As I read and deepened my knowledge, I learned a few things that I will try to summarise here.

First, living within restrictive boundaries of masculinity may mean an inability to live authentically and may be causing men very real pain, yet we socialise our boys and men in a way that means the tools for managing this pain are often missing. The expectations placed upon males may not be achievable, yet the fear of failure may be suffocating. For example, for a man who has constructed much of his identity and self-worth around the expected "breadwinner" role, unemployment and or family breakdown can be devastating. In Chapter 10 we will discuss the impact of gender boxes on LGBT+ people, but it's important to note here the worryingly high rates of suicide among these groups.

We know that people who die by suicide are trying to escape unbearable emotional pain. Being able to express our experience of pain to others allows us to receive help and support. If the prevailing narrative around masculinity is one of strength and invulnerability, and if boys are taught emotional suppression from a young age, it stands to reason that many men find expressing their pain difficult. The drive for self-sufficiency can also lead to a lack of emotionally supportive relationships. Men may not have the language or confidence to describe their pain and seek support. When sensitivity is felt to be a weakness, or a failure of masculinity, is it any wonder that many boys and men will continue to mask their pain and cope alone? It is important to note here that many men do seek help, and that we should be careful not to be seen to be placing blame on individual men. A 2017 study of middle-aged men who had died by suicide in England found that 43 per cent had been in contact with their GP within the three-month period prior to their death, and about 38 per cent of them discussed their mental health and/or self-harm or suicidal thoughts.[13]

Many men find alternative ways of suppressing pain, including the use of alcohol, drugs or gambling, and a variety of other risky or bodily harmful behaviours. These coping strategies may be effective in the short term, but can cause an increase in pain in the longer term while failing to address the root causes of the pain. Many of these behaviours increase the risk of suicide.

People who die by suicide do not want to die – they simply wish to escape their pain and it may feel like the only option they have. Without the tools to effectively manage them, pain levels can quickly get to extreme levels. An inability to cope with this pain may feel like a failure in masculinity. When depression and other mental health issues are viewed through the lens of powerlessness, emotionality and vulnerability, many men may find seeking support difficult. They may feel trapped in their pain and suicide may seem like the only available option. A Samaritans report suggested that suicide could be understood as a way of expressing or regaining control in the face of these threats to masculine identity, which may explain this.[14]

It is interesting to note that women actually attempt suicide in far greater numbers than men. So why are men more likely to die? There is evidence that suggests when men attempt suicide they often choose more lethal methods. Some have argued that this indicates a stronger intent to die. There are various explanations given for this. Routine suppression of pain and pain increasing coping mechanisms may mean that at the point of suicide attempt men are in greater levels of pain and distress, with suppositions that women may attempt suicide earlier when there is less distress, perhaps as a help-seeking behaviour. It has also been suggested that men's choice of more lethal methods may also be a demonstration of masculinity, with "failure" to succeed in taking one's life associated with the more "feminine" practice of self-harm. Researchers who have recently looked specifically at male suicide believe we need a similar detailed understanding of women's suicidal behaviour if we are to truly understand what aspects of suicide are distinctly male in their experience.

When someone prominent dies by suicide, particularly if that person is male, social media is awash with messages encouraging people to reach out, to talk and to seek support. We know that when a person is thinking about suicide, they often (though not always) give clues to the people around them that they are struggling. However, a lifetime of emotional suppression may mean that these clues may not always be what we expect. For example, depression in men can often present outwardly as anger. Is men's pain being misinterpreted or even missed by those around them and the services that are there to help? I think we have come a long way recently in our understanding of and response to suicidality in men. We need to ensure that our universal services meet the needs of all people, ensuring that everyone can access the support they need from their mental and emotional health at the time that they need it regardless of how they present – and this should start with our boys.

What Can We Do?

We need to change the narrative around masculinity and what it means to be a man if we are to stop constructing identities for boys and men that are causing them very real pain and harm. As individuals and practitioners, we need to reflect on whether we are perpetuating stereotypes that push this one-dimensional idea of being a man. It makes sense that if we do whatever we can to reduce gender stereotyping from as early as possible, we can allow boys to grow into men without these limitations or expectations. Allowing boys to grow as their authentic selves is surely one of the greatest gifts that we can offer them. A truly equitable approach to these issues requires us to recognise that, despite our best efforts, without wider cultural and systemic change boys will continue to receive these harmful messages. We need to implement strategies to counteract them.

It is really important that boys and men are not made to feel a sense of shame about their gender. Masculinity is not a dirty word. In the book *The Men and the Boys*, R.W. Connell describes this brilliantly:

> The task is not to abolish gender but to reshape it; to disconnect (for instance) courage from violence, steadfastness from prejudice, ambition from exploitation. In the course of that reshaping, diversity will grow. Making boys and men aware of the diversity of masculinities that already exist in the world, beyond the narrow models they are commonly offered, is an important task for education.[15]

By moving beyond traditional masculinity and teaching children that masculinity can encompass many of the qualities, traits and skills that might be found in the "woman box", we can expand their visions of how real men can be.

Here are a few of our suggestions that may support you as you undertake this work:

- It is important that boys are shown there are many ways to be a boy and a man. Ensure that the visual displays in the nursery show boys and men undertaking a variety of roles and tasks, particularly non-stereotypical ones. Consider how you can utilise men within the nursery setting (staff, dads, granddads and male visitors) for the same purpose. Draw the children's attention to these counter stereotypes – make sure they notice!

- Look at your story books and learning materials. Ensure that they include stories about caring boys and nurturing men. Use these resources to have conversations with children – particularly boys – about gender roles and masculinities that involve care, compassion, respect and love.
- Consider how you can use resources to promote increased emotional literacy in boys. Particularly as they get older, consider ways that you can create spaces for boys to talk together and see that other boys have the same feelings as them.
- Take some time to reflect on how you handle discipline or address poor behaviour. How do you deal with violence and aggression among the children? Consider whether you may be sending messages to young boys (and young girls) about what is expected of them.
- Encourage boys to ask for help when they need it – especially from each other. Discussions about friendship and teamwork may help with this. We know that as they get older, often the need to demonstrate dominance and power (to show that they are firmly in the "man box") and the rejection of anything "girly" can mean that while they may retain friendships, these can be lacking in the emotional connection and supportiveness.
- Consider how we can teach children – especially boys – to challenge negative behaviour in others when they see it. The notion of male solidarity at all costs is harmful, so we can teach boys that challenge is both important and okay. Can we reclaim the word "brave" to mean standing up for what you believe in, seeking help or walking away from negative peer influence? We can role-model this as adults by talking about and taking a stand on issues. As adults, we can help children to develop values and character even at a young age.
- Consider whether there are ways in which we can help boys to develop empathy. For example, are there toys that help develop these skills which boys may have absorbed are "not for boys"?

Notes

1 M. Kaufman, *The Seven P's of Men's Violence* (1999). Available at www.michaelkaufman.com/wp-content/uploads/2009/01/kaufman-7-ps-of-mens-violence.pdf (accessed 2 February 2022).
2 A total of 3900 exclusions compared with 1200. UK Government, *Permanent Exclusions and Suspensions in England* (2021). Available at https://explore-education-statistics.service.gov.uk/find-statistics/permanent-and-fixed-period-exclusions-in-england (accessed 2 February 2022).
3 The Howard League, *Prison Watch*, https://howardleague.org/prisons-information/prison-watch (accessed 2 February 2022).
4 Scottish Public Health Observatory, *Prisoners: Prison Population* (2021). Available at www.scotpho.org.uk/population-groups/prisoners/data/prison-population (accessed 2 February 2022).
5 Office for National Statistics, *Nature of Violent Crime in England and Wales: Year Ending March 2020*. Available at www.ons.gov.uk/peoplepopulationandcommunity/crimeandjustice/articles/thenatureofviolentcrimeinenglandandwales/yearendingmarch2020 (accessed 2 February 2022).
6 National Record of Scotland, *Drugs Related Deaths Rise* (2021). Available at www.nrscotland.gov.uk/news/2021/drug-related-deaths-rise (accessed 2 February 2022).
7 Samaritans UK, *Latest Suicide Data*. Available at www.samaritans.org/scotland/about-samaritans/research-policy/suicide-facts-and-figures/latest-suicide-data (accessed 2 February 2022).
8 M. Pinkett and M. Roberts, *Boys Don't Try? Rethinking Masculinity in Schools* (London: Routledge, 2019).
9 T. Porter, *A Call yo Men*. TED Talk. Available at https://youtu.be/td1PbsV6B80 (accessed 2 February 2022).

10 Kaufman, *7 P's of Men's Violence.*
11 For more on the work of Jackson Katz, see his website, which contains links to his books and films. Available at www.jacksonkatz.com (accessed 2 February 2022).
12 J. Cerel, M. Brown, M. Maple, M. Singleton, J. van de Venne, M. Moore and C. Flaherty, "How Many People are Exposed to Suicide? Not Six". *Suicide and Life-Threatening Behaviour* (2018). Available at https://onlinelibrary.wiley.com/doi/pdf/10.1111/sltb.12450 (accessed 2 February 2022).
13 The National Confidential Inquiry into Suicide and Safety in Mental Health, *Suicide by Middle-aged Men* (2021). Manchester: University of Manchester. Available at https://sites.manchester.ac.uk/ncish/reports/suicide-by-middle-aged-men (accessed 2 February 2022).
14 Samaritans UK, *Men, Suicide and Society: Why Disadvantaged Men in Mid-life Die by Suicide* (London: Samaritans UK, 2010).
15 RW Connell, *The Men and the Boys* (Sydney: Allen & Unwin, 2000), 225–6.

8 Gendered Bodies

Susie Heywood

Why You Should Read This Chapter

As early years practitioners, it's important to be aware of how the messages we send to children about bodies through our language and actions can contain value judgements that reinforce gender ideals. Issues like appearance-based bullying and discrimination, poor body image, low self-esteem and mental health conditions such as eating disorders are exacerbated by the messages we receive from the people and culture around us, which demonstrate the types of bodies that are accepted and celebrated. This chapter describes some of the issues and provides useful suggestions for sensitive and proactive approaches that can ensure children learn acceptance and respect when it comes to all sort of bodies and appearances, reducing instances of appearance-based discrimination within our early years settings.

What do you think of when you hear the phrase "body image"? Perhaps if, like me (and many others), you've had half a lifetime of feeling uncomfortable in your own skin, you might immediately see it as something negative. But, of course, poor body image and negative ideas about our bodies are not inevitabilities: they are the unsurprising outcomes of living in a world where we are constantly sent messages about what ideal bodies look like and do. I want to unpick some of this stuff a bit more in this chapter, explore how such messages are related to gender stereotypes and make some suggestions for how we, as adults, can make changes to our interactions with children to minimise their exposure to unhelpful messages about bodies.

Let's start with some statistics:

- In a 2016 survey, 24 per cent of childcare practitioners noticed signs that children in their care aged three to five years were unhappy with the appearance of their bodies. This figure almost doubles by the time children reach ten years of age.[1]
- Almost one-fifth (19 per cent) reported having seen children reject food because "it will make them fat".[2]

DOI: 10.4324/9781003167921-11

- The 2019 Mental Health Foundation Body Image Report found that among teenagers, 37 per cent felt upset and 31 per cent felt ashamed about their body image. It found that 46 per cent of girls reported that their body image caused them to worry "often" or "always" compared with 25 per cent of boys.[3]
- The same report found that one in five adults (20 per cent) felt shame, just over one third (34 per cent) felt down or low, and 19 per cent felt disgusted because of their body image.

Idealised Bodies

There has always been a societal body ideal. While the shape of this "ideal" body has changed over time, a few things have remained the same: it's always White and able-bodied, it's never scarred, it is young and it's always unattainable by the large majority of the population. In the last century, for women, we've had the curvaceous and womanly body typified by Marilyn Monroe through to the waif-like figures of supermodels such as Kate Moss. Currently, we have a generation of women and girls comparing their bum-to-hips ratio with the Kardashian family and coming up short. While idealised body types have historically been an issue primarily for females, in recent years men and boys have been feeling pressure to keep up with similarly idealised body types. Reality TV shows such as *Love Island* have been highlighted as presenting quite a fixed male body ideal – think muscly arms, six packs, pecs, minimal fat and zero body hair.[4] None of us can escape the pressure – it's literally everywhere: TV, film, fashion and fitness magazines, newspapers, advertising, celebrity culture, social media … the list goes on.

Weight is a huge part of it. We live in a society where to be fat (a word that has become so loaded with negativity that we are often scared to use it) is to be shamed. We stereotype people who are overweight as lazy, messy and disorganised. Weight stigma, which is basically where we stereotype or discriminate against a person because of their weight, is having a very real impact on us all, and has been rightly recognised as a public health issue.[5] We hear many people talking publicly about their experiences of being "fat-shamed". Coming from a background in public health, I've sat in numerous lectures, seminars and meetings where weight is discussed as a barometer for a person's health. I've heard of many women who are tired of their weight being the constant focus of their conversations with the GP regardless of their presenting issue. We've all heard of the "obesity epidemic" and the war that needs to be waged against it. Associating thinness with health (also called healthism) is unhelpful. We can't assume that thin people are healthy and vice versa. Health is about so much more than our physical bodies and whether we have or are at increased risk of an illness or condition. Health is about how we feel about our lives: how happy we are, how fulfilled we are, how connected we are, how sexually fulfilled we are, what we are able to achieve and do … again, the list goes on.

Body shape and weight are only part of it. Skin colour or shade, facial features and hair texture can be a source of dissatisfaction and self-loathing for many people, an inevitable result of a culture that celebrates and rewards whiteness. And many people living with disability, scarring or disfigurement can never hope to live up to an ideal that favours non-disabled bodies. Body ideals feed appearance-based discrimination. Ableism, for example, is discrimination in favour of non-disabled people. Campaigning organisation Changing Faces cites examples of where people with visible difference or disfigurement have faced discrimination and harassment due to their appearance: being turned down for jobs, socially excluded, and experiencing hurtful comments or suggestions.[6]

Gender stereotypes have a role to play too, with clear cultural ideas about what we expect people to look like based on their gender. Even young children are quite clear: if you are a girl, you should have long hair; if you are a boy, it should be short. Simple. From an early age we accessorise young girls with sparkly bags, glitzy hair bows and delicate shoes. Take a walk down the magazine aisle of your nearest newsagent and notice the gendered messaging in the content and freebies of those children's magazines that are beloved and reviled by parents in equal measure. Fake lipstick, hair clips, tiaras and face glitter for girls versus dinosaur tracking GPS watches, cars and tools for boys. The societal expectations here are clear.

Being ladylike or womanly is associated with looking attractive to the opposite sex, having womanly curves, large breasts, long lustrous hair, large eyes and full lips. While for men a toned and muscular physique that exudes strength is seen as the ideal physical embodiment of a masculinity that celebrates power and dominance. Physical attractiveness generally seems to have been placed at the top of the list of important qualities when looking for a life partner, with dating apps allowing people to discount potential matches based on a couple of photographs. Don't like what you see? Swipe on by!

I spoke with Julie Cameron, Associate Director of the Mental Health Foundation in Scotland, who has been researching body image and eating disorders for many years. I asked her what she felt had changed since she started work in the field. Her response was clear:

> We think of that societal pressure as always being external, and what became really clear when we were writing the [body image] report was that in the world that we are now frequenting, so much of that pressure, there's like an internalisation that happens. I know that's always been the case, but it's so apparent now, in a way that wasn't there eight years ago. Young people [then] would never have used filters every single day of their life, so that every time they looked in the mirror it was literally a different representation from what they are used to seeing. That's quite complex, isn't it! How you see yourself on your phone has got filters all over it so when you actually see your real face it isn't how your mind thinks it looks. I mean that's new … it's an additional layer of complexity.

Altered images as a result of photoshopping used to be the domain of the advertising and beauty industry (buy this product and you too can look like this!), but now we all have similar technology at our fingertips by way of filters and apps that we can use to change pretty much everything about ourselves before we upload an image onto social media. Is it any wonder that we often feel we can just never match up to the faces and bodies that we see on our screens - even our own! There are some great videos produced by the Dove Real Beauty campaign that illustrate this perfectly.[7]

And while there is no doubt that much of the pressure around body image has tradition-ally been directed towards females, there is increasing pressure on men and boys too. As Julie describes it:

> Unfortunately it's a bit of a race to the bottom at the minute and we are dragging young boys down with us girls. Girls have already been there for a long, long time in terms of these pressures, and now, rather than trying to move everything up and better it, we are bringing everything down, and young boys are a part of that. But it's still more pronounced for girls – concepts of success are still so wrapped up in our female appearance. And while it's increasingly so with boys, there are many other areas where they can demonstrate success, like sport or business. There are fewer of these oppor-tunities for girls.

This echoes the findings from the Children's Society Good Childhood 2021 report, which demonstrated that while the gender gap in appearance-related dissatisfaction was narrowing, more children were reporting unhappiness with their appearance since the survey began in 2019.[8] Levelling down rather than up.

What's the Harm?

For those of us who cannot hope to inhabit one of these ideal bodies, who never quite measure up, what does it mean? For many of us, it might just mean a lifetime of never feeling fully comfortable in our own bodies. For some of us, it might mean a lifetime of making comparisons, endless weighing and measuring, jumping from one fad diet to the next, or pur-chasing beauty products, lotions, potions, drinks, shakes or pills in the hope that they will be the answer. Helping us to "look good" is a lucrative business!

For some, it can lead to the use of illegal and potentially harmful substances or drugs. According to the 2019 UK Anti-Doping (UKAD) report on Image and Performance Enhancing Drug Use, the most common demographic for the onset of IPED use in 20–24-year-old males, with anabolic steroids being the most popular choice.[9] UKAD suggests that social media, body image influencers, the rise of the *"Love Island* look" are feeding this problem, with men turning to steroids to increase muscle mass and reduce body fat. We know that steroid use is dangerous. As well as the psychological and emotional effects, there are many known ser-ious risks and physical side-effects, including heart attacks, blood clots, and liver or kidney failure. I know of a young lad who experienced severe and painful acne all over his body as a result of usage, meaning he felt unable to leave the house for a significant period of time and experienced deep regret and embarrassment.

Concerns about our bodies and poor body image can limit how we interact and engage with the world. If our head space is taken up worrying about how we look, it stands to reason that this will impact on our ability to focus on other aspects of life. For example, research has shown that a fear of being criticised for their appearance leads to girls changing what they wear, choosing not to be photographed and, perhaps most worryingly, deciding not to speak up in class![10]

Although health is about more than how our bodies look or perform, we also know that moving our bodies brings so many physical and mental health benefits. The ability to participate in physical activity is important, yet we know that by the age of 18 far more girls than boys have dropped out of all sports activity,[11] and participation in exercise among disabled people is significantly lower than that of the general population – and much more so among women than men.[12]

There are a number of factors that could be driving these concerning statistics. While many of these will be personal to each individual and may be the result of a variety of factors, including personal preference, ethnic or cultural background, affordability and physical and mental ability, many stem directly from the gender boxes we discussed earlier – for example, lack of time due to domestic and caring responsibilities, concerns about personal safety, particularly in public spaces or unstaffed gyms, and a lack of investment in women's and disabled sports. On a personal level, concerns around body image, self-confidence in ability and an internalisation of messages about what is and is not appropriate or achievable all interplay and result in these lower participation rates. A 2017 survey by Women in Sport showed that while boys tended to mention practical restrictions to taking part in physical activity at school, such as injury, when it came to girls, low confidence and dislike of being watched were mentioned as significant barriers.[13] Women, girls and disabled people are losing out of the physical and mental health benefits of physical activity as a result.

While we all feel pressures around body image, and experience the negative impacts of this on our wellbeing to different extents, for some groups in society these pressures can be compounded by other aspects of their identity and experience. Sadly, when the focus has often been on culturally dominant groups, our understanding of these experiences is more limited. We have just discussed one specific issue that faces disabled people; however, as Julie again explained, people with a disability or who have visible difference can often feel excluded from wider conversations around healthy body image:

> The concept of "healthy" is quite loaded for anyone with a disability, because immediately you don't feel that you are in that healthy camp. So that's why we very purposely use the language of "good" body image rather than "healthy" body image. For people who have a disability or a visible difference it can feel as though they can't ever have a healthy body image because they are already removed from the concept of health because of their disability. It's also quite important to say that it's not about loving your body all of the time – that's quite a lot of pressure to put on somebody. We need to recognise that it's okay to have ups and downs about how you feel about your body, but what you want is more positives than negatives, and a recognition that even if your body is not exactly as you would want it, it does a lot for you.

Language matters, and we need to ensure that our language around body image is as inclusive as possible. We've already discussed that body image is about more than weight and how this may be particularly the case for people from different racial groups. Another group we know struggle with body image are transgender people or those who are experiencing gender dysphoria, where their experience is that their biological sex does not align with the gender with which they identify. Gay men are also more likely to experience a desire to be thin and can experience higher levels of eating disorder symptoms as a result.[14]

Eating Disorders

For a small number of people, the consequences of these body pressures are very serious indeed. The Mental Health Foundation reported that just over one-third of adults said they had felt anxious or depressed at some point because of their body image, and one in eight had experienced suicidal thoughts or feelings relating to concerns about their body image. I asked Julie to tell me more about what we know about the links between poor body image and mental illness, in particular eating disorders. She explains:

> There will be lots of people in the world who just have poor body image and will never go on to develop a mental health issue as a result, but poor body image will be part of the picture within an eating disorder, although maybe not the main driver. Unfortunately the risk factors for poor body image will also be risk factors for eating disorders, like weight based bullying, or having a personality type that is a perfectionist. This could mean that a person may be more likely to have poor body image because their body might not be meeting the pressure that they put on themselves. That's a risk factor for an eating disorder. So they are aligned, there's no doubt about it. Poor body image in and of itself is not a mental health problem, or a mental illness like eating disorders, but certainly the risk factors attached to both are quite similar.

Culturally, eating disorders are associated with females and, as we have already learned, boys are taught from a young age to reject anything seen as feminine. Another sad outcome of this is that many boys and men may not feel able to admit to or seek help for an eating disorder. Therefore, the studies that suggest up to a quarter of eating disorder sufferers are male may not provide a true reflection of the problem.[15] Julie agreed, explaining that when we look at the statistics around eating disorders we see an over-representation of White, middle-class females. There is a need for more research to understand more about why this might be – for example, is there something in some ethnic groups that acts as a protective factor against eating disorders?

What Does This Mean for Early Years?

So what has all this got to do with the early years? I was struck by the following quote, which I heard recently from Dawn Estofan, a psychotherapist speaking about body image on BBC *Woman's Hour*:

> It's quite a complex thing to unpick, but what I would say is our perception of ourselves or our development of self is embedded in our early years experiences and our relationship with our early care givers. This is gradually built on by societal, familial and community perceptions.[16]

All this stuff that we've just been hearing about – the body ideals, the weight stigma, healthism – we begin to learn about pretty early. We've already learned how young children are exposed to mass media, which peddle idealised body images, but it's useful now to consider the role of early caregivers, and how they can either reinforce or challenge some of this stuff. I think a personal example might help to illustrate this.

I am privileged to have wonderful memories of an enjoyable childhood. My home was full of love, care and fun, and we were happy. My mum, though – like many other women – never seemed to be happy with how she looked. Looking back, I can remember diets or weight-loss programmes (cabbage soup anyone?). I remember throwaway comments about weight – her own and other people's – and while they were never meant in a mean way and were more often self-deprecating, the underlying message about what bodies were preferred was plain as day. And it sunk in. I'm not sure at what age I started being uncomfortable in my body. Up until I was in my teens, I was the "skinny minny" of the family, and even as a young kid I knew this was a good thing. But I do remember at quite an early age becoming aware of my pot belly and then as a teen my quite large breasts (too much info, but why the heck was I worried about droopy boobs at the age of 14?). I remember as a very hungry university student being told that my "eating would catch up with me eventually", like it was something to be feared. And when my body did inevitably change and grow, I embarked on a series of diets and fitness programmes with the sole aim of weight loss over any ideas about health or fitness. Sound familiar? Yes, I was doing exactly what I'd learned to do from what I'd seen growing up, from what I'd read in those glossy teen mags, and fuelled by the messages I was receiving from all around me about what the perfect body should look like. I thought (and sometimes still think) that if I could get that body I would truly be happy!

As adults involved in the care of children, we need to consider carefully what we say and do in relation to bodies, health and fitness in the company of children. Because they are watching and listening. Children are not born with body image – they are unencumbered, free and enviably at ease with their perfect little bodies. It's our role as the adults in their lives to preserve that as much as possible, but also to start equipping them with the confidence, knowledge and tools to question some of the narrative the world will inevitably sell them about what they should look like.

Little girls are particularly vulnerable when it comes to body image in the early years. The pressure on females to present themselves in a certain way starts early. For example, research from the Girl Guiding Association shows that a third of seven- to ten-year-old girls say people make them think that the most important thing about them is how they look.[17] To me this is desperately sad, and a real call to action for those of us who spend time around young children. We've already spoken about the association with princesses, sweetness, cuteness and pinkness that accompanies many young girls from birth. We also know that both Black and White children are more likely to choose to play with White dolls[18] and that the association of whiteness with goodness and purity is laid down early.[19] Constant comments or judgements on how they are dressed, or their hairstyle, or how pretty they look – while done with the loveliest of intentions – reinforce to little girls that the adults around them place great value on these things. And so begins a lifetime of pressure to look and act in a certain way in order to please other people.

The aim of our approach is to create early years spaces where children are not limited. Body image limits us all, including children. This excellent quote from body activist Molly Forbes sums it up perfectly:

> In a world where we're regularly encouraging our kids to "be their best self" or "live their best life", we need to recognise that this is often pretty hard if the vessel taking

our children from A to B every day, enabling them to live their life, is something they are taught to question, distrust – or even hate. You can't embrace every experience and opportunity that comes your way if you're distracted by negative thoughts about your body.[20]

The same goes for adults. What could we achieve if we directed the thinking time, energy and money that we spend worrying about our bodies onto something else?

What Can We Do?

We've included what we think are some useful ways in which we can begin to combat some of these unhelpful messages about bodies and health. Some are inspired by Molly Forbes' brilliant book *Body Happy Kids*,[21] which we would highly recommend if you're looking for a more comprehensive toolkit for taking action around body image and children:

- *Move away from a focus on appearance.* In all our interactions with children, we should try not to comment on appearance – especially with girls, who we know are subjected to appearance-based comments much more than boys. In fact, not commenting on other people's appearance or bodies may be a useful playroom rule. This is a lot harder than it sounds. Everybody loves a compliment, especially about how we look, so they often roll off the tongue without us even noticing, especially when you are presented with a little girl with a wide beaming smile who is clearly delighted with her freshly curled hair and new, sparkly trainers. We need to figure out ways to make children feel seen and validated without including an appearance-based judgement on top.

 Exercise: Consider the difference between these two statements:

"Look how pretty you look in your sparkly new shoes, Emma!"

"Emma! You've got new shoes – those sparkles will certainly help me to see how fast you are running!"

- The first is loaded with appearance-based value – her new shoes make her look pretty, which pleases me as an adult. The second still acknowledges her shoes, but focuses on what they will help her to achieve rather than how she looks. Emma will still feel complimented, but we haven't reinforced the old gender stereotype of "pretty little girls".
- *Teach children to compliment on things other than appearance.* As we learn how to change our own behaviour, we also need to consider how we can teach children to do the same. For example, when we are teaching children to give compliments, which can form a part of early emotional literacy programmes, we need to encourage children to focus on attributes beyond appearance. I'll never forget when my daughter came running out of her nursery clutching a sheet of compliments from the other children

and staff. Every single one of them, including the compliment from her teacher, was about her long hair or her green eyes or some other facet of how she looked. Her cleverness, humour, confidence, bravery and all her other qualities had been overlooked. An opportunity missed to teach her that we value all of these wonderful attributes as much as her face and hair.

- *Address appearance-based teasing.* Talking about other people's bodies is generally not a good idea. As adults, we need to address appearance-based teasing among the children in our care and ensure they are clear that this is never acceptable.

- *Focus on function.* As part of our teaching, we will inevitably talk about bodies; however, keeping the focus on function rather than appearance may be a helpful rule. We could focus on how our muscles help us to run fast, how our stomachs help us to digest our food or how our eyes and face help us to see the world and express our emotions. When we talk about exercise and movement, we should focus on how it makes us feel, how it helps our bodies, without talking about how it can change how we look.

- *Consider how we talk about disability.* While we advocate for a focus on function over appearance, we need to be careful how this is framed in the context of disability. All bodies are good bodies, so we need to become comfortable with talking about disability with children.

- *And race and ethnicity.* Be confident about how you respond to questions and discussion about race and ethnicity. The early years is a great time for conversations about difference and uniqueness: children notice these things, it matters to them, and it's our job to help them explore it further. If you lack confidence around this, it is vital that you spend some time on it. There are useful books and resources that can help.[22] You may want to consider whether the toys, objects and dressing-up clothes you have in play settings take into account racial and ethnic diversity or reinforce messages about idealised beauty.

- *Avoid equating "unhealthy foods" with weight gain.* While some might argue that we should avoid talking about "healthy" and "unhealthy", or "good" and "bad", foods altogether, part of our role in the early years will be to discuss food and nutrition with children. I don't think it's helpful to pretend that eating several doughnuts is healthy, but the problem for me is when we equate that with weight gain. Instead of discussing which food might make us fat, we should talk about what different foods offer us in terms of their nutritional value and how they make us feel, teaching children about the importance of diet for our health and wellbeing without sowing the seeds of "diet culture".

- *Ensure you use body diverse resources.* Can you imagine how it feels to a young child if all you see in the books and displays around you are people who look nothing like you and your family? Consider the books you use. Are there representations of all body types, sizes and colours? Are people of different body types shown doing normal everyday things and in a positive light? For example, *My Hair* by Hannah Lee is a fun kids' story that celebrates afro hair.[23]

- *Model body acceptance.* And, of course – as I mentioned earlier – the impact of how we talk about our own bodies with children needs to be acknowledged. As their caregivers, children will turn to us for information about the world around them, what they should do and how they should act. We should wherever we can role-model an acceptance of and appreciation for our own bodies. The self-deprecating humour and throwaway comments about our appearance, body shape or weight that can often mask our personal deep-seated insecurities have to go. And this might prove to be the hardest step of all.

Notes

1 PACEY, "Children as Young as Three Unhappy with Their Bodies" (2016). Available at www.pacey.org.uk/news-and-views/news/archive/2016-news/august-2016/children-as-young-as-3-unhappy-with-their-bodies (accessed 2 February 2022).
2 PACEY, "Children as Young as Three".
3 Mental Health Foundation, *Body Image: How We Think and Feel About our Bodies: A Research Report* (London: Mental Health Foundation, 2019). Available at www.mentalhealth.org.uk/sites/default/files/DqVNbWRVvpAPQzw.pdf (accessed 2 February 2022).
4 R. Moss, "*Love Island 2019*: Is the Reality Show Affecting Male Body Image?" *Huffington Post*, 5 June 2019. Available at www.huffingtonpost.co.uk/entry/love-island-2019-is-the-reality-show-affecting-male-body-image_uk_5cf61f85e4b0a1997b702181 (accessed 2 February 2022).
5 *The Lancet*, "Addressing Weight Stigma (Editorial)", April 2019. Available at www.thelancet.com/action/showPdf?pii=S2468-2667%2819%2930045-3 (accessed 2 February 2022).
6 Changing Faces website. Available at www.changingfaces.org.uk (accessed 2 February 2022).
7 This is the most recent one: Dove US, *Dove: Reverse Selfie* (2021). Available at https://youtu.be/z2T-Rh838GA (accessed 2 February 2022).
8 The Children's Society, *The Good Childhood Report 2021*. Available at www.childrenssociety.org.uk/information/professionals/resources/good-childhood-report-2021 (accessed 2 February 2022).
9 UK Anti-Doping, *Image and Performance Enhancing Drugs: UKAD's status Report on IPEDs in the UK* (2019). Available at www.ukad.org.uk (accessed 2 February 2022).
10 Girl Guiding UK, *Girls Attitudes Survey 2020*. Available at www.girlguiding.org.uk/globalassets/docs-and-resources/research-and-campaigns/girls-attitudes-survey-2020.pdf (accessed 2 February 2022).
11 Women in Sport, *Women in Sport: Reframing Sport for Teenage Girls* (2019). Available at www.gmmoving.co.uk/media/2544/women-in-sport-teenage-girls-dropping-out-of-sport-and-pa.pdf (accessed 2 February 2022).
12 Sport England, *Active Lives Adult Survey: May 2020/2021 Report* (2021). Available at www.sportengland.org/know-your-audience/data/active-lives (accessed 2 February 2022).
13 Youth Sports Trust, *Key Findings from Girls Active Survey* (2017). Available at www.womeninsport.org/wp-content/uploads/2017/11/Girls-Active-statistics-1.pdf (accessed 2 February 2022).
14 Mental Health Foundation, *Body Image: Sexual Orientation and Gender Identity* (2019). Available at www.mentalhealth.org.uk/publications/body-image-report/sexuality-gender-identity (accessed 2 February 2022).
15 Beat Eating Disorders, *Do Men Get Eating Disorders?* (2021). Available at www.beateatingdisorders.org.uk/get-information-and-support/about-eating-disorders/do-men-get-eating-disorders (accessed 2 February 2022).
16 *Woman's Hour*, "Body Image. Caring for an Abuser. Bafta lookahead. Mrs Sri Lanka Beauty pageant controversy". BBC Radio 4, 9 April 2021. Available at www.bbc.co.uk/programmes/m000twt5 (accessed 2 February 2022).
17 Girl Guiding UK, "Girls Fear Criticism for Being Themselves". Available at www.girlguiding.org.uk/what-we-do/our-stories-and-news/news/girls--fear-criticism-for-being-themselves (accessed 2 February 2022).
18 A 1940s study by psychologists Kenneth and Mamie Clark, commonly called "The Dolls Test", is often quoted as evidence of this. I like this piece from Toni Sturdivant in *The Conversation* (2021), which discusses it in more depth and suggests that there is more we can learn about watching how children interact with dolls with different skin tones. Available at https://theconversation.com/what-i-learned-when-i-recreated-the-famous-doll-test-that-looked-at-how-black-kids-see-race-153780 (accessed 2 February 2022).
19 P. Agarwal, *Wish We Knew What to Say: Talking with Children About Race* (Boston: Little, Brown, 2020) contains a really comprehensive and nuanced discussion around this, and has some really helpful suggestions and tips for discussing issues of race with young children.

20 M. Forbes, *Body Happy Kids: How to Help Children and Teens Love the Skin They're In* (London: Vermillion, 2021).

21 Forbes, *Body Happy Kids*.

22 We like Agarwal's previously mentioned *Wish We Knew What to Say*. For more in-depth information, including useful scenarios and case studies to prompt reflection, we would also recommend Jane Lane, *Young Children and Racial Justice: Taking Action for Racial Equality in the Early Years – Understanding the Past, Thinking About the Present, Planning for the Future* (London: National Children's Bureau, 2008).

23 Available at www.youtube.com/watch?v=oNet1W_TMqM (accessed 2 February 2022).

9 Parent Pressure

Susie Heywood

Why You Should Read This Chapter

The transition to parenthood is difficult for everyone, but there are very specific pressures that face men and women, which stem from the gender stereotypes and binary gender roles we are taught from an early age. It is vital that early years settings are inclusive of and welcoming to all parents, and in this chapter we suggest that specific strategies to engage with fathers can form part of an equitable response to a world where parenting continues to be primarily defined as "women's work", hearing from the experiences of Thomas Lynch from Dads Rock. We also explore the pressures women can experience as they become mothers, which can lead to difficulties with mental and emotional wellbeing. Early years practitioners can support all children to learn the emotional and practical building blocks to support caring and parenthood.

In Chapter 17, we will touch upon the key role parents and carers can play in minimising the impact of gender stereotypes in the lives of their children. However, parents will likely have experienced the very real impacts of gender stereotyping themselves as they made the leap into parenthood. This chapter explores what the transition to parenthood is like and the ways in which gender stereotypes may be increasing the pressures society already places on parents, and in turn they ways in which parents may unwittingly be reinforcing some of these ideas with their own children.

A Delicate Balance: Becoming a Parent

I've often said that it was only after becoming a mother that I really began to truly understand the inequalities facing women who chose to have children. From an intellectual point of view, I knew about things like the gender pay gap and sex discrimination in the workplace, and had seen other women trying to juggle the demands of motherhood with the desire to continue to progress and demonstrate success in the workplace. However, it was only once I experienced it myself that I truly understood what it felt like to make the decision to return to work, to experience the guilt that went along with knowing there was no way I would ever be happy remaining at home and that I needed and wanted to have a successful career as

DOI: 10.4324/9781003167921-12

well as being a mother. I had hoped that returning to work on a part-time basis might allow me a balance between work and home life, but for much of the time it just felt as if I never felt truly successful in either sphere. The impact on my mental health was not great, and I have experienced many ups and downs.

It often feels like there is a double standard that is simultaneously judging mothers who choose to return to work yet displaying a lack of respect and status for those who choose to remain at home. We know that following maternity leave, many women choose either not to return to work at all or to work reduced hours. Research by Understanding Society in 2019 showed that fewer than one in five new UK mothers return to full-time work in the three years after maternity leave and 17 per cent of women leave employment completely in the first five years, compared with 4 per cent of men.[1]

There are some very practical reasons for this. The cost of childcare has risen to unaffordable levels, meaning that many parents are unable to afford return to work, which places some families into poverty. A survey of parents conducted in 2020 by Pregnant Then Screwed found that over one-third of those returning to work after having a baby either only just break even or are financially worse off as a result of childcare costs.[2] Who says work pays? Figures from the OECD suggested that the average worker in the United Kingdom may spend around 35.7 per cent of their income on childcare – meaning that for many the figure will be significantly higher.[3] And that's if there is even childcare available – in some areas, lack of provision, long waiting lists and inflexibility of current models of provision can be a huge barrier for parents who wish to return to work.

Yet the default in most heterosexual families appears to be that when one parent needs to stay home, it tends to be the mother. Hopefully by now the link between this and those gender boxes is pretty clear – the female carer and homemaker, and the male breadwinner. As women's equality and opportunities in the workplace have advanced, we have seen more men taking a more equal and occasionally leading role in day-to-day childcare. This is not to suggest this is the only reason, but it doesn't feel like a stretch to assume that in many cases economics trumps traditional gender roles. Interestingly, there is lots of evidence suggesting that when women do work outside the home, they continue to bear most of the load of domestic duties. Cordelia Fine describes how in families where both parents work full time, women do around twice the amount of domestic labour as their male partner (the "second shift"), and while this gap decreases as she earns more, it never equals out (in fact, when she earns more than her male partner, the amount of housework she does actually increases again!).[4] Why this might be the case is up for debate: I wonder whether good old fashioned guilt (based, of course, on those stereotypes of the good wife and mother) is to blame?

In recent years, there has been a move to promote the idea of shared care, with initiatives such as paid or shared maternity leave becoming available for many couples. While uptake remains low,[5] it does feel that we are beginning to see a change in societal attitudes towards men who are taking active and even leading roles in childcare at home, though there is still some way to go.[6] I spoke recently to Thomas Lynch, service manager and co-founder of Dads Rock, a Scottish organisation that aims to improve outcomes for children by providing supports to dads and families, and promoting the vital roles fathers play in the lives of their children and families. He spoke of dads who had decided to leave work to look after their children being met with disbelief, questions and assumptions, and a general sense that it still isn't fully accepted by society – and perhaps only an option available to a privileged few. These are men who do not fit the archetypes of manhood found in the gender boxes, and can face prejudice as a result. We still belittle the idea of men who care. Around the idea of shared care, he said:

> In the ten years that we have been doing this there are definitely more dads taking more time off and wanting to take time off, career breaks or whatever. Sometimes I think it's a very middle-class thing, because sometimes middle-class families are more likely to be able to afford it or they have jobs where they can take career breaks compared with the dad who has three jobs or it's not the type of job where you can have that conversation. I think the class thing is really interesting and unfortunate. The vast majority of men do want more and do understand that it's better to be with your family and to be around your kids. Dads I have spoken to believe that lockdown has helped with that because they have been able to see their kids do things that they would never have seen if they had been at the office.

Of course, there may be many women who are resistant to the idea of shared care for a variety of reasons. It was never really on the cards in our house, partly because I was reluctant to give up that precious time with my babies – and yes, I recognise now how unfair this was on my partner, who deserved to have some of this time too. In a patriarchal world, the home and the care of children is one of the only spheres of life where traditionally women have really held any significant power, so it feels understandable to me that there might be some reluctance to give that up, even though it might move us towards a more even distribution of power in other spheres. Again, some thoughts from Thomas:

> I do feel that there is still so much inequality for women, so we need to be careful about how we push at those doors where we think there is inequality for men. But ultimately the focus needs to be on the child and the family and that's what we are trying to improve. Yes we'd love it if maternity services could be more geared towards the needs of the men for example, but we are doing that for the child as much as we are doing that for the man.

Equitable approaches need to consider the needs of all people and groups, recognising the range of inequalities and being careful that these are all addressed. Placing the needs of the child at the centre, as suggested by Thomas, seems like a useful approach. The positive benefits of involved fathers on the outcomes of children have been well evidenced,[7] and the benefits for women and girls of domestic and workplace equality too are clear. A study conducted by the Harvard Business School in 2015, for example, showed that compared with mothers who were not in employment, the daughters of mothers who were went on to have better, higher paid careers themselves, and the sons of those mothers took more responsibility for caring within families.[8] In the case of "the domestic load", and to paraphrase the words of the inspirational Ruth Bader Ginsburg, women will only have achieved true equality when men share with them the responsibility of bringing up the next generation.

The Emotional Toll

From a young age, we are socialised to understand what our roles within the family should be – what type of parent we are expected to be, and despite the advances of women in the workplace, many men continue to feel pressure to take on the breadwinner/head of the family role. The pointers towards these roles appear early in life. While there is no doubt that things have improved, we still see toys of a more "domestic" nature being marketed heavily towards girls (think aisles of pink prams, baby baths, ironing boards, kitchen sets and shopping trolleys), while "toys of the world" are pushed towards boys (vehicles, action sets, science kits). As a young girl, much of my early play experiences involved dolls, prams, kitchens and houses – although as I grew older and had more autonomy over my choices, this quickly expanded and have always been grateful that my parents didn't take issue with a daughter who would spend hours playing with her giant car mat.

We've spoken about toys and how they are marketed and presented to children in an earlier chapter. What's clear, though, is that it's the toys that are pushed on little girls that provide the opportunity to learn and role-play the domestic, caring and empathy skills associated with raising children. When, as a society, we continue to discourage boys from stepping outside their gender box, this is particularly problematic. We are much more likely to take the doll off a little boy than the car off a little girl.[9] How can boys learn the skills which will support them as they become partners and fathers if we never give them the opportunity to develop these in their formative years?

I am sure you are very familiar with the concept of the "natural mother" and the idea that women have innate child-rearing skills in a way that men, who tend to have to "learn on the job", don't. For many women, this idea that they should take to motherhood like a duck to water is problematic because, let's face it, motherhood is hard. While, as young children, we are often given the tools to help us learn the skills we will need – dolls, prams, bottles, etc. – nothing can really prepare anyone for the difficulties of breastfeeding, the lack of sleep, the loss of a sense of self and the impact on relationships. Parenthood is a steep learning curve, so the idea that somehow it all just happens as if by magic is not only nonsensical, but also harmful.

The emotional toll on both men and women cannot be understated. While a temporary bout of the baby blues is normal for many mothers, according to the Maternal Mental Health Alliance around one in ten women develops more serious mental health issues, including anxiety and depression, in the year after having a baby.[10] I think we are getting better at speaking about this stuff generally,[11] but from the time I spent working on various projects related to perinatal mental health, I am aware that there continues to be a reluctance on behalf of many women to admit that they are struggling as mothers, partly due to the stigma surrounding mental health but also because of these gendered pressures and the idea that women should take to motherhood easily. Men too are not immune – in recent years, the mental health of new fathers has been spotlighted by organisations such as Fathers Network Scotland and Fathers Reaching Out, which have been working with perinatal health care providers to ensure that the mental health needs of dad are discussed.

Including Dads

A few years ago, I conducted a research project looking at the support needs of new fathers. I spoke with 14 new dads about their experience. Despite an acknowledgement of the changing nature of fatherhood from previous generations, and for many a desire to be a different kind of father from their own, many of the dads felt constrained by traditional gender roles that impacted their ability to seek support. They spoke about being unable to talk about the emotional and mental health impacts of fatherhood, with some reporting feeling worry, stress, fear, pressure and even depression, and some describing situations of relationship strain and breakdown with the baby's mother. In addition, the dads described a sense that society, service and support prioritised the needs of mothers. This extended into social experiences, with men often feeling uncomfortable being in the minority when it came to parent-child activities. Thomas reflect on his own experiences of becoming a dad and men seeking support:

> I think in some respects it's changing. I think it is easier for men to ask for support but there is still an expectation that you will be strong and you will be competent. I remember a midwife saying to me and another dad in antenatal classes "You two have to be like swans for mum - you can be paddling away furiously under the water, but on the surface you need to be calm, she needs you to be calm." At the time I thought, "That's true, that's how I want to be", but it just puts pressure on dads that they have to be strong and they have to be a certain way. It tells them that because they are not going through labour it's not about them.

It is likely that same-sex parents may face similar experiences, and perhaps even further exclusion. For example heteronormative ideas about parents may lead to lesbian mothers being excluded from services geared towards the birthing mother, while having no place in those built around the needs of fathers. Research by Stonewall in 2015 looked at the LGBT+ issues in health and social care services and found that among staff there was a lack of consideration, understanding and confidence in meeting the needs of LGBT+ service users.[12] In Chapter 10, we will explore the higher levels of depression and anxiety amongst LGBT+ people compared with the general population. Add to that the assumptions made about family makeup, and incidences of inappropriate or discriminatory comments from staff and others, and it's not difficult to see why parenthood for LGBT+ people may bring additional pressures. Chapter 10 explores how early years settings can ensure that LGBT+ families know they are welcomed and supported.

When it comes to fathers, the work of Dads Rock and similar organisations is slowly making a difference, but from chatting with Thomas his frustration at the slow pace of change is clear. There is clearly a need for anyone involved in work with children and families to consider their practice in relation to overcoming some of these challenges for male carers, and early years settings are no exception. There are loads of ways in which early years settings can support fathers. I asked Thomas what one thing he felt would make the most difference:

> Just invite dads in. Have something specific for them. I know that there's a worry about saying it's for dads because some families don't have dads, but I think it's important for

staff to know who the important males are in that child's life. And again I know that there will be some children who don't have an important male in their life, but most of them do have somebody. It doesn't have to be rocket science - it just needs to be something that says "Dads, men - please come and do this with us, please come and help us with something, or please come and play with your kid and have some fun." Because we need to get the dads in early, and once we get them in they are a lot more comfortable.

Dads are more involved in the lives of their children than ever before, so it's vital that settings consider how they can meet their needs, being mindful of some of the gendered challenges they may face. We can look at our settings with a "dads lens" and ask ourselves whether we have created an environment where dads are comfortable and visible. We can consider the parent-facing activities that we deliver to ensure they are dad friendly. We provide some concrete suggestions at the end of this chapter, but organisations such as The Fatherhood Institute and Fathers Network Scotland have resources and suggestions that can help you.

Role Model Pressure

Parents often feel pressure in their role as those responsible for raising healthy and happy citizens of the world. As parents, we hope to be positive role models for our children, but this too brings with it gendered pressures. I have found myself choosing to do activities that I would normally avoid because I want my children to see a woman who "can do it all". I'm trying to be kinder to myself now - it's better that my children have a mother who isn't laid up with another sprained ankle after climbing on those slippery beach rocks!

For men, too, the pressures to model ways to be a man can be difficult and can often be wrapped up in societal pressures around maintaining that masculine ideal. We have often heard early years staff speak of times when a dad has been upset to see their son playing with a doll or wearing a princess dress. While the inherent homophobia/transphobia needs to be probed, for some the concern may also arise from a worry that their child may become a target of bullying because they are pushing gendered norms feels understandable. Tackling homophobia and transphobia, and creating early years environments where LGBT+ people and families are represented is vitally important and, as practitioners, the gently challenging conversations you have around these topics can be important in allaying any fears.

I can't help but wonder whether, for some of these parents, their own masculine identity is tied up in that of their sons, so any threat to either needs to be challenged. As parents, we see ourselves as role models, so the desire to demonstrate to our children the type of person they should or could aspire to be feels important - that's what I was attempting to do by climbing those rocks! For those of us who may have been socialised to place our value in traditional gender norms (the gender boxes), this can mean pressure to embody these ourselves. For some it's the opposite - a need to demonstrate that women or men can be different from the stereotype. For some, it's both. I know that as a mother, particularly to my daughter, I put a lot of pressure on myself to demonstrate to her that women can have a fulfilling and rewarding career and still be the best mother possible. Unfortunately for me, the reality is that I am probably failing in both areas (or at least it feels like it sometimes), so the guilt and pressure this brings can at times be overwhelming. Thomas's experience is that many dads are attempting to break the mould and model a different sort of masculinity to their children:

> There's some really great examples of dads being silly, and dressing up with their daughters and doing things with their hair and make-up and I actually think that's really important. I think that it can take a lot of confidence, but men need to continue to do it to challenge the old fashioned stereotypes.

I also know of many men who feel it's important to demonstrate that they are not the "hapless father" stereotype that we have seen in many places (Homer Simpson anyone?) Of course, parents cannot be expected to be all things, and we also must not be made to feel guilty when we get things wrong, or even when we choose to do it our own way.

It is clear that children learn from what they see, and the learning they get from us as the adults in their lives is important. As part of the film we helped to develop for the Gender Friendly Nursery, we asked nursery-aged children to point to male and female dolls in response to some "Who does what?" type questions, replicating an older film that we found on YouTube.[13] This was in no way a scientific experiment, and we recognise the inherent binary of the male and female dolls, but what we found was that while often the children's responses referenced traditional stereotypes about who plays with what and who dresses in what when it came to the child dolls, when it came to the adult dolls the responses were quite varied and our assumption was that children were responding based on what was normal for them in their own family life. Role modelling is important, and while the influence of parents and families is clear, early years professionals can support parents by ensuring that children see (including by specifically pointing out) domestic and workplace equality in the resources, stories and songs shared in the nursery setting.

Of course, the way children are parented is influenced by the bias and stereotypes of parents. We don't want to place any further pressure or guilt on parents, who are very often held accountable for many of the world's ills. However, though all of us are products of our own experiences and have absorbed the messages and biases of the environments in which we grew up, parents can proactively make changes to try to minimise what they pass on to children. Chapter 15 looks in more detail about the ways we might challenge our own biases and help children to grow up free from bias and Chapter 17 talks more about how parents can be engaged in reducing gender stereotypes in particular.

What Can We Do?

In early years settings, there are so many things that we can do to minimise the stereotypes, provide a balance to the messages that the world is sending to children about gender roles and parenthood and help support the parents who are coming into our settings and who may be feeling the pressures of parenthood, or barriers to fully participating in nursery life:

- We need to move away from the stereotypes and recognise that families come in all shapes and sizes, that mums and dads are not an homogenous group, and that not all families have both a mum and a dad. We need to ensure that our organisations and systems recognise this and meet the needs of all kinds of parents. It is my experience that early years settings are pretty good at this already.

- We can teach children that when it comes to child-rearing and domestic chores, both parents can undertake any of these roles. For example, it may be that in their home it's mum who does all the cooking, but we can show them that men can do these things too.
- Nursery staff can support and nurture parents, recognising the pressures they are facing.
- We can ensure that we are fully aware of the family circumstances of the children in our care, such as parental separation, lone parent families, LGBT+ families, kinship care arrangements and so on. By knowing each family, we can be comfortable talking with and about them with children without making assumptions.
- Some ways to ensure that LGBT+ parents and families are welcomed and included in nursery life are included in Chapter 10.
- It is important to recognise the vital role that dads play in the lives of their children. Nurseries should consider proactive ways in which dads can be made to feel welcome and a key part of nursery life.
- It is also vital to ensure that dads and other male carers are visible in nursery materials, websites and displays. If we really want to counteract the stereotypes, we need to see lots of dads in lots of places. One picture of a dad on the website or on one display will easily be missed, dismissed or forgotten!
- Consider how welcoming your family areas are to dads. I was involved in setting up a parents group at one point and it was only after receiving some training on involving dads that it struck me that the pink polka dot cake stands and table cloths might be sending out a message about who the group was for!
- Ensure that dads are made to feel welcome at nursery events – in fact, as Thomas suggested, consider running specific events for dads and inviting them to come.
- When writing home, think about how you are addressing parents. Fathers Network Scotland has suggested that when people read the word "parent", they can often sub-consciously assume it means "mum". Are there better ways that are more inclusive to dads (and all parents and carers)?

Notes

1 S. Harkness, M. Borkowska and A. Pelikh, "Employment Pathways and Occupational Change After Childbirth" (2019). Available at www.understandingsociety.ac.uk/2019/10/22/how-womens-employment-changes-after-having-a-child (accessed 27 February 2022).

2 Anyone with an interest in the impacts of parenthood on mothers in the workplace could do worse than spending some time on the Pregnant Then Screwed website! Available at www.pregnantthenscrewed.com (accessed 27 February 2022).

3 Found at https://data.oecd.org/benwage/net-childcare-costs.htm (accessed 27 February 2022).

4 C. Fine, *Delusions of Gender* (New York: W.W. Norton, 2010). Chapter 7 explores gender equality in detail and is well worth a read.

5 E. Howlett, "Shared Parental Leave Uptake Still 'Exceptionally Low', Research Finds". *People Management UK*, September 2020. Available at www.peoplemanagement.co.uk/news/articles/shared-parental-leave-uptake-still-exceptionally-low#gref (accessed 27 February 2022).

6 A. Burgess and J. Davies, *Cash or Carry: Fathers Combining Work and Care in the UK* (London: Fatherhood Institute, 2017). Available at www.fatherhoodinstitute.org (accessed 27 February 2022).

7 For a summary of some of the evidence, see www.fatherhoodinstitute.org/2021/revealing-fathers-impact-on-their-childrens-learning-and-development-our-new-study (accessed 27 February 2022).

8 K.L. McGinn, M.R. Castro and E.L Lingo, *Mums the Word! Cross-national Effects of Maternal Employment on Gender Inequalities at Work and at Home*. Working Paper 15–094 (Cambridge, MA: Harvard Business School, 2015).

9 J.H. Langlois and A.C. Downs, "Mothers, Fathers and Peers as Socialisation Agents of Sex-Types Play Behaviours in Young Children". *Child Development*, 51(4) (1980): 1237–47

10 The Maternal Mental Health Alliance website is a trove of information about perinatal mental health. Available at https://maternalmentalhealthalliance.org/about/perinatal-mental-health (accessed 27 February 2022).

11 Initiatives such as the brilliant PNDandMe who run the weekly PND hour on Twitter support people struggling with perinatal mental health to connect with others and access peer support and help.

12 Stonewall UK, "Unhealthy Attitudes: The Treatment of LGBT People in Health and Social Care Services" (2015). Available at www.stonewall.org.uk/resources/unhealthy-attitudes-2015 (accessed 27 February 2022).

13 *"Gender Roles: Interviews with Kids.* Available at https://youtu.be/-VqsbvG40Ww (accessed 27 February 2022).

10 Sexuality and Gender Identity
The Pressure to Conform

Barbara Adzajlic

Why You Should Read This Chapter

Even if you aren't aware of it, many of the children with whom you work will either have family members who are LGBT+, or may grow up to be LGBT+ themselves. All children will go out into the world and encounter people of different gender identities and sexualities, and hopefully they will be inclusive and accepting of all those people. Now is the time to lay the groundwork for those positive attitudes that will help people to feel comfortable in their skin and able to express themselves without fear. Here we look at how gender stereotypes prescribe what we see as "normal" relationships and gender expression, and how this impacts on people who are LGBT+, and those who aren't. We will conclude by giving some tips and strategies to reduce the impact of those stereotypes and to make it easier for children to be themselves.

In this chapter, we take another look at the gender boxes we introduced in Chapter 5, which are so powerful in upholding unrealistic and restrictive ideas about the ways men and women, and boys and girls, should be. We'll look at what this means for Lesbian, Gay, Bisexual, and Transgender (LGBT+)[1] people and others who don't fit neatly into binary categories because of their sexuality or gender identity, and what early years settings can do to help. We'll hear from two Scottish educators who are leaders in promoting LGBT+ diversity and inclusion in their early years and primary settings, and from a public health practitioner on why inclusion is so important.

A gender equitable approach recognises that the pressures from the outside world restrict what children believe about who and what they can and can't be. It recognises that this impacts many aspects of their lives, including who they might one day love and what their family might look like, now and in the future. So if you have doubts about the importance of this in early years, bear the following in mind:

- The children with whom you work with now may have friends or family members who are LGBT+, whether or not you are aware of it, and they need to know that this is accepted and reflected in your childcare setting.
- You might have staff members who are LGBT+, and they need to know they are respected and protected from discrimination.

DOI: 10.4324/9781003167921-13

- For children who may realise at some point in their lives that they are LGBT+ themselves, this time is crucial for them to know that they are loved and accepted regardless, and that they will be protected from discrimination.
- Homophobia, biphobia and transphobia affect people who are heterosexual and cisgender too, by policing their behaviours (more on this below).
- Whether or not any of the children in your care now grow up to be LGBT+, they will certainly at some point in their lives come across people who are. It is important for children to understand that there are different kinds of relationships and different ways of identifying so they can grow into kind and tolerant members of society.

We want every child to have the freedom to explore their own personality and to be the person they want to be without facing prejudice from others – and we want them to grow up allowing others to do the same, as allies.

How Do Gender Stereotypes Contribute to Homophobia, Biphobia and Transphobia?

Gender stereotypes affect the way society reacts to lesbian, gay and bisexual people, and people who identify as trans or non-binary or any of the other identities under the LGBT+ umbrella. Despite the fact that sexuality and gender reassignment are protected characteristics within law in the United Kingdom, LGBT+ people still face a lot of discrimination, which limits their freedoms, rights and opportunities.

Why is this still happening in today's, supposedly much more open and accepting, society? What exactly is the perceived "problem" with same-sex relationships, and why do we need people to express their gender using only those binary categories – the stereotypical male or the stereotypical female? Let's return to the gender boxes and think about some of the expectations we found there: men should be strong, dominant, breadwinners, protective. What happens to men and boys who aren't? What are some of the words and phrases that are used about boys who like to dance or who like cute, fluffy animals? Very often the language that is used to keep boys and men in the man box is language that questions their sexuality: "that's so gay" being probably the most commonly used insult against boys who dress in the "wrong" way, or who like, don't like, are good or not good at the "wrong" things. The other type of insult thrown at them is language that questions their gender: "you throw like a girl"; "girly swot"; "don't cry like a girl". So immediately children get the message that certain behaviours are associated with a gender and a sexuality, and that – particularly for boys – being associated with the "wrong" gender or sexuality is bad.

Anita le Tissier and James Cook are educators in Scottish primary schools with early years settings, and are the co-founders of Scottish Educators Connect. Anita described an early experience in her career that motivated her to do more to promote LGBT+ inclusion:

At a parents evening, one parent was talking about how concerned they were about their son having all female friends, he was very particular about his handwriting, was very obsessive about being neat and tidy, and his mum had very jokingly said, "I've got three sons, he's probably going to be the gay one" … in a really dismissive way, but she'd said it in front of the child, and I just felt that if her son were gay he'd just been laughed at by his parent, and second, if he weren't, he's having all of his, for him normalised behaviours, stereotyped, because he didn't fit the mould of his two older brothers who were quite the opposite.

Increasingly today, we also have adults making assumptions about whether a boy in this situation is really a boy at all, or actually a girl in a boy's body – again because they don't seem to fit the stereotyped idea of what a boy should be like. The same is true for girls who don't fit the girl stereotype: assumptions can be made about their sexuality or gender identity, although perhaps less so in the early years at least, because the types of insults levelled at these girls are less derogatory. Calling a girl a tomboy or bossy carries more of a suggestion that they are trying to be something "better". This goes back to the higher value that is placed upon stereotypical "boy" behaviours, over stereotypical "girl" behaviours. When delivering training to early years settings, we have sometimes been asked for advice on how to support children, or the parents of children, who are "presenting" as a different gender – more on this later in this chapter.

Research shows that around the age of four, children have fixed notions of gender identity based firmly on gender stereotypes – so if a man puts on a dress, he becomes a woman.[2] So we can see how a boy who understands that girls wear dresses, and who wants to wear dresses, and who is told repeatedly that dresses aren't for him because he's a boy, might want to be, or believe he is, a girl. It is also worth noting that some of the grown-ups in the life of this child might also question whether a dress-wearing, ballet-dancing, pink unicorn-loving boy is actually a girl in a boy's body. This is not to suggest that all parents of gender non-conforming children hold stereotypical views about what girls and boys can do, or that gender reassignment is an easier option than letting your son do ballet or your daughter play with trucks, but just a way to explain how gender stereotypes can influence this thought process.

James has worked with groups of young people looking at homophobic bullying, and explains more about how, within peer groups, even heterosexual boys are forced to conform to stereotype: "Quite often homophobia is a way of gender policing. The use of homophobic language is a way to gender police heterosexual boys and men because it's seen as a negative, so it's seen as a way of policing the way in which they express their gender, not about the way in which they identify." Anita agrees that a huge number of young people have been subjected to homophobic bullying and that young people themselves were able to identify that at least some of this was down to simple, throwaway comments like "you're so gay". Although a comment like this is rarely meant literally, it is part of the everyday language used to gender police children and young people, and it reminds them that being gay is still associated with something not-quite-right, or to be laughed at.

In the United Kingdom, we probably like to think we have moved on from all this and that our attitudes, as well as our laws, have changed. Certainly the evidence suggests that younger generations are more accepting of LGBT+ people.[3] But that doesn't mean this group doesn't face challenges.

Nicky Coia, Health Improvement Manager for Sexual Health with Glasgow Health and Social Care Partnership, has been involved in commissioning and responding to research into the needs of the LGBT+ population for two decades, including, early on in his career, the first local assessment of the health needs of young lesbian, gay and bisexual people.[4] Used alongside other excellent qualitative research by LGBT Youth Scotland and others, Nicky explains that:

> the qualitative themes were telling us about the experiences of discrimination and how that translated, in the views of the young people themselves, into poor mental health outcomes, into risky behaviours, into self-harming and eating disorders, experiences of depression and indeed suicidal ideation.

Knowing that outcomes – and particularly mental health outcomes – were poorer, and also realising that public health systems were not necessarily either acknowledging or responding to these different needs, Nicky was keen to improve on this evidence base in order to effect change. When, in 2016, Glasgow began to include the topic of sexuality within a process of routinely surveying the health and wellbeing of secondary school pupils, this allowed a more census-type, in-depth analysis of the specific issues for LGBT+ pupils compared with health outcomes for their peers.[5] A few headlines from the report show that, compared with hetero-sexual pupils, LGBT+ young people were:

- less likely than their peers to report feeling positive about their overall health (50% versus 70%)
- more likely to report experiencing a range of physical illnesses and conditions
- less likely to participate in physical activity, eat breakfast or lunch, and get enough sleep
- much more likely (22 per cent versus only 4 per cent of heterosexual pupils) to experi-ence a range of mental, emotional or learning difficulties
- more likely to say they had worries, and less likely to say they had someone they could talk to about those worries
- much more likely (44 per cent versus 20 per cent) to say they had been bullied in the last year, as well as saying they had bullied someone else (21 per cent versus 15 per cent)
- more likely across all age groups to have used or to regularly use cigarettes, drugs or alcohol; and more likely to have engaged in other risky behaviours (74 per cent versus 53 per cent)
- more likely to have engaged in sexual activity, and less likely to have used contraception when doing so.[6]

It is also interesting, and important, to note that across most of these areas, outcomes for LGBT+ girls generally tended to be worse (mirroring worse outcomes for girls in the hetero-sexual population), and that in the original research to which Nicky referred, bisexual women fared worst.

So what has all this research achieved, and how have things changed in the years during which Nicky has been doing this work? For one thing, Education Services in Glasgow have signed up to the LGBT Charter operated by LGBT Youth Scotland.[7] Nicky says that while this isn't "job done", it sends a strong signal to all those involved with a school that it is trying to be more inclusive. Within the schools survey process, "We can now ask the questions [about sexuality and gender identity] directly." There are also many wider cultural changes – par-ticularly, Nicky says, in terms of society being more welcoming towards lesbians and gay men, although acceptance of bisexuality has been trickier, and the trans "debate" continues.

Another area of progress is Scotland's new Relationships, Sexual Health and Parenting curriculum,[8] with which Nicky's team has been heavily involved. At its foundation, it aims to take a preventative approach to a number of issues like gender equality and LGBT+ inclusion, which Nicky says is about:

> giving children permission to be any kind of boy or any kind of girl or any kind of child that they want to be, and building in a recognition that if someone tries to put you in a box that you're not comfortable with, whatever that box is, that that's not ok. If you do that, at the youngest age, even at the pre-5 age where you dismantle those gender related norms, then you set a permission for a child to play in the way they want to play, achieve what they want to achieve. Those blocks that they're going to have to come to terms with at some point: the more we can shove some of those blocks out of the way, the better their journey into adulthood will be, and hopefully the safer and healthier they will be as a result of it.

Nicky reinforces the point that was mentioned by James and Anita about heterosexual and cisgender people also being negatively impacted by homophobia, biphobia and transphobia, referring in particular to the "masculinity straitjacket": the fear of being "outed" or being called any of those names that question masculinity, leading some boys to feel pressure to visibly demonstrate their masculinity in unhealthy ways that don't reflect who they actually want to be.

Too Early for the Early Years?

James Cook and Anita le Tissier both agree that things have changed enormously for the better since they, as members of the LGBT+ community themselves, were growing up. But progress is still patchy; it depends on the area, the school, the individual practitioner. Additionally, says James, "there is less of a fear to address this in a secondary context than there is in an early years and a primary context because of the positive work in secondary schools, and on occasion conversations I have had are, 'Are our kids aren't ready to have these conversations? If we talk about this, are we encouraging exploration of sexuality and gender identity?'"

This is a fear and a discomfort that we have experienced from practitioners with whom we work – the worry that being LGBT+ inclusive means talking about sexuality and gender, and taking away children's innocence. There are a few things worth noting in response to this:

• Just like early healthy relationships education, LGBT+ inclusivity is not about introducing adult ideas. We already talk about healthy relationships and consent in the early years through topics such as friendship, families and sharing; in the same way, we can encourage children to be open and accepting of different types of families, and dismantle the gender boxes that encourage homophobic attitudes, without going into inappropriate levels of detail. Some of the fear, says Nicky Coia, is down to adults viewing things through an adult lens. "If we take the 'sex' or 'sexuality' bit out of sexual orientation, it's about who you are attracted to rather than what you do!"

- Children aren't growing up in a political vacuum! They are already being exposed to prejudice in the world around them (the gender stereotypes and lack of representation in television, books and toys being a prime example). Most children still grow up in a heteronormative culture – that is, one that holds on to the idea that only heterosexual relationships are normal. For so much of our history, in most of the world's cultures and religions, heterosexuality has been the "norm". Some religious leaders still state outright that marriage between a man and a woman is the only "right" kind of relationship, and there are still countries today where homosexuality is illegal, with punishments including execution. Faced with all this, it is important that we provide our children and young people with a counter-narrative that reassures them that it's okay to be LGBT+.

- Finally, as already noted, members of staff, the children's families and friends, and, one day, the children themselves or their friends may be LGBT+. Creating an environment where everyone feels accepted and included is core business for early years settings. As Anita le Tissier says, it all comes back to the values that you establish: "our values are that we are kind, we are fair, we are gentle, we are respectful and we belong ... your child can't belong if they feel like there are parts of this nursery that they can't interact with". Your staff and families also can't belong if they feel they can't be open and honest about their own lives.

What Can We Do in Early Years to Promote Acceptance of LGBT+ People?

We can't say with absolute certainty that if we got rid of gender stereotypes and the restrictions they impose, homophobia, biphobia and transphobia would disappear altogether, or that everyone would be free to love who they want and be comfortable in the body they were born with. But it's safe to say that gender stereotypes do have an impact on how children, young people and adults see themselves within a society dominated by gender boxes, and that they place limits upon their freedom to be anything other than a particular kind of boy or a particular kind of girl.

There are lots of ways that early years practitioners can support with LGBT+ issues, and none of them is about taking away children's innocence – just promoting inclusion and acceptance of every child and family. This is about supporting children, families and staff who fall into this category, and also about building children's resilience to challenge gender stereotypes.

What Do We Do When a Child is Gender Non-conforming?

You may come across children in your work who don't accept the gender identity that corresponds to their sex: girls who say they are boys and want to be called by a boy's name, or vice versa. It is really important to note that children who do this might continue in this way as they get older and may actually be gender non-conforming; however, they might also just be going through a "phase", exercising their imaginations or reacting to gender stereotypes in their family (a girl who notices that she isn't allowed to climb trees or play football like her brothers might respond by deciding she wants to be, or simply is, a boy in order to do these things).

So do we have to start calling every child in the nursery "they" in order that that child feels okay? We would suggest this is neither necessary nor helpful. Unless it is being done in a carefully planned way (see the Swedish nursery example in Chapter 16), you run the risk of upsetting other parents, drawing attention to this child and also confusing children who are being called "he" and "she" everywhere else. It's more likely the child in question will want to use one gender pronoun or the other. Do we encourage the child who wants to be a girl to play with the girls and "girl" toys? Hopefully if you've got this far you'll agree that this is just reinforcing gender stereotypes – it is better to encourage all children to play with each other and with a range of toys and materials. Finally, be carefully about labelling children as transgender. If a parent suggests their child is trans, listen to what the parent wants and try to ascertain what the child wants, do what you can to make the child feel comfortable in your setting (which may mean using the name and gender pronouns they prefer), and try to talk about the child as "gender non-conforming" which is more accurate than "trans" at this very early stage. Have a look at the case study mentioned at the end of this chapter for a parent's perspective of supporting a child to explore their gender identity.

What Else Can We Do to Promote LGBT+ Inclusion in Early Years?

Below are some of our top tips and areas to consider, with some additional resources you may find helpful noted at the end.

- *Ask* specific questions of LGBT+ families in a sensitive way that respects their right to privacy. What names do the children use for you? How should we refer to you? How should we describe your family to the children/others? How should I respond to questions about your family?
- *Reflect* on where you stand as a practitioner and an organisation regarding LGBT+ issues. Are staff aware? How is it addressed in the curriculum? Do you have same-sex family resources? Is your work a gesture, or is it truly embedded across your organisation?
- *Audit* your resources. You may have openly same-sex families or families that include a transgender person in your nursery; you may not have any; or you might have some who haven't told you. Whatever your experience in this area is, children will grow up and move on to school, further education, jobs and social lives, and will meet people from all kinds of backgrounds. They need to know that all kinds of families exist and that this is okay. Many nurseries are already great in this respect and have books, posters and dolls that are representative of different types of families. If you don't already do this, take a look at your resources and think about whether every child who is now in your nursery, and any child who might join your nursery at some stage, could see their lives reflected in your resources. This means thinking wider than same-sex families to making sure your dolls, book characters and poster people aren't all White, able-bodied, two-parent heterosexual families. The more your displays and resources reflect the real world, the better you prepare your children to go out into that world (our audit tool in Appendix 2 can help you with this).

- *Communicate* with families in ways that don't make assumptions, or exclude people. For example, when you are generalising about all children, talk about families and homes rather than referring to "mummy and daddy" verbally, in letters, newsletters and social media. This also means single-parent families, kinship carers and other care arrangements are all catered for and everyone is included.
- *Challenge* discrimination. Be prepared to challenge any homophobia or transphobia. There is great advice available from organisations such as Stonewall and LGBT Youth Scotland.
- *Be visibly inclusive.* Inclusion doesn't just mean being reactive when someone steps out of line. Openly stating that your nursery welcomes people of all sexualities and gender identities as well as all races, religions and other characteristics, sends a message that you recognise there are challenges for same-sex families and for trans people and that you want to offer support.
- *Reassure* any worried staff and parents that this isn't about teaching sex education or confusing children with theories about gender identity. In the same way that early years settings are beginning conversations about child protection, consent and healthy relationships in an age-appropriate way, this is about setting the foundations for inclusion and acceptance.
- *If* you still can't bring people with you, you may have to remind them that you have a legal obligation regarding inclusion under Scottish or UK equalities legislation, as well as Scotland's GIRFEC (Getting It Right For Every Child) framework and other policies.
- *Treat* each child as an individual with their own personality and interests, and encourage them to enjoy a wide range of experiences and opportunities, regardless of their biological sex or gender identity.
- *Use "teachable moments"* to allow children to explore the reality that there are same-sex relationships. For example, discussions about getting married (young children sometimes talk of marrying their best friend) are an obvious situation where the idea of a same-sex marriage could be either ridiculed and discouraged, and the foundation set for homophobia; or discussed in an open way that allows children to feel just as comfortable with it as they would with the idea of heterosexual relationships.[9] Some staff may need to work on their reactions and responses so they are ready for these situations.
- *Finally, challenge gender stereotypes!* For any children in your care who are now exploring, or who may in future explore, their gender identity, you have an opportunity right now to make this process easier for them. By encouraging children to be themselves, you can remove the gender boxes that reserve some things for boys and others for girls, and give all children the opportunity to explore and develop free of those limitations. You can provide a safe space where children don't have to question whether their behaviour fits with what girls or boys are supposed to do. You can even go so far as to counteract stereotypes, as we'll discuss in Chapter 16. By reducing gender stereotypes, we can reduce the pressure to conform and work towards a more tolerant society.

Useful Resources

- Stonewall's Getting Started toolkit (Early Years) www.stonewall.org.uk/resources/getting-started-toolkit-early-years (accessed 2 March 2022).

- Highland Council's Equalities Improvement Group and LGBTI+ sub-group published a series of lesson plans to support the development of equality and diversity across the curriculum. There are 18 picture books with lesson plans created for early to fourth levels (Curriculum for Excellence) driven by the Literacy and English and Health and Wellbeing Experiences and Outcomes. Available at https://highlandliteracy.com/equal ity-and-diversity-picture-books (accessed 2 March 2022).
- LGBTQIA+ Early Years hosts ideas, resources and blogs about including and supporting LGBT+ people in early years settings. There is a case studies page including a lovely example (from a parent's perspective) suggesting how a gender non-conforming child can be supported. Available at https://lgbtqearlyyears.org.
- For primary and secondary resources, see Scotland's TIE (Time for Inclusive Education) campaign. Available at www.tie.scot (accessed 2 March 2022).

Notes

1 Some people and some organisations prefer to use LGBTI+, LGBTQ+, LGBTQIA+, or other acronyms. At the risk of offending anyone we are going to use LGBT+ here and we mean it to include anyone who considers themselves to be within any of these categories.
2 We looked at theories behind this, including Kohlberg's theory of gender, in Chapter 3.
3 For example, LGBT+ Youth Scotland carries out five-yearly surveys on life in Scotland for LGBT young people, and comparisons over the years show attitudes are slowly changing and becoming more accepting. You can find the reports at www.lgbtyouth.org.uk (accessed 2 March 2022).
4 At that point in time, gender identity was not yet identified or recognised as widely as it is today.
5 NHSGGC, *Key Findings in NHSGGC Schools Surveys by Sexual Identity: Final Report* (2016). Available at www.stor.scot.nhs.uk/handle/11289/579795 (accessed 2 March 2022). Interestingly, in the early surveys indicators of sexuality were used, such as asking young people whether they were mainly attracted to people of the same or a different sex, rather than using the terms lesbian, gay, bisexual and so on, as this was agreed to be more acceptable to schools and parents at the time. The format of questions in later surveys reflects changing attitudes towards the acceptability of talking about sexuality, and questions about gender identity are now also included.
6 There were also a small number of questions where outcomes for LGBT+ pupils were better than those of heterosexual pupils. For example, they were more likely to have participated in some positive behaviours such as volunteering and cultural experiences, and gay and bisexual boys were more likely to have expectations of positive destinations than heterosexual boys.
7 See www.lgbtyouth.org.uk/the-lgbt-charter (accessed 2 March 2022).
8 See https://rshp.scot (accessed 2 March 2022).
9 We have seen primary school classes learning about religious ceremonies and acting out a "traditional" wedding scenario between a boy and girl, with wedding guests, religious functionaries and so on. This feels a bit uncomfortable and like a step back towards reinforcing traditions and norms that don't reflect the lives of many people. We would suggest that these activities are undertaken with care to ensure there is time and space for discussion about different ways of doing things, so no one feels excluded.

11 Learning, Working, Earning

Barbara Adzajlic

Why You Should Read This Chapter

There are stark gender differences in the subjects that children and young people choose when they get to secondary and tertiary education, and in the career paths they follow. From the very early years, children are receiving messages about what girls and boys "can" and "can't" do, what they are good at and what are appropriate careers for them. Some workforces are highly gendered (the early years workforce being a prime example!) and the little girls with whom you work now will probably still have a gender pay gap and other forms of employment discrimination to contend with by the time they enter the workforce. This chapter will help you to consider how, at this early stage, you can help all children to have the opportunities, experiences and encouragement they need to open up a world of educational and employment options in the future.

It would be nice to think that, in this day and age, a wide range of career paths is open to every child and young person. There are now many high-profile women in politics and other powerful positions, in science and sport careers, and it's now more acceptable for men to work in caring professions like early learning and childcare and nursing, and to take time off work to care for family members. Things have changed a lot – haven't they?

Well, yes and no. There are certainly high-profile women in those positions, but in 2021, only 35 per cent of science, technology, engineering and mathematics (STEM) students in the United Kingdom, and 34% of MPs in the House of Commons, were female.[1] And despite decades of effort to diversify the professions, in 2019 just over 10 per cent of registered nurses in the United Kingdom[2] and only 3 per cent and 4 per cent of those working in the early years in England and Scotland respectively[3] were male.

What's going on here? In this chapter, we'll look at the reasons for these gender disparities in subject choices and career paths, which – as you will have guessed – are rooted in gender stereotypes and inequalities. From children's own beliefs about what they can and should do, to the attitudes of teachers, parents and peers, to the various barriers they encounter when they enter certain types of careers, the world, as usual, is very much divided into pink and blue. And, as usual, early years practitioners have an important role to play in changing this.

DOI: 10.4324/9781003167921-14

Before We Go Any Further ...

We know that one of the most important factors in children's attainment is socio-economic status. Much work has gone into closing the attainment gap in Scotland and the rest of the United Kingdom with programmes like the Cost of the School Day,[4] Scotland's Attainment Challenge[5] and targeted funding like the Pupil Equity Fund in Scotland and the Pupil Premium in England. These recognise the disadvantage with which many children start school because of living in poverty and all that this implies: a lack of adequate nutrition; poor housing and related health conditions; and a lack of funds to pay for school uniforms, trips and other educational experiences. Children with disabilities, and children whose parents have disabilities, are more likely to be living in poverty,[6] and children from ethnically diverse communities face educational barriers. So, as always, gender isn't the only factor at play here, but we will focus here on the specific ways that gender impacts this area.

How Do Gender Stereotypes Impact on Children's Self-belief and Aspirations: Who Thinks They are Really, Really Smart?

Gina Rippon showed us earlier on that there really is nothing innate in our brains that can explain maths and science being "boy" things, and languages and caring being "girl" things. Along with Cordelia Fine, whose work we also examined in Chapter 3, she discusses many examples of how gender influences what people *think* they can do. A well-known study by Bian et al.[7] showed that gender stereotypes lead to associations of brilliance with men more than with women. The authors found that, while at age five boys and girls were equally likely to associate people of their own gender with being "really, really smart", by age six this had changed, with girls less likely to believe that they and other girls were "really, really smart", and also less likely to select activities that they were told were for children who were "really, really smart". Rippon also highlights a prevailing belief in society that success in scientific discovery is related more to having an innate "spark of genius", rather than to hard work and perseverance, and that this spark is more often associated with men while perseverance is associated with women/[8].

To back this up we have evidence that children still associate the word "scientist" with men, as children asked to draw a scientist still mostly produce artwork depicting men rather than women, in a study that has been repeated over many years.[9] (Try it in your nursery!)

Meanwhile, a study looking at boys' poorer engagement at school explored the link between the stereotype of academic engagement and hard work as a feminine trait, and the pressure on boys to adhere to masculine stereotypes – in other words, it isn't manly to work hard at school.[10] In his brilliant book, *How Not to Be a Boy*,[11] the comedian Robert Webb tells us exactly how this played out in the grammar school he attended:

> a boy and a girl who came top of their class would each need a different excuse: if accused of intelligence, the girl would be expected to shrug it off and say that she just worked very hard. If accused of diligence, the boy would be expected to claim that it was all done at the last minute and he just happens to be quite good at that particular subject. It's OK as long as you didn't make an effort. It's not OK to be a "girlie" swot.

We also know that stepping outside of your assigned gender box often carries harsher punishments for boys than for girls,[12] so that a boy expressing interest in a caring career like nursing would experience more social barriers, or gender policing, than a girl would if she talked about becoming a scientist. All of these restrictions and limitations are being seen in children from the early stages of primary school, meaning that even before then, the stereotypes to which they are being exposed are causing their brains to make these associations.

There is also the issue of stereotype threat. This is where awareness of negative stereotypes about your own group reduces your confidence, clogs up your working memory and negatively influences your performance. In Chapter 3 of *Delusions of Gender*,[13] Cordelia Fine discusses lots of examples where, before taking part in a study, participants are told this is an area where boys tend to out-perform girls; or that it's part of an effort to understand why boys don't have the same language skills as girls. In those studies, the stereotype appears to come true, whereas if participants are told something different (for example, students at your school do really well at this subject and we are trying to find out why), the same thing doesn't happen.

And while it's useful, and important, to show children examples of people not conforming to stereotype, there is evidence that this alone doesn't work, because the stereotype is usually so entrenched that the child will misremember what they were shown so that the people do appear to conform. Martin and Halverson first showed this in 1983 and there are more recent studies showing the same result, with children either changing the gender of the person or the activity they were doing, or even adding details to the scenario to make it more stereotype-consistent.[14]

So we can easily see how societal expectations and internalised stereotypes are leading children to have gendered expectations of their own abilities. Once children have spent several years getting used to all this, what happens when they reach the stage where they are actually choosing subjects?

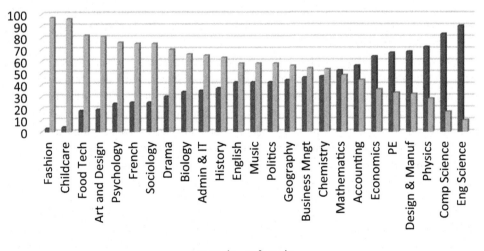

Figure 11.1

The Scottish Qualifications Authority's 2018/19 Higher Entry Statistics (Figure 11.1) show us there are still huge differences in the types of subjects girls and boys are choosing to study, with boys massively over-represented in certain STEM fields and girls over-represented in caring and creative subjects.[15] So we can see how the pool of candidates for working in particular fields is already being narrowed, not because of ability but because of gender stereotypes.

Girls continue to out-perform boys academically, even in the early years, although the gender gap is closing[16]. Despite this, girls experience a confidence gap. For example, when presented with the statement, "When I am failing, I worry about what others think of me", 73 per cent of girls in Scotland agreed, compared with 57 per cent of boys.[17] And in a study showing that children reported being shouted at more in disadvantaged schools, it was also observed that boys tended to see this as "unfair", while girls tended to make excuses for the teachers and blame themselves to a degree.[18]

How Do Gender Stereotypes Impact Educators?

But what about the educators? Maybe teachers are more gender aware and can help children to overcome their gendered expectations of themselves?

Again, research shows that teachers respond differently to similar behaviours in boys and girls, and that this is happening right from the early years onwards. A study by Yale University[19] asked early years practitioners to observe interactions between a group of four children who were filmed playing together in a series of interactions. The group consisted of one White boy, one Black boy, one Black girl and one White girl. The practitioners were told they would witness some challenging behaviour and were asked to report afterwards on what they had observed. In addition to their recorded observations, their eye movements were tracked electronically to see on whom they focused most attention while looking for challenging behaviour. In fact there was no challenging behaviour in any of the films, but most of the attention was on the Black boy, followed by the White boy, the White girl and the Black girl, and challenging behaviour was reported to have been observed in that same order. While this study was done in order to look at racial profiling and has important implications for school exclusions and criminal justice for ethnic minorities, it also clearly shows that the practitioners expected to see challenging behaviour from boys, but not from girls.

Later, in school, we also see that girls tend to be noticed and praised for good behaviour and working hard, but criticised for work content, while boys are called out for their behaviour but praised for work content, ideas and understanding (that "spark of genius" again).[20]

In schools, we also sometimes see the phenomenon whereby girls are seated strategically between boys to prevent boys from misbehaving, thereby making girls responsible for regulating boys' behaviour (a trait we also see in the world of violence against women, where women are expected to take responsibility for preventing men's anger and violence (see Chapter 6). In 2018-19, boys in Scotland accounted for 79 per cent of total exclusions,[21] and similar patterns are seen in other countries. How much of this is down to boys' more aggressive behaviour, which as we have seen, is allowed/tolerated/encouraged to a certain extent as part of their socialisation – "boys will be boys" – and how much to different expectations of those in authority is impossible to say, but the end result is that boys are not engaging in education to the same extent as girls. For a really good discussion about the many issues affecting boys' engagement and attainment, Matt Pinkett and Mark Roberts' *Boys Don't Try?*[22] is a great source of information and guidance for educators and parents alike.

Let's not forget that parents and carers are the primary educators of their children. They set expectations at home, role-model what life can be like and want their children to be able to achieve. As always, we must be careful not to blame everything on parents, who have the hardest job in the world; as a parent myself, I know the many pressures we face just keeping things running on a daily basis. But, having read the research, I also know that I have been guilty of falling into traps around expectations on girls versus boys. So, as we saw in Chapter 3, even parents who profess to be fully signed up to gender equality display subtle disapproval of boys playing with "girl" toys.[23] Further research has shown that parents' responses to the question "What type of job would you most like your child to pursue when they finish their education?" show gender biases. Parents were more likely to wish for careers in fashion, hairdressing, nursing and teaching for their daughters, while careers in STEM, policing and sports were seen as more desirable for sons.[24]

For a full and more academic look at the various influences of gender stereotypes on learners and teachers, Education Scotland's Improving Gender Balance and Equality programme has a comprehensive literature review.[25]

Careers

So we now have girls out-performing boys and being more engaged in education. Once these children and young people grow up and start their careers, or the higher and further education that will lead them into careers, gender stereotypes continue to play a role in how things develop. Remember that statistic at the top of this chapter about STEM students? Thirty-five per cent of them were female, but by the time they graduate, this figure falls to 26 per cent. Similarly, the percentage of men *studying* early learning and childcare in Scotland[26] is higher than those actually *working* in the profession. Something is causing more women to leave STEM professions, and men to leave the childcare profession. Something is also bringing about the gender pay gap and preventing women from excelling in a number of professions to the same extent as men.

Sexist work practices, "old boys' clubs'", family-unfriendly policies, the "motherhood penalty", the glass ceiling and elevator – these are all hugely important factors that are preventing many women and men from progressing in the careers of their choice. There isn't scope here to do justice to each of these, but Cordelia Fine and others have written about them (see the Further Reading section at the end of this book). For now, let's just get some insider knowledge from two people who are bucking the trend in a very gendered professions.

Case Study: Women in Intensive Care Medicine

We have talked quite a lot about STEM in general, but we are going to look at one very specific field where women are under-represented. Dr Rosie Baruah is a Consultant in Intensive

Care Medicine and was the inaugural Chair of Women in Intensive Care Medicine, an organisation set up to improve women's position in a field that is dominated (80 per cent) by men. Rosie was also the first woman with a child to undertake Intensive Care training in Edinburgh, and had to fight to be allowed to train part-time despite there being a precedent for men training part-time. She explains that medical school outputs have been around 55 per cent female for the last 25 years, but that only 36 per cent of hospital consultants in the United Kingdom are female overall, with certain specialties having even fewer women.

Rosie was instrumental in the actions WICM took to support women in this field:

> We set up a national mentoring scheme, and an emerging leadership programme where women can attend board meetings and get experience of chairing boards and setting agendas and doing all those kind of leadership tasks that you may not have been given an opportunity to do.

Rosie has since moved her focus to researching what it is about the culture of certain fields of medicine that is preventing women from getting there in the first place. Looking back at her training, Rosie can clearly see that female students are encouraged in a very different direction from males:

> At medical school there was a lot of that low level benevolent sexism ... saying, "You need to think about your future family and your future career and how you're going to balance the two." And it came from a good place, but it was still delivered predominantly to women, and in retrospect it's very clear to me that by giving women that advice, you cut off their ability to see themselves in positions that perhaps not many women have succeeded in so, "You want to have a family, have you thought about general practice?' ... it's very easy to then see yourself as a general practitioner but, "You want to think about your family so have you thought about orthopaedic surgery' ... no one would ever say that to a woman.

What is it about some types of medicine that make them seem more of a natural "fit" for men than for women? Rosie says:

> A lot of that is to do with the stereotype that to do intensive care you need to be the toughest of the tough, you deal with the sickest of the sick, so you need to work the hardest of the hardest, and there's that kind of idea that that is not compatible with being female. And all of this benevolent sexism I think comes down to the fact that that the toughest of the tough, sickest of the sick, hardest of the hard, doesn't align with that female stereotype that people have in their heads, and therefore they can't see you as an intensivist, so they just cut off your ability to see yourself.

Of her own experience with part-time training, Rosie says the attitude was "mothers don't do intensive care".

On the subject of differential treatment of girls and boys by educators, I talked to Rosie about what happens when girls shout out in class rather than putting their hands up, a trait generally seen as "masculine" so therefore tolerated in boys, while girls are told they are "bossy":

> I do think it starts there. As a little girl you very quickly learn that you don't shout out the answer – I got told I was bossy all the time because I was just like, you know, "I know the answer, why don't I just tell everyone?!" And as soon as I got a bit older you get … inhibited from doing these sorts of things. I think it does need to start from the very, very early stages … again, my experience in training is that boys would always shout out the answer, and that would be expected, and were always allowed to dominate the conversation, felt extremely comfortable doing that, just owning the space in a way that women didn't, and there's that sense of decisiveness and authoritativeness that's expected and nurtured and encouraged and applauded in men, but the same was not seen in women and I think that was very clear throughout all my medical training.

This culture has an impact on men in the profession too:

> Interestingly, a lot of my participants so far have talked about men having to affect this aura of over-confidence because it's so difficult for them to accept that they don't know everything, and they don't have the answer to everything. They almost over-compensate to the point where it becomes problematic. Whereas women kind of do the opposite and no one's happy and it's because of the culture.

Added to that is the outright sexism that female students and practitioners experience. At the time of writing (September 2021), social media and the national press are commenting on a case raised by the friend of a female medical student who received a yellow card (a system used during an exam situation to feed back to the student that they have displayed behaviour that is unprofessional or raises a serious concern about their fitness to practise).[27] The student's crime? Wearing a dress that came to below the knee,[28] which was described by a role-play patient, passed on by the examiner and backed up by the university as "the most inappropriate dress they had ever seen". How can this still be happening in 2021? Probably in the same way that Rosie tells me of a clinic sign-in area where the symbol for doctors is a man, and the one for nurses is a woman, and where a profession that was designed by men, for men still features many militaristic terms (house officers; doctors' mess). And all this in the wider context of a society still dominated by gender stereotypes.

What can be done? Rosie is particularly interested in the feedback that is given – not just to medical students, but to children of all ages and genders. She mentions an activity she undertook with first-year medical students, one of whom reported receiving feedback where

> a consultant said that because she hadn't smiled that day the consultant didn't have any idea if she even wanted to be there and what was the point of her being there. And she had done everything to a very high standard … this was such gendered feedback.

The same goes for all the micro-interactions we have on a daily basis: "Changing culture is really hard and I think culture starts at the micro level." If adults and educators were more aware of the impact such gendered feedback could have on children's and students' aspirations, self-belief and comfort levels in different spaces, Rosie believes we could avoid some of the negative impacts.

Case Study: Men in Childcare

When we developed the Gender Friendly Nursery for NHS Greater Glasgow & Clyde, we paid special attention to the topic of men in the childcare workforce, discussing the reasons why we need more of them, the barriers they face and what nurseries can do. We came across many examples of difficulties that male practitioners, and their colleagues and managers, faced, including one nursery that told us their only male practitioner, a wonderful young man who the children loved, was leaving that day. The manager and staff had tried hard to support and encourage him to stay but the backlash he had faced from his own peer group, who continually questioned his motives, eventually became too much for him to the point where he felt he couldn't continue.

Shaddai Tembo is a Postgraduate Research Student at the University of the West of Scotland who has worked as an early years practitioner and has been a strong voice advocating for men in the early years. Shaddai tells me that some of the barriers in place for men in this field

> are often put in place throughout their early childhood and schooling experiences. From being discouraged from engaging in caring activities through to the subtle messages that position the early years as an easy or feminine role, boys are rarely inspired to enter this profession in the same way that girls are. All too often, even the suggestion that a boy may want to work with young children is met with accusations of one the "three Ps". That is, you are a paedophile, a "poof" or a pervert. I know this because I've experienced it myself, along with many others I worked to support as male practitioners.

For those who do make it into the profession, Shaddai says:

> Further barriers remain in place. Often, these take the form of a lack of support from other staff members who themselves may hold prejudices against men, parental perceptions of who should look after their child, and a lack of a support network for the men themselves.

Why the need for a specific support network for men? This is

> especially important since there remains a general lack of knowledge within settings about how to support staff through situations where their practice is called into question because of their gender. For instance, when parents or carers request that the male practitioner do not change their child's nappy, or that they do not become their child's key worker.

Shaddai is clear that there are situations where settings may have to consider the circumstances of individual families when such requests take place (more on this in Chapters 13 and 18). But in a general sense:

> Could you even imagine a parent asking for their child not to be cared for by a woman? Once we start to unpick the argument against male practitioners, it becomes clear that a level of prejudice is often at play. Early years settings have a duty to stand behind their male staff on these issues.

Is the current push for more men in the early years working to break down these barriers? Not if by doing so we are perpetuating gender stereotypes!

> For me it's really important that when we think about men in early years, we avoid envisaging a single type of man. The image of men working with young children often stirs up ideas about rough and tumble play, outdoors activities, being a "father figure" and generally being there "for the boys". My own experience as a male practitioner reminds me of how often I was burdened with the role of doing outdoorsy activities and seen as less suited to working with babies and younger children. However, this is problematic because it's a stereotype based upon very traditional ideas of who men should be and what kinds of things they should be doing. It also suggests that the existing practitioners, implicitly women, are not doing these things – positioning them as deficient or lacking something in their practice because of their gender.

In Chapter 13, we will take a closer look at gender in the early years workforce, why we need a more diverse workforce generally and what practitioners and managers can do to bring this about. For now, it's also worth remembering that many of the barriers we have looked at here can be applied to men in other female-dominated professions such as nursing, hair and beauty, and dance. Once again, gender stereotypes are limiting our children's aspirations.

What Can We Do?

As we've said before, the early years are a critical period for the development of basic skills, attitudes, confidence-building and learning about our place in the world. So there are many, many opportunities for early years settings to support and encourage children to believe they can aspire to a whole range of future career paths, and to begin developing the skills they will need to get there. The following suggestions will almost certainly include things you are already doing, although perhaps not with an awareness of their importance in bridging the gender gaps we have looked at in this chapter. So please bear in mind the principle of equity: we're trying as always, to recognise which children aren't likely to get these opportunities from society at large, and to offer those opportunities and encouragement. This doesn't mean assuming that all girls will have poor spatial awareness or that all boys are emotionally stunted, but it does mean we can be aware that gender stereotypes make it more likely that grown-ups believe this, that they project these beliefs onto children and that children will internalise them. It also means we need to look out for other characteristics – stereotypes that may be limiting children' opportunities, like ethnicity, poverty or disability, and at how these might intersect with sex and gender.

- Consider your displays and resources and how they model career possibilities. Make sure you show children that women can be firefighters and men can be carers.
- If you invite people in to talk about their jobs, find out whether it's possible to get female scientists and male hairdressers rather than only the gendered "norm".
- Think about how you can promote early skills in the areas where men, and women, are under-represented. Support girls (and other under-represented groups) with early STEM skills such as spatial awareness, questioning, tinkering and experimenting by

promoting play with loose parts; promote confidence and assertiveness in potential future politicians and business leaders; help boys to access their emotions in healthy ways by using the tips we discussed in Chapter 7; encourage them to be creative using arts and crafts, and to improve literacy through storytelling.

- Undertake continuing professional development (CPD). The Scottish Government produced STEM CPL modules for early years and childcare learning practitioners that can help you understand how to promote these skills for all under-represented groups.[29]
- Think about your use of resources such as PATHS to see whether there are ways in which they can be used equitably to support boys' emotional literacy.
- Role model! Make sure any men in your setting aren't used for stereotypically male activities like IT and outdoor play, and that they are seen by all to be involved in story-telling, cuddles and other nurturing activities. And ensure that women are also seen by the children being involved in all sorts of aspects of childcare and education.
- Think about the feedback and micro-interactions that Dr Rosie Baruah discussed in this chapter. What aspects of children's behaviour and abilities do you pick up on, or not pick up on? Why? What impact could this have?

Notes

1 Women in STEM, "Percentages of Women in STEM Statistics" (2021). Available at www.stemwomen.co.uk/blog/2021/01/women-in-stem-percentages-of-women-in-stem-statistics (accessed 13 January 2022); House of Commons Library, "Research Briefing: Women in Politics and Public Life" (2021). Available at https://commonslibrary.parliament.uk/research-briefings/sn01250 (accessed 13 January 2022).
2 M. Ford, "Focus: Men in Nursing: Tipping the Gender Balance", *Nursing Times*, 6 March 2019. Available at www.nursingtimes.net/news/workforce/focus-men-in-nursing-tipping-the-gender-balance-06-03-2019 (accessed 13 January 2022).
3 GenderEYE, *End of Project Report: Gender Diversification of the Early Years Workforce: Recruiting and Supporting Male Practitioners* (2020). Available at https://gendereye.files.wordpress.com/2020/10/gendereye-final-end-of-project-report-28-oct.pdf (accessed 13 January 2022).
4 See https://cpag.org.uk/cost-of-the-school-day (accessed 13 January 2022).
5 See https://education.gov.scot/improvement/learning-resources/scottish-attainment-challenge (accessed 13 January 2022).
6 Joseph Rowntree Foundation, *UK Poverty 2019/20* (2020). Available at www.jrf.org.uk/report/uk-poverty-2019-20 (accessed 13 January 2022).
7 L. Bian, S.J. Leslie and A. Cimpian, "Gender Stereotypes About Intellectual Ability Emerge Early and Influence Children's Interests". *Science* 355(6323) (2017): 389–91.
8 G. Rippon, *The Gendered Brain* (Harmondsworth: Penguin, 2019): Chapter 10.
9 D.I. Miller, K.M. Nolla, A.H. Eagly and D.H. Uttal (2018). "The Development of Children's Gender-Science Stereotypes: A Meta-analysis of 5 Decades of U.S. Draw-A-Scientist Studies". *Child Development*, 89(6): 1943–55.
10 U. Kessels, A. Heyder, M. Latsch and B. Hannover, "How Gender Differences in Academic Engagement Relate to Students' Gender Identity", *Educational Research*, 56(2) (2014): 220–9.
11 R. Webb, *How Not to Be a Boy* (Edinburgh: Canongate, 2017), 84.
12 A.M. Koenig, "Comparing Prescriptive and Descriptive Gender Stereotypes About Children, Adults, and the Elderly", *Frontiers in Psychology*, 26 June 2018, https://doi.org/10.3389/fpsyg.2018.01086(accessed 13 January 2022).
13 C. Fine, *Delusions of Gender* (London: Icon Books, 2010).
14 C.L. Martin and C.F. Halverson . "The Effects of Sex-typing Schemas on Young Children's Memory". *Child Development*, 54(3) (1983): 563–74.

15 SQA, *SQA Annual Statistical Report* (2019). Available at www.sqa.org.uk/sqa/91419.html (accessed 13 January 2022).

16 Department for Education, *Early Years Foundation Stage Profile Results in England, 2019* (2019). Available at https://assets.publishing.service.gov.uk/government/uploads/system/uploads/attachment_data/file/839934/EYFSP_2019_Main_Text_Oct.pdf (accessed 13 January 2022).

17 Scottish Government, *Programme for International Student Assessment (PISA) 2018: Highlights from Scotland's Results* (2019). Available at www.gov.scot/publications/programme-international-student-assessment-pisa-2018-highlights-scotlands-results/pages/8 (accessed 13 January 2022).

18 G. Horgan, *The Impact of Poverty on Young Children's Experience of School. Joseph Rowntree Foundation* (2007). Available at www.jrf.org.uk/report/impact-poverty-young-childrens-experience-school (accessed 13 January 2022).

19 W.S. Gilliam et al., *Do Early Educators' Implicit Biases Regarding Sex and Race Relate to Behavior Expectations and Recommendations of Preschool Expulsions and Suspensions?* (New Haven CT: Yale University Child Study Center, 2016). Available at https://medicine.yale.edu/childstudy/zigler/publications/Preschool%20Implicit%20Bias%20Policy%20Brief_final_9_26_276766_5379_v1.pdf-(accessed 13 January 2022).

20 M. Kollmayer, B. Schober and C. Spiel, "Gender Stereotypes in Education: Development, Consequences, and Interventions". *European Journal of Developmental Psychology*, 15(4) (2018): 361-77.

21 See www.gov.scot/publications/school-exclusion-statistics (accessed 13 January 2022).

22 M. Pinkett and M. Roberts, *Boys Don't Try?* (London: Routledge, 2019).

23 N. Freeman, "Preschoolers' Perceptions of Gender Appropriate Toys and Their Parents' Beliefs About Genderized Behaviors: Miscommunication, Mixed Messages, or Hidden Truths?" *Early Childhood Education Journal*, 34(5) (2007): 357-66.

24 *Improving Diversity in STEM: A report by the Campaign for Science and Engineering (CaSE)* (London: Kings College 2014), 23. Available at www.sciencecampaign.org.uk/static/uploaded/50c4b928-d252-4ce8-825065f92d8deca3.pdf (accessed 13 January 2022).

25 Education Scotland, *Improving Gender Balance: Literature Review* (2019). Available at https://education.gov.scot/media/asOhl3fz/sci38-igb-a-literature-review.pdf (accessed 13 January 2022).

26 A. Malcolm, "The Scottish Perspective: Men in Early Years Challenge Fund" (2019). Presentation to Men in the Early Years conference). Available at https://miteyuk.org/2019/09/17/mitey2019-conference-presentations/ (accessed 13 January 2022).

27 C. Duncan, "Newcastle University Apologises to Medical Student 'Who was Told Her Skirt was Too Short". *Independent*, 10 September 2021. Available at www.independent.co.uk/news/uk/home-news/newcastle-university-student-skirt-sexism-b1918026.html (accessed 13 January 2022).

28 I mention the length of the skirt, which was also shown on social media, not because it matters (the point being that no one would accuse a male student of inappropriate behaviour based on the wearing of normal clothes!) but to pre-empt any questions about whether it actually really was inappropriate: it definitely wasn't! In Chapter 6, we looked at the blaming of women and girls for men's thoughts and behaviours, including the policing of their clothing: this is another example.

29 See www.gov.scot/publications/training-modules-for-all-elc-practitioners (accessed 13 January 2022).

12 Mental Health

Barbara Adzajlic

Why You Should Read This Chapter

We have touched on the issue of mental health across a few of these chapters. Children are being fed a diet of messages that contribute to their feelings about masculinity, femininity, body image and their role in the world, and the restrictions and limits imposed by these messages can take a toll on their mental health as they grow older and realise they can't always conform to stereotypes. In this short chapter, we'll briefly look at some other starkly gendered issues in mental health and explore why these differences exist and what we can do to support all children to have the foundations for good mental health.

Girls' and Boys' Mental Health Statistics

Let's start with some statistics. According to the Mental Health Foundation[1]:

- Today, women are three times more likely than men to experience common mental health problems. In 1993, they were twice as likely.
- Rates of self-harm among young women have tripled since 1993.
- Young women are three times more likely than young men to experience post-traumatic stress disorder (PTSD).
- Young women are three times more likely to experience eating disorders than young men.

Some other data worth noting:

- Girl Guiding UK produce an annual survey of girls' attitudes and opinions on a range of topics. The 2021 report, produced during the COVID-19 pandemic, suggests 67 per cent of girls aged seven to 21 years feel more sad, anxious or worried as a result of the pandemic.[2]

DOI: 10.4324/9781003167921-15

- Glasgow's School Health and Wellbeing survey, data for which were collected just before the pandemic, compares self-reported health data for girls and boys aged 11–16 years. Using a well-known mental health scoring tool it shows that 24 per cent of boys and 43 per cent of girls aged 13–16 years had probable depression, while 9% of boys and 18% of girls experienced loneliness often or always.[3]
- Boys are much more likely to be diagnosed with neurodiversity, like Autistic Spectrum Disorder, ADD and ADHD – but recently discussions have turned towards an under-diagnosis of girls, who are much more likely to mask their symptoms, while disruptive behaviours in boys are more likely to lead to referrals.[4]

There is also the fact that, while men are more likely to *complete* suicide (as we discussed in Chapter 7), women are more likely to make suicide *attempts*.[5] Moreover, more males are detained under the Mental Health Act because of suicide attempts, but those females who are detained are more likely to be detained multiple times.[6] So while male suicide is a really important area that needs to be addressed, we also need to look at what is happening with women and girls, because mental health problems often start young.

Why the Difference?

There isn't scope here to go into the suicide paradox in any depth, and others have already done the work in this area, but it's worth asking ourselves just what is happening to our girls' mental health? How does this relate to gendered expectations and gender stereotypes? What's happening to boys? And, of course, what can we do?

In 2017, in a report aptly named *While Your Back Was Turned*, the Mental Health Foundation warned that not enough attention had been paid to the mental health of women and girls.[7] It links deteriorating mental health to issues like austerity (which hits women hardest because they are more likely to be in low-paid, part-time or insecure employment, to be single parents, to be disabled or to care for someone who is, or to be in an abusive relationship); online culture (which we discussed in Chapter 4 in terms of the pressures from the music and fashion industries, social media and pornography); and the impact of domestic abuse. It argues that policy-makers have not been paying enough attention and calls for gender-specific data and policies that take gendered issues into account.

To understand more about how some of these interlinking issues result in depression for women, we can take a look at some really interesting work by Jack and Ali on the concept of "self-silencing".[8] Self-silencing is an internalised response to rejection, and can include withdrawal, a loss of self-esteem and of a sense of self – all early symptoms that can lead on to depression. Studies show that while some people respond to rejection with aggression, women and people from minority groups are more likely to respond with self-silencing. Why? The answers lie in historical power dynamics and silencing of these groups, continuing social inequality and devaluing of traits that are seen as "female" (back to those "you throw like a girl" and "pink stinks" attitudes), as well as societal pressure for women to be self-sacrificing within their close relationships ("stand by your man", "behind every great man is a great woman" … the expectation to sacrifice career for family and so on). All this leads to women being more likely to self-silence and to experience depression. And this is a pattern that is seen increasingly across the globe, as the work by Jack and Ali illustrates.

We also touched briefly on micro aggressions in Chapter 5. Microaggressions are the small, often unrecognised and unremarked-upon incidents of discrimination that can be experienced on a daily basis by women, people from minority ethnic groups, people with disabilities and others. They are the "harmless", or "jokey" comments we see at the bottom of the Allport Scale: asking someone where they come from because of their skin colour; assuming someone is helpless because they are disabled; assuming that the woman in the white coat is a nurse and the younger man with her is the consultant. We know that discrimination has an impact on health, particularly mental health.[9] If we think of micro aggressions as a dripping tap effect, wearing away gradually at a stone, we can understand how detrimental the effect can be over time.

And what about the boys? The data we looked at above might suggest that boys are doing much better than girls overall. But we always have to consider the gender boxes and what they do to boys' and men's ability to express their emotions and talk about any difficulties they are experiencing. The fact that women are more likely to self-silence leaves us with men who are more likely to have the opposite reaction – aggression – and we looked in Chapter 7 at how this can manifest as harming others or harming oneself. We also need to think about the boys who don't use the aggression route to cope with their difficulties. And, among all of this, we need, as always, to consider intersectional issues. We saw in Chapter 10 that of all the LGBT+ categories involved in a piece of research, bisexual young women were most likely to experience mental health problems. Black girls and women, girls and women of colour, and disabled girls and women are more likely to experience the double (or more) impacts of their minority status, so we need to pay special attention to mitigating all the factors at play here.

What Can We Do?

Early intervention is really important, but we know that professionals often fail to spot the signs of mental health problems when they are internalised – as they often are in girls – rather than externalised. So there is an issue here for professionals who work with children and young people to become better at spotting the early signs that a girl might be struggling with her mental health, or be neurodiverse. There are gendered issues at the early intervention stage: whether talking therapies work for boys who aren't used to talking about emotions and who see it as a sign of weakness, or whether play and art therapy might work better (and indeed, whether this approach also discriminates against girls by assuming *they* don't need access to these alternative approaches). There are issues at the treatment stage (there's an argument that women and minorities are more likely to be medicated for certain conditions that are a natural response to the trauma and discrimination they have experienced). And, of course, there are the issues that are contributing to all of this: the gendered pressures, expectations and stereotypes that are the root cause of at least some of these differences.

So, while it's a huge and complex issue and there is work to be done at every level, what you can do at the crucial early years stage is actually quite simple, and consistent with the messages we have been promoting throughout this book. It's about reducing gender stereotypes wherever you can using an equitable approach: giving boys the opportunities they need to talk about emotions in healthy ways, and giving girls permission to be seen and heard rather than feeling they have to self-silence. Wherever possible, it's also about supporting families as well: supporting parents and carers to be emotionally literate; encouraging them to talk about mental health; and helping them to do the same with their children. Jack and Ali[10] promote the idea of healing women's depression through recovery of voice. What you can do is help children to have that voice in the first place.

Top Tips for Promoting Good Mental Health

- Promote emotional literacy in boys through resources such as PATHS[11] and by normalising the idea of boys and men talking about emotions through play, books and the example of your male staff, if you have them.
- Give girls permission to have a voice: to say when things are bothering them and to have those things addressed, to voice their opinions, to know that their thoughts and feelings matter.
- Watch out for examples of self-silencing in your resources and everyday interactions. If you notice an example in a story of a woman or girl keeping silent about an issue, use it as a teachable moment to remind children that they can all speak up about things, whoever they are.
- Support families to reinforce these messages by telling them how important this is, by inviting them to come in and learn more, and by sharing resources that they can use at home.
- Support parents and carers, and staff, to look after their own mental health. Consider training staff in basic mental health so they can support conversations with families, and make sure you know where you can signpost people if they need help (see the list of support services in Appendix 3).

Notes

1 Mental Health Foundation, "While Your Back Was Turned: How Mental Health Policymakers Stopped Paying Attention to the Specific Needs of Women and Girls", Policy Briefing, December 2017 Available at www.mentalhealth.org.uk/publications/mental-health-young-women-and-girls (accessed 12 January 2022).
2 Girl Guiding, *Girls Attitudes Survey 2021*. Available at www.girlguiding.org.uk/girls-making-change/girls-attitudes-survey (accessed 12 January 2022).
3 NHS Greater Glasgow and Clyde, *Glasgow City Schools Health and Wellbeing Survey 2019/20* (2020). Available at www.stor.scot.nhs.uk/handle/11289/580310 (accessed 12 January 2022).
4 The reasons for this are varied, and more research is needed to properly understand it, but it certainly looks as if gendered expectations are involved. This article gives a good summary of the issues for ADHD: K. Oakes, "Why is ADHD Missed in Girls?", BBC Future (2019). Available at www.bbc.com/future/article/20190530-why-is-adhd-missed-in-girls (accessed 12 January 2022).
5 D.L. Schrijvers, J. Bollen and B. Sabbe, "The Gender Paradox in Suicidal Behavior and Its Impact on the Suicidal Process", *Journal of Affective Disorders* 138(1-2) (2012):19-26.
6 C. Warrington, "Repeated Police Mental Health Act Detentions in England and Wales: Trauma and Recurrent Suicidality". *International Journal of Environmental Research and Public Health*, 16(23) C. (2019): 4786.
7 Mental Health Foundation, "While Your Back was Turned: How Mental Health Policymakers Stopped Paying Attention to the Specific Needs of Women and Girls', Policy Briefing, December 2017. Available at www.mentalhealth.org.uk/publications/mental-health-young-women-and-girls (accessed 12 January 2022).

8 D. Jack and A. Ali, *Silencing the Self Across Cultures: Depression and Gender in the Social World* (Oxford: Oxford University Press, 2010).

9 There are some brilliant studies looking at the direct impact of racist incidents on mental health, as well as the impact of racist micro aggressions, including: D. Williams, H. Neighbors and J. Jackson, "Racial/Ethnic Discrimination and Health: Findings from Community Studies". *American Journal of Public Health*, 98 (2008): S29-S37.

10 Jack and Ali, *Silencing the Self Across Cultures*.

11 See www.pathseducation.co.uk (accessed 12 January 2022).

13 Gender and the Early Years Workforce

Susie Heywood

Why You Should Read This Chapter

We have already touched on how gender stereotypes are limiting career paths, why we might see such low levels of men working in early learning and childcare settings, and the issues facing women who return to work after having children. This chapter highlights the gendered issues facing early years staff in more detail, and in particular what we can do to increase diversity within the workforce.

It is important right at the outset of this chapter to note that neither of us has worked directly in early years settings. Many of you reading this may have your own thoughts and opinions about the issues facing your workforce, which are informed by your own experiences as a person working in the sector. Our hope is that this chapter will provide some context for these issues, or may inspire you to reflect on them more, either as an individual or as a staff team. We have also included some thoughts from Shaddai Tembo. As well as his experience as a male practitioner within various early years settings and roles, he brings a wealth of knowledge and research experience regarding the importance of diversity in early years settings.

Is a Gender-balanced Workforce Important?

Let's begin by returning to the lack of men in the early years workforce – one of the most obvious and glaring gendered issues we face. Before we consider why we might see such a huge gender imbalance and look at what could be done to tackle this, it feels important to briefly establish the benefits of a gender-diverse early years workforce. You will recognise themes that we raised earlier in the book, but it's useful to remind ourselves in this workforce context.[1]

Children need to be exposed to diversity in all aspects of their life. All children need to see that all kinds of people can be caring, gentle, playful and fun. A female early years workforce reinforces the message (stereotype!) that caring for children is "women's work". A diverse workforce demonstrates to children that this is not the case, and allows young boys to be able to see themselves in these kinds of roles as they grow older. This can be supported by

DOI: 10.4324/9781003167921-16

the increased participation of men and dads in domestic life and childcare. It also means that children are able to have positive and varied interactions with both men and women in the nursery setting and that the conversations we have about gender equality and stereotypes can be done in a place where we can see diversity in action. While we know that the early years is not the only female-dominated workforce, we know the importance and influence of those early years, so making changes here feels important.

The more men we have in our settings, the easier it is to attract and retain more! Many men already do want to work in early learning and childcare settings, but there are many barriers preventing this from happening. Why would we want to limit the talent pool to only half of the population when we can attract a diverse range of highly motivated and skilled individuals when we open it out to all?

Barriers to a Gender-balanced Workforce

So what are the barriers facing men entering the early years workforce? The clash between traditional masculine identity and the childcare role is clearly a factor. Our current working-age men are much more likely to have grown up without men in childcare or child-rearing role models – we hope that this will change as men increasingly take on active fathering roles, but as we have already discussed, it's hard to aspire to be something that you didn't realise was an option. Despite efforts to diversify the workforce, the majority of courses in childcare and recruitment for childcare roles are not proactive in seeking men, and can even perhaps suggest that only females are being sought. We have seen posters in pink and purple, feminine imagery and pictures of female-only staff groups. It is unlikely any of this was done intentionally – it's that unconscious bias coming into play again – and it isn't just an issue for early years. We came across an advertisement for a medical secretary that used the female pronoun in the job description!

Even for those men who do develop an interest, there are further barriers. Being the only male in a female staff group or training cohort can be the reality for men who enter the workforce. For some, this is not an issue, but for others it can prove uncomfortable, and we have heard some men describing feelings of loneliness, isolation and lack of support. Staff areas in nurseries may appear feminine after years of female-only use, and female staff may find it difficult to adjust to a male member of staff coming into what has always been a female-only space. People can and will adjust – staff are, of course, professionals who treat others with respect and dignity – but some teething difficulties might be expected and may need proactive effort to overcome.

I am sure you will have heard of, or even encountered, parents who express concern about having male members of staff change nappies. We have heard stories like this in almost every training we have delivered. Men in early years spaces can be treated with suspicion and their motivations for being there can be questioned. This association of men with abuse is not acceptable and deeply sexist. Shaddai faced this situation himself in his career in early learning and childcare and reflects:

> Clearly, we have to consider religious reasons and should treat this on an individual basis. However, as per the Equality Act 2010, in general you cannot choose who carries

out different activities based on a person's gender, any more than you can choose based on a person's age, race, sexuality, faith or any other of the protected characteristics. If a parent were to say that they didn't want their child to be cared for by a black person, a gay person, or a disabled person, think about how you would react to that. So why is gender any different?

This feels pretty clear and nursery staff and managers should be supported to approach these situations and discussions with respect and confidence. In most cases it should be made clear that all members of staff can undertake all duties within the nursery.

And this of course is important. We would be missing out on a great opportunity to show children that men too can be caring, soft and kind if we divided up the tasks in the nursery into male and female tasks, if we assigned the male staff the "rough and tumble" or tasked them with organising the dads events. By doing this we are making assumptions that men and women will have certain skills and attributes. Likewise the idea that male staff can be role models for little boys is limiting and places value on their gender rather than on the skills, qualities and knowledge that they have as individuals.

Increasing All Kinds of Diversity

While a more gender diverse workforce is an important and admirable aspiration, other forms of diversity are also lacking, are of equal importance and should form part of the conversation we are having about men in childcare. Shaddai is a loud and welcome voice in the sector around this. As he explains:

> I'm keen to push the argument for 'More Men of All Kinds in The Early Years'. In recognising the diversity of men, including those who actively challenge conventional assumptions of masculinity, Black and racially minoritised men, LGBT+ men, transgender men, and disabled men, we can really disrupt gender stereotypes and begin to normalise other ways of being a man.

This is not rocket science, yet it is sometimes absent from the discourse. Men of all kinds, who bring their own identities, experiences, abilities and bodies into early years settings, can demonstrate that there are so many ways of being a man! The same applies to women - do we see diversity across the workforce more generally?[2] It's not simply about numbers, as Shaddai quite eloquently explains in this paragraph, which sums it up better than we ever could:

> I believe that the ultimate number [of men in the workforce] matters a lot less than the actual practice of the men themselves. What if we had 30 per cent men, but all they wanted to do was play superheroes and build fires? What if we had a 50/50 split of men and women, but both conformed to traditional mother and father figure roles within the nursery? My argument is that this issue isn't one of brute percentages, but rather about social justice. It is about actively challenging the inequality that has arisen out of historical gender norms, hence why I advocate for more men of all kinds in the early years - as a means of unsettling conventional perceptions of what counts as a man within Western societies. I also believe that we need to focus our attention on supporting all

practitioners already within the profession to reflect on their gender identity critically and consider how they may be conforming with or resisting gender stereotypes.

It's what we do with our workforce that counts – the force for social change that we can create – not simply who is included in the numbers.

The Most Under-appreciated Workforce?

There is no doubt that when it comes to pay and career progression, the early years may not seem like the most attractive sector in which to work. This is not just an issue for male staff – nobody likes to feel under-paid and under-valued – but very often it is cited as one of the reasons for the low number of males in the workforce. I would expect that there is some truth in this, particularly when coupled with the continued pressure on men to earn and provide for families; however, we do see many men in many other under-paid workforces and job roles, so we would argue that it's the stereotype of child care as women's work that is having the greater impact here. Low pay is not just an issue for men either. Shaddai again:

> Suggesting that men will only come into the profession when pay and conditions increase is dismissive of the 96 per cent of women in the profession who have his-torically had to deal with low pay and poor working conditions, implicitly suggesting men need better conditions to work. A sounder logic would be that both pay and conditions need to be improved irrespective of engaging more men in early years, not because of them.

I don't think we need to tell you the importance of those early years of children's lives. Public discourse around early childhood, the first 1001 days, the impact of adversity in childhood, the discourse around play, and the importance of placing the children's rights and needs at the centre of all our decision-making are all demonstrations that in general society gets it. What happens in early childhood matters! So the fact that it sometimes feels like we don't treat our early learning and childcare workforce with the respect and reward it deserves suggests we are not always following through on that. As a society in general, we seem to continue to under-value softer, more caring and (what are seen to be) more feminine skills.

Things do appear to be improving. There have been moves to professionalise the work-force, to offer higher level qualifications for nursery staff that recognise the knowledge and skills they hold. While these are seen as desirable and offer the chance for practitioners to develop specialisms and improve practice, as well as learning useful and transferable skills such as research and inquiry, there is a sense from within the workforce that these types of qualifications are not recognised in terms of gaining promotion, increased pay or add-itional responsibility or leadership around specialisms. This raises the issue of whether, at present, there is any value for individual practitioners in terms of the financial, time and effort costs of achieving these qualifications. Despite this, there are higher paid roles up for grabs within the sector, from nursery teachers, supervisory roles, nursery and chain man-agement to training, teaching, academic and specialist development roles – but are these open to everyone? More on that later!

Is a Female-dominated Workforce a Female-friendly Workforce?

We have looked at the issues for men in the early years and the reasons why it's so important to address them. But what about the majority of the workforce? Does being in the majority mean they get an easy ride?

Let's not forget in all the discussion about the need for more men in the workforce, that current statistics tell us that between 96 and 97 per cent of the workforce is female, so there is a need to recognise the issues and pressures affecting females too. Women in early years settings are subject to the same pressures (and stereotypes) as all women everywhere while working in an under-valued and demanding setting. We have already touched on the pressures facing women as they become mothers, or take on other caring responsibilities within the family (as older women in particular often do). In addition to the burden of balancing caring, domestic roles and careers, which women tend to experience more than men, research also shows that when it comes to hiring, women face a "motherhood penalty", making mothers less likely to be hired and less likely to be highly rated in terms of their performance, a phenomenon not seen with fathers.[3] We don't know if the motherhood penalty is seen to the same extent within the childcare profession (and indeed we would hope that having children would not disadvantage anyone interested in a career working with children!), but flexible working to support people to carry out caring roles is an important consideration for nursery managers, particularly for a workforce that is lower paid and therefore carries a greater risk of women and their families falling into poverty if they are unable to find a happy balance.

It is useful here to consider a phenomenon that has been termed the "glass escalator effect,"[4] which describes how (White) men in majority female workforces or professions both face pressure to, and just tend to, rise through the ranks to higher positions quite quickly. Cordelia Fine describes it as being like a red carpet has been rolled out for them, leading to better paid positions in the field.[5] We come from a health and social care working background, and this phenomena is seen here too – certainly in proportion to the gender breakdown of the lower paid staff, there is a far greater proportion of men to women in most management type roles across the sector.[6] Why this might be is up for debate: perhaps we assume men are more suited to these roles; perhaps we think if we don't pay them more or reward them for being there that they will leave, assuming that they can't be happy in lower paid and more "feminine" roles. Casual sexism in recruitment and progression perhaps? Or perhaps it's just a coincidence? Whatever the reason, this needs to be looked at in early years workforces to ensure that nobody is unfairly advantaged or disadvantaged.

Returning to intersectionality, it's worth noting that women are more likely than men to be affected by disability.[7] There is now a long overdue recognition of specific conditions that women experience – such as endometriosis, which affects 10 per cent of women worldwide[8] – and of the challenges the menopause can present and how it can disrupt women's career progression. We need to make sure that women, whether at the start of their career or with years of experience in the profession, don't miss out on recruitment, retention and progression because of a lack of support to cope with disability and health issues, compounded by caring responsibilities, the glass escalator or the motherhood penalty.

Professionalising the Workforce: Possible Pitfalls

Efforts to professionalise the early years workforce have brought with them expectations and requirements for further study and training in order to achieve seniority in position. There is no doubt that the costs – both financial and in terms of time required – are harder for people who have additional caring responsibilities. I have no doubt that nursery managers will want to support their staff to develop and progress; however, this also means trying to balance this with the needs of the day-to-day running and, for privately owned businesses, the financial capabilities of the nursery. I recently attended a session with a higher education provider who offered undergraduate, postgraduate and masters level qualifications in early childhood education. Several nursery managers also attended and there was a discussion about how staff are supported to achieve these qualifications. It seemed that practice differed between nurseries. Some staff were allowed to attend lectures and seminars in their paid time, which meant that cover was needed within the nursery. Others were expected to use annual leave or unpaid leave. For those with caring or family commitments, this is time that could be used for family activities and such education is often unachievable, both financially and practically. The education provider was challenged to consider whether the way they currently offered their qualifications was stretching the capabilities of nursery managers and failing to meet the needs of their 99 per cent female student population.

What Can We Do?

So what can be done to support and increase recognition for the current workforce as well as to improve the gender balance and attract men of all kinds into the early learning and childcare profession? Clearly a lot of what needs to happen is at a societal level – moving away from the idea that caring is solely women's work, ensuring that early years staff are paid a salary worthy of the importance of their role and so on. Much of it too is particularly relevant for those with management responsibility within nurseries. However, all staff can contribute by continuing to reduce and provide a counterbalance to the gender stereotypes that lie at the root of much of this.

It is also vitally important that everyone understands the issue and is on the same page, particularly when it comes to increasing diversity. For that reason, considering what training or discussion might be needed is vital. Shaddai feels as if this should be a first step for any nursery looking to make changes:

> There is little value in placing the burden on the single man to fly the men in early years flag, everyone needs to get involved – not just management and even those members of staff who may express reluctance. Discussing what gender actually is and what it means, the current profession statistics, reasons why men don't want to work in early years and looking at barriers within one's own setting is a really useful starting point. Ask questions like: is the man/are the men in the setting only working with older children and not seen as capable of working with younger infants and babies? (Conversely, are the women within the setting challenging conventional ways of being women?) Is our practice based on traditional notions of how men and women should be?

Open, honest and reflective conversations, where we increase our understanding and challenge our own stereotypes and biases, are important.

Other actions that could help include:

- Consider whether your recruitment materials and practices send particular messages about who should apply for the job. If you are female, you may want to involve men or male practitioners in preparing these – sometimes they will notice something you might not. If you are keen to increase the number of men in your setting, then you should say you are actively seeking applications from men (of all kinds!) seeking to work in the early years.[9]
- Consider what you can do in your setting to make it more welcoming to all staff. For example, even if you don't have any male staff currently, this could change and it's better to have considered it now. If you are female, reflect on how it would feel to be the only female in a male-dominated workplace. Ask yourself what might help.
- Be clear to everyone – staff, parents and children – about the benefits of men in the early years. If you have male staff, celebrate them and make sure they feel welcomed, included and valued.
- Look for peer support options for lone male staff within your setting. Of course they can be supported well by their female colleagues, but being in a minority can be hard. Having someone to talk to who has experienced similar things is always helpful. There may be online groups, or you may be able to reach out to other nursery managers who may have male staff, who would also welcome that support.
- Avoid pigeon-holing members of staff, particularly male staff, when it comes to the activities they lead and roles they take in the playroom.
- Consider how male nursery staff, particularly young staff and those who may have had less experience of caring roles in their day-to-day lives (remember that this can be the case for female staff too!), can be encouraged and supported to undertake those activities and roles in the early years settings. Work with the staff member to identify any areas for development or training.
- If you don't have any male staff in your nursery, could you invite a male staff member from a partner or other local nursery in to talk to the children about his job and why he enjoys it?
- Consider how you can support staff, particularly those who have caring responsibilities, to access education and training opportunities. There will be no "one-size-fits-all" approach, so including a range of options such as day release or evening study can help.
- When it comes to opportunities for more senior positions or promotions within the nursery, nursery managers should look to support and encourage all staff to apply.
- In general, family-friendly policies support all staff to feel more valued and appreciated, and can attract staff to join and stay with your setting. Initiatives such as the Mum Friendly Workplace[10] can help you consider whether there is more you can do to support parents among your staff.
- Ensure staff feel supported with any health issues, particularly topics that have traditionally been hard to talk about and have tended not to be recognised or supported, such as mental health and the menopause.

- Celebrate the achievements of your staff – I am sure you already do, but having seen first-hand as a parent and through my work with nurseries just how dedicated, skilled and caring the staff are, they deserve to be recognised and celebrated!

Notes

1 We have attempted to summarise what we have learned here, but if you want to delve into this in more depth, we would highly recommend paying a visit to the Men In The Early Years (MITEY) website. Their "10 Myths about Men and Early Years Education" download is particularly useful. Available at www.miteyuk.org (accessed 2 March 2022).

2 We have been watching the development of The Early Years Black List with interest. Efforts to recognise the experiences of Black practitioners, and to ensure that their voices and expertise are included and valued, are vital to developing a workforce that reflects society and that can challenge racial and gender (and other) bias within the system. See www.theearlyyearsblacklist.com (accessed 2 March 2022).

3 S.J. Correll, S. Benard and I. Paik, "Getting a Job: Is There a Motherhood Penalty?", American Journal of Sociology, 112(5) (2007), https://doi.org/10.1086/511799. cited in C/. Fine, C. (2010) *Delusions of Gender* London: Icon Books. p57

4 This term was coined by Sociologist Christine Williams in 1992 in a paper called "The glass escalator: Hidden advantages for men in the "female" professions." (*Social Problems*, 39(3), 253-266)

5 Fine, C., *Delusions of Gender* (London: Icon Books, 2010), 64.

6 For example, Geoffrey Punshon and colleagues show that, in nursing, men are over-represented at senior bands compared to their overall proportion in the UK nursing population. There also seems to be an advantage in terms of faster attainment of higher grades from the point of registration. See G. Punshon et al., "Nursing Pay by Gender Distribution in the UK: Does the Glass Escalator Still Exist?" *International Journal of Nursing Studies*, 93 (2018): 21-9.

7 Women's Budget Group, *Disabled Women and Austerity: Briefing from the UK Women's Budget Group on the Impact of Austerity on Disabled Women.* Available at https://wbg.org.uk/wp-content/uploads/2018/10/Disabled-women-October-2018-w-cover-2.pdf (accessed 2 March 2022).

8 See the list of facts and figures on the Endometriosis UK website at www.endometriosis-uk.org/endometriosis-facts-and-figures (accessed 2 March 2022).

9 MITEY (www.miteyuk.org) and GenderEYE (www.gendereye.org) both have useful guides to support recruiting men. GenderEYE also have a really practical toolkit to support early years setting recruit, retain and support men in the workforce (accessed 2 March 2022).

10 See www.mumsreturningtowork.org (accessed 2 March 2022).

PART 3

14 Auditing Your Practice

Barbara Adzajlic and Susie Heywood

Reflecting on our practice is always a good idea. We hope that by this point you will be convinced of the need to ensure that practice across our early years settings not only minimises gender stereotyping, but also actively provides a new narrative that promotes equity. We have previously mentioned the need for whole setting approaches, which take into account the various facets and areas of practice and nursery life.

In this section, we want to introduce you to a tool we have developed that can help you to apply a broad lens to work and practice. You can find the tool in Appendix 2. I am sure the concept of an audit tool is not new to you – they are well used for a reason. In our tool, we have broken down early years settings into four areas: People; Place; Practice; and Planning and Policy. Under each there is a series of reflective questions. We suggest that as a first step you consider your current practice in relation to each area – because experience has taught us that early years staff are very often already doing a lot of this stuff either intuitively or because of the existing knowledge they have around equalities and child-centred practice. It is worth taking the time to reflect on and celebrate this stuff, and realising that you are already further ahead than you think. You can then look at areas for development or improvement.

Key Principles

As you work your way through the audit, bear in mind the key principles of gender equitable practice, which can help to guide your approach. These are:

- **Equity:** Remember that this is about the ways we can provide a counterbalance to the messages that children will be receiving from the world around them about gender and what is or is not appropriate for them and others. This means that there may be times when you may want to tailor your approach to certain groups of children. Chapter 16 provides more details and examples.
- **Inclusivity:** Remember that gender stereotypes affect everyone, though sometimes in different ways. It is in everyone's interest that we take action in this area and we can *all* be part of the solution. If you are completing this on behalf of a setting, we recommend involving everyone in the discussions and reflections – as well as all staff, this could also include parents, children and the wider community. Can you organise training on the

DOI: 10.4324/9781003167921-18

issues, or use this book to lead discussions with your colleagues? Help them to find the motivation to change practice.

- **Holistic:** We have tried to chunk up nursery life and early years practice into manageable areas to allow you to work through them a bit at a time. Making progress in any area is good - but real change will only happen if we can look across the whole setting, so we encourage you to complete the whole audit - even if it takes you quite a while!

- **Preventative:** Knowing why it is important to do this work can provide the motivation we need to keep us going, so understanding and revisiting the relationship between these seemingly harmless stereotypes and the very real harms can help us stay on track.

- **Intersectional:** While the focus of the audit is on gender equitable practice, we always have to remember that there are many other characteristics and experiences that may impact children's opportunities in the early years and in our early years settings. This includes race, ethnicity, disability and class. While an equitable approach may at times require us to tailor specific responses for boys and girls in order to "level the playing field" when it comes to messages about gender, we also need to be mindful that within each group, certain children may have additional needs by virtue of these other characteristics and experiences.

- **Rights-based:** The right of children to live lives free from discrimination and unlimited by harmful gender stereotypes is at the heart of this whole approach. Putting children's rights at the heart of everything we do can help us to stay on the right track.

- **Informed:** As you visit each section of the audit, you may want to consider whether there are areas where you or your colleagues require further training or knowledge, and seek these out. We have been working on this topic for over seven years and we are still learning new things almost daily. Find ways to remain engaged in the topic - to keep your passion for this work alive.

- **Action-focused:** The purpose of the audit is to identify areas for development, so it's really just the beginning. From your findings, you may wish to develop a set of actions to take forward either as an individual or as a whole setting. We have included some suggestions for this at the end of this chapter.

We hope that you find this tool useful. It is fairly comprehensive, but there will be additional areas or actions that may be specific to you or your setting which you may want to add, so we've left a few rows blank under each section. We would suggest taking some time over it. Talk things over with others in your setting. Come back to it at a later date when you have had a chance to reflect a bit more. There may be areas that are of less relevance to you, your practice or your setting, and there are likely areas where you are already doing excellent work with little room for development. Depending on your role, there may be areas of practice that feel outside your sphere of influence - perhaps if you aren't part of management you may feel you have no control over recruitment policies, for example. Don't be disheartened by this - there will be plenty of areas where changes can be made and practice developed, which is why the audit process is only the first step. We would encourage you to consider whether you feel able to bring these other areas to the attention of those who may be able to make changes should you feel comfortable doing so.

Action Planning

We suggest that your next step would be to create an action plan based on the findings of your audit. It may be that you find there are several clear, obvious actions that need to be taken forward, but it's equally likely that there are many areas where action could support improvement, and that's where some focused action planning can help you achieve clarity around the way forward.

We have not provided a comprehensive action plan tool, but the action checklist in Appendix 1, which you will hopefully have completed while reading this book, may be a useful place to start. Below we have listed some things you might want to consider as you develop your action plan.

- You may wish to consider which of the actions are most achievable for you and/or your setting. Things to consider include the resources that will be required for each – that could be time, money, materials or the requirement for additional training.
- You may also want to consider the balance of effort and impact of each action as you decide where to place your focus. Not all actions need to be huge to have a big impact!
- We know that early years staff and settings face a number of demands and competing priorities, so it's important to consider where this work fits, and what is realistic for you.
- It is good practice to set yourself timescales for your actions and celebrate your achievements when you have completed them. In our experience, things often take longer than you think they will, so be kind to yourself.
- It can be easy to be overwhelmed, particularly if there are lots of areas for development, so setting short-, medium- and long-term goals can be useful.
- If something doesn't feel achievable right now, it doesn't mean it never will be. We would recommend that you revisit the audit tool periodically and set yourself new actions and goals.

We also want to provide a few suggestions for actions that we believe can play a fundamental role in changing organisational culture and individual practice. You may wish to consider these alongside your own.

- Where possible, training for all staff within a setting, which includes an exploration of the reason for adopting this approach, can ensure that everyone is on board and understands the need to change practice. We know that accessing training can be expensive and time-consuming, but we truly believe that having the time and space to learn about and discuss these as a staff group is valuable. This is not a tick box exercise.
- Consider developing a specific gender- or gender stereotype-focused policy for your setting. A specific policy relating to gender equity should be a strong statement of commitment and intent to implementing gender equitable practice and minimising gender stereotypes in your setting. It should clearly state your aim of ensuring that nobody is limited by gender stereotypes and should also make clear to all what this means for your setting. If you already have a strong equality and diversity policy with which you are happy, you may want to consider adding something specific to it in relation to gender equality.

- If you are undertaking this process as a setting, it is important to communicate with your wider nursery community, letting them know you are working in this way and why. This can include parents, partner agencies and associated schools. We would suggest that including information on gender equitable practice in your nursery handbook, website or information sheets is a useful start.

Inspiration

Finally, some inspiration from nurseries who have undertaken a similar process. The NHS Greater Glasgow & Clyde-owned Gender Friendly Nursery project includes an audit and action planning process whereby nurseries work towards "Gender Friendly" accreditation. The evaluation of the project included examples of actions taken forward by nurseries who were involved in the pilot.[1] Here are a few of them:

- Development of specific posters and leaflets to communicate with parents about the Gender Friendly approach.
- Carrying out an audit of books in the nursery library to ensure a range of non-stereotypical gender roles and family types were included.
- No longer buying gendered birthday cards or graduation gifts for the children.
- Moving away from routinely dividing the children by gender for nursery activities.
- Conducting a staff peer observation and feedback exercise focused on language use and interactions with the children.

Note

1   S. Heywood, *An Evaluation of the North East Glasgow Pilot of the Gender Friendly Nursery Programme* S (2018). Available at www.stor.scot.nhs.uk/bitstream/handle/11289/579834/Gender%20Frien dly%20Nursery%20Evaluation%20Report%202018.pdf?sequence=1&isAllowed=y (accessed 7 January 2022).

15 Bias, and How to Get Over It!

Barbara Adzajlic and Susie Heywood

A bias is a preference or inclination for or against a particular group. It is based on a stereo-type, which as we know is an unfair belief about that group having certain characteristics. While we're pretty confident that by this stage in the book (if not well before!) you are convinced of the harms of stereotypes and the biases they produce, you may not have had the opportunity to explore your own biases or those of the people around you. There is a lot of discussion these days about "unconscious bias" - the kind that is so deeply entrenched we aren't even aware of it, even when we act upon it and it affects our ability to treat people fairly. So it's important to come to terms with our biases, whether conscious or uncon-scious, and to know what to do with them. Taking a gender equitable approach also means supporting children to navigate their own biases.

But I'm Not Biased!

Just in case you haven't considered before whether you hold any bias, there are some easy activities you can try. You may know this little story - it has been around for a long time (since at least 1984, when Barbara heard it for the first time) but it still manages to catch people out (regularly, on our training courses!). If you haven't seen it before, think about it for a moment and then turn to the end of this chapter for the answer.

> A man and his son are driving along a winding mountain road when the man loses control and the car plunges down a cliff. The man is killed instantly but emergency ser-vices arrive and take the boy to hospital, where a surgeon is called on to perform an emergency operation. The surgeon sees the boy and says, "I can't do this - that's my son!" How is this possible?

If you didn't fall for this one, congratulations! If you did, chances are you won't fall for that particular scenario again because you will have been alerted to your unconscious bias, but hopefully you get the point. We have caught ourselves many times making assumptions about a situation based on stereotypes, despite working for several years on this topic! It's tricky, but worth working on because of the impact it can have.

DOI: 10.4324/9781003167921-19

STATEMENT	QUESTION
A doctor and a nurse are talking about the nurse's daughter, who is married to an engineer.	Which of the characters did you picture as male and which as female?
On the way to dance class, Alex is shouted at by the driver of a white van.	Which sex did you imagine Alex and the van driver to be?
In the canteen three scientists are arguing about the results of an experiment, while the catering staff clear up after lunch.	What kind of scientists did you picture? What did they look like? (Did they wear uniforms?) Were they male or female? What was their ethnicity? What about the caterers?
There are two boys outside the headteacher's office. One is East Asian, the other Black. The headteacher comes out and thanks the headboy for coming, then tells off the other child for being disruptive in class.[1]	In your mind's eye, which boy was the headboy and which had disrupted the class?
...and finally, did you imagine any of these people having a physical disability?	

Figure 15.1

[1]This scenario is adapted from a scene from the Netflix series, *Sex Education*

Here are some other examples that might bring your unconscious biases to the surface. Read each statement first (try covering up the questions so you don't prime yourself!) and then think about the questions:

Another way to test yourself is with the Harvard Implicit Association test, which looks at gender, racial and other biases.[1]

Okay, so Maybe I Do Have Unconscious Bias ... But Where Does It Come From?

Unconscious, or implicit, bias is a mental short-cut to quickly process information and make a decision. It used to be, and sometimes still can be, a survival technique. In situations when our survival depended on being able to access scarce resources and knowing the difference between friendly and unfriendly neighbouring groups, we had to make rapid decisions about new people or things that we encountered. Friend or foe? Likely to be strong and fast, or weak and slow? Someone I can trade with and learn from, or need to run from? Even if our world today is less full of dangers, survival is still about learning about one's social group, its rules and norms, and what we need to do to fit in, to make friends, to be loved and protected. So when we meet others who don't fit with those rules and norms, we see them as group outsiders, and if we rely on our unconscious bias and the knowledge and experience we have gained about our own group, then we may treat them as outsiders.

As we saw in Chapter 3, from the very start of our lives we are busily picking up signs and cues about those rules and norms. And sometimes the knowledge we pick up is based on stereotypes, which as we know are inaccurate and over-generalised. You can probably think of quite a few examples of stereotypes: racial stereotypes, stereotypes about people with glasses, stereotypes about people on benefits, or those about footballers' wives and girlfriends. We will all be aware of some of these stereotypes, and by this stage in the book you are probably pretty conscious of any gender stereotypes you may hear, if you weren't already! But others may be ones we haven't realised we hold, or that we haven't stopped to think about for long enough to realise they simply aren't true. These are the unconscious ones and they are often deeply ingrained.

Having unconscious bias isn't a bad thing, but *not addressing it* is. Unconscious bias is a product of the environment we grow up in, that everyone has to some extent, which is not only no longer useful in most situations but actually has harmful consequences. It can greatly limit our social circle,[2] cause us to inflict micro aggressions on other people (as we discussed in Chapter 12) and lead to unfair decisions. We only need to look at the top of the Allport Scale in Chapter 5 to be reminded of some of the worst consequences.

A fascinating example of early years practitioners' unconscious bias in action can be seen in a study by Yale University that we looked at in Chapter 11, where practitioners were asked to view some short films of the same group of four children playing and interacting, and to identify any challenging behaviours they observed. The group of children consisted of a Black and a White boy, and a Black and a White girl. Despite there being *no challenging behaviours* in any of the film clips, practitioners were significantly more likely to report observing them in the Black boy, followed by the White boy, the White girl and finally the Black girl.[3] This is really significant when we look at the likelihood of Black boys in particular experiencing school exclusions and encounters with the justice system.

What Can We Do About It?

So how do we go about addressing unconscious bias? You can attend training, but there isn't great evidence that this actually works and some actually suggest it can do more harm than good, by highlighting and reinforcing stereotypes (remember stereotype threat, which we discussed in Chapter 11!) and by allowing people to think they have the moral high ground. The first step is acknowledging your bias; the harder part is changing your behaviour, and looking at what, both personally and in the structure of your organisation, is allowing discrimination to take place. We suggest you embed a model of reflection like the one in Figure 15.2, and use it as a staff group so that you can help each other out.

1. *Recognise* when your unconscious bias has caused you to act unfairly (or work with supportive friends or colleagues to help each other recognise it).
2. *Correct* yourself straight away if possible to prevent your action from influencing how someone else thinks, or from causing unfairness. For example, "Oops, I shouldn't have said that, let me just re-phrase it …", or "I'm sorry, I've just realised that wasn't fair. Let's do it this way instead …"
3. Once the immediate situation has passed, *reflect* on what made you think or act that way.
4. *Plan* how you can avoid this particular bias from tripping you up in future. You might ask a colleague to help you out if they notice it, or run through practice scenarios in your head.
5. This process should help you to slow down your thinking next time you are in a similar situation, which will help you to *do it right* … but if not, make sure you recognise it and go through the cycle again, until you do get it right.

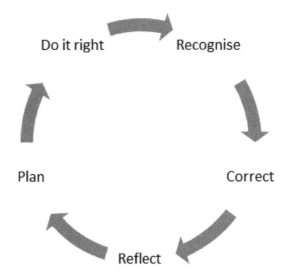

Figure 15.2

By slowing down our thinking, reflecting, learning, unlearning and relearning, we can catch ourselves in a thought or an action at earlier points, and eventually begin to make a difference. And while we shouldn't punish ourselves for *having* bias (especially at the beginning of this process), we should remember that unconscious bias is still bias and we need to do better.

We can put all the strategies in this book in place, teach gender equality, create neutral spaces and buy all the new resources in the world, but if our unconscious bias creeps out in our language and behaviours, then we risk sending contradictory and confusing messages to children. We need to be all in. We need to be focused.

Watch Out for Cognitive Dissonance!

Cognitive dissonance is the tension or discomfort that people experience when they want to stand up for what they believe in, but societal pressure or inconvenience makes it difficult. For example:

- You are earning more money than someone else who has done exactly the same job as you for exactly the same length of time, and who you believe to be equally competent. It doesn't feel right, but you invent a reason for it ("They mustn't be as good as me").
- You accept an invitation onto an all-male, or all-White discussion panel, knowing there should be better representation. You say nothing and tell yourself it's for the greater good because what you have to say is really important.
- You find yourself laughing along with friends at a joke that is racist or sexist even though you believe this is wrong. This distresses you, so you reduce the distress by telling yourself that the person telling the joke didn't mean it in a bad way.

Figure 15.3 Cognitive dissonance

We have to watch out for moments of cognitive dissonance because they can trip us up: we're aware of our unconscious bias; we're trying to be anti-racist or anti-sexist; but a moment of cognitive dissonance can lead us to minimise or justify what has just happened, rather than taking the harder path of acting to make amends or change our behaviour next time. It can be hard to admit you've done something that goes against what you believe, or to tell a colleague or friend they have done so. So just take a moment to reflect, forgive yourself this time round but then decide what you're going to do about it.

Tackling Bias in Children

Our approach is rooted in prevention, and as such it's worth considering whether there are things we can do to tackle bias among young children and perhaps stop it from developing in the first place. Children are not born with prejudice, but they *are* born into a prejudiced world. They begin to learn about the world through categories and look to others around them to learn more about what these categories mean. As such, they are learning from others' biases (conscious and unconscious) and very quickly can learn to stereotype themselves and other people as a way of simplifying a complex world.

There are some great books about bias, how it affects us and how to address it with children. We have learned a lot from *Unravelling Bias* by Dr Christia Spears Brown,[4] *Young Children and Racial Justice* by Jane Long[5] and *Talking with Children About Race* by Dr Pragya Agarwal,[6] which we have summarised into some key points below.

- It's important when embarking on conversations with others about their bias to do the work with ourselves. Self-reflection, a better understanding (and reduction of) our own bias and confronting the stereotypes that we hold will put us in a better position to discuss and consider these with other people.

- Don't assume that young children are free from bias and excuse or minimise prejudiced behaviour – we need to address it with confidence, and help children to understand and learn from it. Be clear to the children about what is and what isn't acceptable, and stick to it.
- Dr Christia Spears Brown says we should teach children to be "critical consumers of the world" around them. Instil the building blocks of critical thinking: help children to ask why, to question truths and untruths, and to consider what is fair and unfair.
- Model to children that it's okay to make a mistake, and that we can recognise, admit and learn from these. We never stop learning and unlearning!
- Create opportunities for children both to see and interact with as diverse a variety of people as possible, learning about other people's perspectives and ways of empathising with them. It's more than just seeing ourselves reflected in the world; it's also about seeing people who are different from us, seeing them as individuals rather than as groups (which can lead to stereotypes) and learning to understand and respect difference while also recognising all the things we have in common. Persona Dolls can be useful for this. Think about the examples you use in your teaching and learning, the people who come into the nursery, the places you take the children – all these are chances to help them learn and experience diversity. Simply ensuring that children participate actively, enjoyably and successfully in mixed-sex groups when it comes to nursery activities can be important, particularly when we know that children very quickly self-select playmates of the same sex.
- Don't be afraid to have conversations about this stuff, even with very young children. We know that stereotypes and bias are learned very early, so it's never too early to start to talk about and challenge them.
- Consider how we can support children who may face discrimination and bias to develop a positive self-identity. Help them to feel that they belong, and know that they are valued and celebrated.

Creating Moral Rebels

The next step up from recognising and challenging bias in ourselves and others is supporting children to feel able and comfortable to do this themselves – to actively challenge bias and discrimination against others, to be moral rebels. Parents and carers, we're looking at you in particular here! While early years practitioners can create safe spaces and lead by example, and while they can certainly do some of what follows, this is an area where you have a tremendous amount of influence. We might worry that it's too early to start encouraging children to speak out, and certainly it's important to make sure they can do so in ways that are safe, but there is a lot of information and support out there to help us foster activism in age appropriate ways in children. We have seen children of all ages involved in climate activism in recent years, so it's worth thinking about how we can do this for other areas of injustice.

Bystander theory, first proposed in 1964, explores the factors that encourage or inhibit people from intervening in an emergency situation. As you can imagine, there are many different factors at work here, including the competence of the bystander, the environment, possible consequences of helping or not helping, and their relationship to the person needing help. Various strands of work have emerged from bystander theory, including Mentors in Violence Prevention (MVP), which was mentioned briefly in Chapter 6.[7] MVP aims to build people's capacity to be active rather than passive bystanders by building confidence and providing a range of options for intervening. Intervening can simply mean *not* bowing to social pressure to laugh at that sexist/racist/homophobic joke; or making sure a friend who has had too much to drink gets home safely; or approaching someone else who might have more influence to call out discriminatory language or behaviour. It's also about building male, and White, and straight, and able-bodied, and many other types of solidarity; having allies among people who belong to the groups that have the power and privilege; working towards that critical mass of people who don't tolerate discriminatory language or behaviour, which ultimately makes calling it out easier and safer for everyone. Graham Goulden, who we met in Chapter 7 and who helped bring MVP to Scotland, says, "We need to help people to step into the spotlight. How do we help them to move from the doing nothing to the doing something? Because the standard that you walk past is the standard you accept."

For young children, developing these capabilities is based on the same principle: that doing something is better than doing nothing, and that there is a range of things you can do. It's also about realising that bravery isn't just about the Avengers using their physical strength to defeat the baddies; it's also about having moral courage to stick up for others even when it might not make you popular (we can help to reframe bravery - especially for our boys!). Dr Christia Spears Brown provides more ideas about creating active bystanders - or, as she calls them, "upstanders": people who use their words and actions to help others and themselves. This is about being the child who steps in when someone else is being treated unfairly, when unkind words are said, or when incidents of discrimination happen. In order to support children to be "upstanders", Spears Brown suggests five steps:

1. Give them the knowledge to be able to spot discrimination through conversations about stereotypes, discrimination and privilege.
2. Build empathy for others in order to be able to understand more subtle forms of discrimination including comments or exclusion.
3. Create a sense of personal responsibility and help children to understand that by doing nothing they are part of the problem.
4. Build confidence in helping. Spears Brown suggests using role-play and scenarios. This could also be part of the discussion you have with children when reading books and stories.
5. Help children to know helping strategies - what they could do (tell a teacher, use humour, diffuse the situation, tell someone to stop ...).

Ultimately, as well as removing the unfair limits on children's potential, we want to help them to become great citizens and brave and powerful allies. Our job as the grown-ups in their lives is to help children to be reflective and to identify their values, and to equip them with the tools to make decisions based on these values and to challenge their own choices when needed.

Answer to the first unconscious bias question: the doctor is the boy's mother.

Notes

1   See https://implicit.harvard.edu/implicit/education.html (accessed 7 January 2022).
2   If you're in any doubt about this, here's an exercise Susie did on a training course recently. Participants were asked to take a minute or so to list between ten and 15 people (not immediate family) to whom they were close enough or trusted enough to invite into their homes. They were then asked to look at their list in terms of sex, gender, race/ethnicity, religious background, educational achievement and disability. It was a powerful insight into how much we tend to stick to what we perceive as "our" people.
3   W.S. Gilliam, A.N. Maupin, C.R. Reyes, M. Accavitti and F. Shick, *Do Early Educators' Implicit Biases Regarding Sex and Race Relate to Behavior Expectations and Recommendations of Preschool Expulsions and Suspensions?* (New Haven, CT: Yale University Child Study Center, 2016). Available at https://medicine.yale.edu/childstudy/zigler/publications/Preschool%20Implicit%20Bias%20Pol icy%20Brief_final_9_26_276766_5379_v1.pdf (accessed 7 January 2022).
4   C. Spears Brown, *Unraveling Bias: How Prejudice Has Shaped Children for Generations and Why It's Time to Break the Cycle* (Dallas, TX: BenBella Books, 2021).
5   J. Lane, *Young Children and Racial Justice* (London: Jessica Kingsley, 2008).
6   P. Agarwal, *Wish We Knew What to Say: Talking with Children About Race* (Boston: Little, Brown, 2020).
7   See www.svru.co.uk/mvp (accessed 7 January 2022). MVP has been rolled out widely across Scottish secondary schools and many other settings in the United Kingdom and beyond.

16 Equitable Practice

Barbara Adzajlic and Susie Heywood

This chapter explores in more depth what an equitable approach to gender stereotypes in the early years looks like. We defined what we mean by equity in Chapter 1 (remember the people peeking over the fence?) but to summarise, an equitable approach is one in which everyone is given what they need to achieve the same outcomes or to allow them to have the same access. It is rooted in the knowledge that people do not start out with the same levels of privilege or opportunity, and that society is full of inequalities, which means certain groups and people are at a disadvantage and face additional hurdles or barriers.

There are many examples of where equitable approaches are important in relation to a range of issues. Just the other day, we attended a meeting at a university where one of the senior teaching staff spoke about how they were confident that they were "colour blind" when it came to the curriculum they taught. The notion of passive colour blindness, in a society where people of colour face daily discrimination and disadvantage supported by the reality of structural racism, is laughable. Proactive, anti-racist approaches are required. The voices and experiences of people of colour need to be centred. Likewise, physical alterations to buildings allow equitable access for disabled people. Bursaries and ring-fenced places, which ensure that young people from lower income families can access expensive higher education, provide a level of equity. All-female shortlists in elections have been relatively successful in ensuring more of a gender balance among elected officials. These are all examples of equity in action.

The focus of this book is gender, and the inequalities we see resulting from gender stereotypes and prescribed gender roles. By now you should be well versed in these, so they do not need explaining again, but it is worth reinforcing the impact that these are having – even in the very early years. Children come to you with their own biases because they have already absorbed messages that influence their actions, expectations and aspirations. Because of this, we firmly believe it's not enough to treat all children the same if we want to ensure that they have equal access to all experiences in the nursery. Our approach is a proactive one, which is grounded in the concept of equity. While there may be elements that take a gender-neutral approach, they are part of a response recognising that, for children in our settings, gender stereotypes are very much a part of how they have been taught to understand the world, and which therefore faces this head on. We cannot challenge something that we are afraid to talk about.

DOI: 10.4324/9781003167921-20

Although the mass media will have a key role to play in a dominant cultural narrative, and many of the suggestions we make in this book are about providing a counterbalance to that narrative, children will also be exposed to gendered messages specific to individual areas or families. For example, there may be a unique prevailing narrative about what it means to be a man in an area traditionally dominated by heavy industry. Likewise, individual families may have their own ideas about gender roles, which may be influenced by things like religion, ethnicity or varying cultural norms. All children are unique and our approaches must also take this into account.

 Reflection

Take some time to reflect on what messages the children in your setting might already have been exposed to and the biases they might hold.

- What ideas about gender and gender roles might they hold?
- Where or from whom might they be receiving this information?
- How might these ideas be impacting the choices they make in your setting?

An Unusual Education: The Hjalli Model

But what does this mean in practice in a nursery setting? Let's explore an example of nursery-based gender equity in action. This example comes from Iceland, a country that ranks among the most gender equal in the world. We first came across the Hjalli model of education several years ago and have since been lucky enough to meet and spend time with Margrét Pála Ólafsdóttir, who developed the model in 1989, learning more about why and how it was developed and what it looks like in practice. Margrét Pála is an educator and philanthropist, and has been awarded many honours for her work, including the Icelandic Order of the Falcon and the EU Women Inventors and Innovators Network award. Hjalli is now a well-established provider of nursery and primary level education in Iceland, with long waiting lists, particularly for some of its nurseries, suggesting that the model is well accepted, at least among these parents.

For the majority of their time in Hjalli nurseries, children are divided into small, single-gender[1] groups where they work, with the same teacher, through a curriculum focused on both social and individual skills. The curriculum aims to ensure that children experience all aspects of nursery life in ways that meet the needs of individuals, yet compensate for the difference between the genders that we already see at this age. I'll let Margrét Pála explain where the model came from:

> It's really simple. If it's not working having them together, if you can see girls back out of situations and you can see boys that are not really robust and active, seeing them back also out of situations and not finding themselves … I have seen it again and again … So if it's not working, what is the opposite way? It's as simple as that. Let's at least try to teach them apart and see what will happen.

By dividing the children in this way, as well as through a rich and varied curriculum, staff can ensure that children have equal access to learning, activities and experiences. The social skills curriculum teaches discipline, cooperation, helpfulness, solidarity, intimacy and helping. As individuals, children are taught independence, choice, problem-solving, positivity, joy, courage and risk-taking among other things. It's this training that Margrét Pála believes sets her model apart from other single-sex settings.

Woven through this curriculum is what Margrét Pála calls "compensation work". She talks about the need to understand the things boys need and the things girls need because of the differences we see even at this young age. Doing this in single-gender groups eliminates the need for constant comparison or competition. This is not about training girls to be like boys and vice versa, but rather about recognising the strengths and weaknesses of both, and providing the opportunity to develop those skills or have those experiences that they may have been denied because of their gender. As Margrét Pála says, "If we do not train it, it will not be there." This is quite a long quote, but it's important to hear about the model in Margrét Pála's words:

> Some gain is automatic, just by the simple fact of having them in two groups. Girls will start to run first, to go out first when you are going outside for a walk, and the boys, they will automatically start asking their friend, "Can I borrow your gloves, I've left mine at home" you know, because we know if you have girls there … the boys will ask the girls for help. Because the girls are always ready for everything, they are always prepared, they have everything they need you know and are so happy to share. So [boys are asking girls for help and] are not asking their [male] friends … but if you are having only boys [in a group], they are doing it. So they start occupying roles that they didn't try out before … but then I started to see that that was not enough, just splitting them … the "pink haze" and the "blue haze"[2] was more visible than before … So I started to try out what we call the compensation work … when we are with the girls, strengthening them, helping them to raise their chins and saying out loud what they mean rather than [whispers behind hand] talking behind others' backs and so on. And we are training them in using their bodies in more active and stronger ways than they would do otherwise. And by strengthening them we see how they are coming away from this extreme behaviour that we call the "pink haze". And vice versa.

A vital element of the model is the everyday interaction in mixed-gender groups. During this time, children are taught how to work together, to show respect for one another and how to be friends. Again this is proactive work that Margrét Pála believes does not happen naturally because of the tendency for girls and boys to see each other as different:

> You have to mix every day, even if it's just for a few minutes or an hour, I do not care, as long as it's positive, both groups are good at what they are doing, and they are communicating and working together. Because just keeping them apart is not solving everything, we also need to put them together every day.

She speaks about "the reverse mirror", which is the tendency for boys and girls to look at each other not to learn, but to learn what they should NOT be, how they should NOT act and what they should NOT play with.

There are elements to Hjalli nurseries which are very gender neutral, and Margrét Pála believes this is fundamental to the success of her model. There are no traditional toys. Recognising the importance of intrinsic child-led play and in an attempt to eliminate competition, children are provided with open-ended materials such as blocks, paper, dough, blankets, materials, water, sand and crafting materials in order to stimulate their imagination and promote original and innovative thinking. The nursery environment is uncluttered and neutral in colour. Children are provided with an unfussy and practical uniform, or "workwear", in a choice of red or blue trousers, leggings, t-shirts or jumpers. The idea is not about eliminating individuality, but fostering a sense of belonging to the same team, as well as eliminating the gender bias that is inherent in a lot of this stuff and sends messages we know children are absorbing.

One of the questions Margrét Pála is often asked, and one we asked her the first time we met, is what happens to children who do not identify as either boy or girl, or whose biology does not match the gender with which they identify? For Margrét Pála – who believes that, at nursery age at least, children very firmly understand whether they are a boy or a girl even if that does not align with their sex at birth – the answer was very simple, and was tested pretty early on when a child who was born female yet identified as a boy came to one of her nurseries. Her answer was to let the child choose – spend a day with each group and decide which group they wanted to spend their days with. On this occasion, the child realised that while each group was doing pretty much the same thing, the boys group was a lot noisier, so they opted to join with the girls. None of this phased the children in the nursery – all the anxiety and questions lay with the staff.

The Egalia Model

Of course, Hjalli is only one approach to gender in the early years. Another that many will have heard of is the Egalia model of kindergarten provision in Sweden. Egalia kindergartens were developed in Stockholm, Sweden in 2010. Sweden already recognised the important role that pre-schools had to play in striving for gender equality, including this in the country's Education Act and ensuring that all settings had a gender specialist; however, there was little guidance as to what this looked like in practice.

Egalia (Latin for equality) uses a gender-neutral pedagogy that teaches equal rights, freedom from gender role expectations, personal identity, democracy and citizenship. It is based on the principle that everyone, regardless of sex, should be able to experience the "whole life spectra" (every colour, every emotion, every quality or behaviour, every type of clothing). It celebrates difference yet advocates that everyone should be treated in the same way, regardless of sex.

As well as (most famously) eliminating the use of gendered pronouns (the neutral term "hen" is used as well as "children" or "friends") in the belief that when we assign something or someone a gender it immediately affects our perceptions of it, the nursery environment and the resources used are set up in a way that encourages children to play together and to try activities that are not normally associated with traditional gender roles. Staff are there to ensure neutral language, encourage mixed play, select songs and stories that challenge stereotypes, role-model for children and challenge and talk about gender issues.[3]

The director of Egalia, Lotta Rajalin, explained that the approach they take is attempting to remove the barriers that can prevent children doing what they want to do because of the gendered expectations:

> We want children to have equal opportunities in experiencing their emotions, explaining themselves, loving the colours they want, and playing the games they want to play.[4]

We asked Margrét Pála how the Hjalli model differs from this approach. She explained:

> They are addressing gender ... but they are taking quite the opposite [approach]. We are born two sexes, and somehow it is affecting everything right down to children who are two years old, putting everything into two boxes, male and female. But [at Egalia] they are trying to avoid it as best they can. The last time I paid a visit I saw that just a simple thing like not having school uniforms or nursery clothes, [the children are] still coming in presenting their gender. And they are still having gendered toys and so on. Our method is lifting up the two sexes, ... at least until they are seven or eight years old, and saying "how can we help them to resist sliding into the two boxes" – while [Egalia] are saying "let's make one box".

In case this quote comes across as overly critical, we want to be clear that Margrét Pála states very clearly that she does not believe that her model is the ONLY solution – far from it. She believes that settings and practitioners can find ways that work for them, but she is clear that gender differences are something we can't ignore and need to take action on.

What Can We Learn from These Approaches?

We created The Gender Friendly Nursery before we learned about the Hjalli model, and our thinking has developed and matured as a result of learning about this, and other, approaches. However, even then we recognised that children are not growing up in a gender-neutral world, and were clear that the approach we were advocating was not about creating gender-neutral settings (although we did borrow from these types of approaches). We believed (and still do) that early years settings can be a challenge to these narratives – an opportunity to teach children that anyone can be or do anything regardless of their gender. A chance to practise equity.

It's surprising that the Egalia model, which is widely understood to be a "gender-neutral" model, continues to use traditional toys and allows children to dress as they please, yet the Hjalli model, with its single-sex settings, actually takes the more gender-neutral approach in this regard. Our approach does not ask nurseries to get rid of anything specifically – we are not saying get rid of all the dolls, the cars or the traditional fairy tales, though we do encourage settings to consider open-ended and natural play materials wherever possible. It's important that settings make their own decisions around this; however, as we have previously outlined, we believe that if settings choose to have these types of resources then they need to be prepared to use them to challenge, develop critical awareness, and start conversations with children about the stereotypes and the messages they might be conveying. We know that having these toys and books, and being exposed to these stereotypes, does have an effect on children – so proactive discussions about stereotypes are absolutely vital if you choose to have these types of resources in the nursery!

Hjalli nurseries refrain whenever possible from wall displays, opting for play areas decorated in soft neutral and natural colours. This is not just about removing stereotypes (although when, on occasion, displays are used they ensure that these do not reinforce gender bias) but about removing visual stimuli in an attempt to create calm environments. This is quite different from most UK early years settings, and would be quite a big change for some, but Margrét Pála believes it's just another element to her model that makes a difference. If you do use wall displays, however, you can do your best to ensure that these do not perpetuate stereotypes, and include counter-stereotypical examples wherever possible.

The Hjalli position on uniform feels worth considering – although nurseries must take great care to ensure that any directives on uniform take low-income families into account. The choice of a gender-neutral uniform has a number of benefits. As well as minimising difference and the presence of gendered messages on clothing, it ensures that children are coming to nursery in practical clothing that will not restrict their movement around the nursery. As we've mentioned, for Margrét Pála it's also about fostering a sense of team-building, belonging and body confidence, added to by the fact that staff wear a similar uniform. Food for thought!

It's our understanding from our reading and from conversations with practitioners that children know from a young age whether they are a boy or a girl (though we know this can change as they get older), that they understand gender in a binary way at this point, that it forms a key part of their early identity and that they even begin to police each other around these categories. We know that for a small number of children their gender identity does not match their biological sex – but that even in these cases they are usually very clear about which of the two binary categories they belong to, and in general young children do not seem to question other children when these situations occur. We think, then, that it's okay to call children who are boys [and who are content to be boys] "boys" and vice versa (though we would encourage settings to consider whether the use of more neutral terms at times, particularly when addressing all the children collectively, may be helpful in combating the way that society and the gender boxes set boys and girls up in opposition to each other). If we want to provide the counter-message to what young children are learning from the world around them about what it means to be a boy, then we need to be able to talk about boys, and we may sometimes need to direct our efforts specifically to children who are boys. Margrét Pála's approach may seem pretty radical, yet we can absolutely see the logic in it if it allows that "compensation" work to be done in ways which mean all children can thrive and fully benefit.

The compensatory approach feels important. Margrét Pála describes the purpose of this as ensuring that every child has the chance to experience and develop mastery of every human quality and skill, rather than remain limited to those at each end of the gender scale. Though the approach they take is quite different, this feels similar to the Egalia aim of ensuring that children are able to experience "the whole life spectra". In our nurseries we ought to consider ways in which we too can achieve this. How can we help our little girls to develop confidence, initiative and self-assurance? How can we help little boys to communicate, understand and name a whole range of feelings and emotions, and show care and compassion?[5] And how can we do this while we give them the same experiences of nursery by gently tailoring our approaches, our words, actions and conversation with the children?

As practitioners, having an awareness of the different ways in which boys and girls interact with and use the nursery environment is also important. The same goes for staff attention and time – often we find that boys can dominate. One of the reasons Margrét Pála decided to try dividing the children initially was because she had observed the way that little boys dominated certain play spaces and crowded out the little girls. She noticed well-behaved little girls playing quietly in corners being further encouraged in their "good behaviour" by the staff. It's worth undertaking observations of your own about the ways that children use play areas and the ways staff interact with the children. Is there truly equality of access – or do you notice that there are certain areas that girls or boys tend to avoid? While we may not be able, or choose, to separate our children in the way of Hjalli, we can consider ways that we can try to minimise this kind of thing. If you find boys or girls gravitating towards certain areas of the room, then consider whether you can alter how play areas are set up. One way to do this is to blend areas together, incorporating elements of one into the other. Can we incorporate more traditionally "boyish" toys or activities (if you have them) into the home corner if that's a place you notice that boys tend to avoid? Can we encourage girls who favour the home corner to design and build an even better home corner?

We feel that, in many respects, the approach that we have outlined in this book is quite different from Hjalli and Egalia, yet we have also learned a lot from both. We also want to be clear that we know we don't have all the answers. We have changed and adapted some of our own thinking through meeting people like Margrét Pála and reading about approaches like Egalia. What we have written in this book is quite different in many ways from the early thinking that informed the development of The Gender Friendly Nursery. Equity has always been part of our thinking – it's a huge part of the public health agenda when it comes to addressing inequalities – but we have learned how powerful it can be, and how many ways it can be done in early years settings.

It is probably worth mentioning here that we understand that our approach, like that of Hjalli and Egalia, may be met with condemnation or outrage from some people and certain groups. We know that some people may feel as if we are trying to upset the natural order of the world (we hope we have done a good enough job of convincing you that the current order is far from natural!). People will often hook onto one aspect of a model in particular as an example of why it is problematic (for Egalia, it was the elimination of gender pronouns; for Hjalli, it was the single-sex groupings). To paraphrase something we heard from Margrét Pála and from others when we received criticism of The Gender Friendly Nursery: "If you are doing something important you will always get this kind of resistance." We like to think it means we are doing something right!

So we believe that we need to take equitable proactive approaches to address gender stereotypes as long as we live in a world where they are so prevalent. This, however, begs the question of whether we should just accept these differences and train children to compensate for them, or should be going a step further and fighting against them at a societal level. Prevention rather than cure? This is something we wrestle with in relation to many issues, in fact: to what extent do we strive for and celebrate and champion examples of the ideal, versus accepting the reality of the situation we are currently in and putting measures in place to compensate for the inequalities it brings? For example, thinking back to parenting pressures (Chapter 9), should we be celebrating and presenting as "the norm" those stay-at-home dads or the dads who take an equal share in the parenting, or should we be accepting the reality of the situation: that the lion's share of childcare still falls to women, and ensuring that the support and policies are put in place so women are not disadvantaged by that? It feels like right now we need to do both, and finding the right balance is key.

Intersectional Equity

Of course, gender inequality is only one of the many inequalities that children can face. Gender stereotypes are only one of many types of stereotypes. Sexism is only one of the many "isms". We have touched on the concept of intersectionality at various points in this book. The term was coined by Professor Kimberlé Crenshaw to describe the, at the time, unnamed concept of the crossover of two different types of discrimination – for example, racism and sexism – and was based on her observations of the multiple discrimination faced by workers who were both Black and female, and were locked out of jobs on account of both.

It feels really important that we find ways to incorporate gender equity into our work that do not ignore, and that in fact help to address, these other issues. We were interested to hear Margrét Pála's thoughts on this, aware that Iceland is quite different culturally and demographically from the United Kingdom. We had been reflecting on whether the division of children into single-gender groups, and the large focus on the gender curriculum and compensation work, may come at the expense of these other issues. Margrét Pála disagrees:

> Gender will always be the biggest variable … and so it's always a help to take the biggest variable away, and that's the gender groups … But in our discussion and in our training with the compensation work, like working with two boys holding each other's hands and watching each other's eyes, two girls holding each other's hands when they are jumping down, and all this friendship training, all this working with closeness and courage, it's always connecting this group together … because when you are holding the hand of another [person] of a different colour, or maybe with special needs or something like that (and we discuss it, it's not a secret), I think that's more powerful than having one book out of two hundred.

The idea that spending time and building relationships with people who are different from you is a powerful way to overcome bias would support this view, and the fact that children spend the whole nursery year with the same small group of children and the same teacher would certainly help with this relationship-building. The key here is the role of the teacher in making sure children are encouraged to work together and find the things they have in common, so the absence of a gender variable doesn't serve to highlight other variables. Of course, like gender stereotypes, the stereotypes we have about other groups of people are also learned and ingrained early, so it's important to consider what proactive approaches we can take. Having that one book out of 200 is better than no books – although we know from our experiences of working with early years settings that most are much further ahead than even this, and have a good selection of books, dolls and other resources featuring all kinds of people.

We have spent much of this book unpicking the discrimination faced by children based on their sex and gender, and at various points have included reflections on where certain children may be further disadvantaged because of an additional aspect of their identity. We need to be able to recognise the impacts on certain groups if we are to implement equitable approaches to support them. We need to ensure that our understanding of the experiences of and challenges for various groups is up to date. We need to do the work. And then we need to consider how equity can also be used as a tool to address these.

How Can We Incorporate Equity into Our Settings?

For many, both the Hjalli and Egalia models of education might seem quite extreme. Margrét Pála continues to face many questions about her approach, although the positive experiences of the children and feedback from the parents (as well as positive outcomes of former Hjalli students) suggest that she might be on to a good thing. We have already made some suggestions about how elements of her model could be incorporated into other settings. Interestingly, a couple of years ago Hjalli purchased a nursery in Glasgow and, despite the setback of the COVID-19 pandemic, are taking steps towards testing how the model works in a Scottish setting. We are watching with keen interest.

How else might we incorporate equity into our early years settings? A good example of equity in action comes from the BBC documentary *No More Boys And Girls*. For those of you who haven't seen it, it's a two-part documentary from 2017 that sees Dr Javid Abdelmoneim work with a teacher (Graham Andre) and his class of seven-year-olds to, as he describes it, "turn their class gender neutral". The idea is to see whether this can make a difference to some of the attitudes and ideas about what boys and girls, and men and women, can and can't do or achieve.

The programme described the evidence, which showed girls having lower self-confidence and scores around maths, and the class undertook an experiment in spatial awareness (a key component of STEM subjects) where on average the girls scored lower than the boys in the class. They also demonstrated by way of another experiment (which we described in Chapter 3) that when adults choose toys for children, these are often along very gendered lines, which see little boys being given the toys that are more likely to help them develop these spatial awareness skills – building blocks, robots, cars (things that can be manipulated). By providing the girls in the class with the opportunity to practise tangrams to support the development of the skills required to do well in the test, they saw the scores level up. The seemingly "natural" difference between the boys and the girls could easily be overcome by providing the opportunity to develop and practise these skills. (We often return to this example when we realise our daughters have spent the last two hours playing Minecraft – it certainly helps relieve parental guilt if we tell ourselves it's an exercise in levelling up!)

The programme demonstrated that exposure (or lack of it) to tasks affects ability and brain development, and how ability and performance can be improved through practice. In the programme, Gina Rippon, the neuroscientist who we heard from in earlier chapters, said something that I think is really important. She said (to paraphrase), "If you are better at something, you enjoy doing it more." Stereotypes that limit children's exposure to certain tasks or experiences create a self-perpetuating cycle like the one in Figure 16.1.

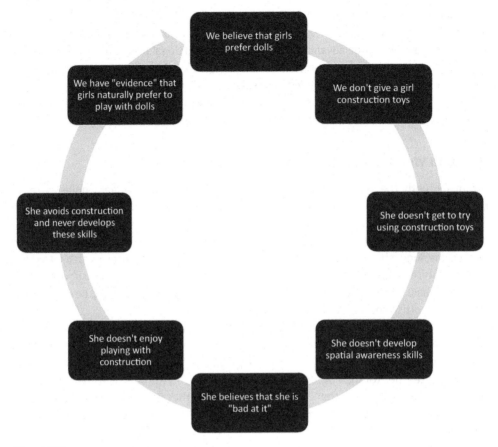

Figure 16.1

Equitable approaches that allow children the opportunity to try things they might not normally be encouraged to attempt (because of the stereotypes) are one way we can break this cycle.

But, as we have already noted, every child is unique. Not all boys will have had the same experiences; not all girls will have grown up in homes with the exact same beliefs about gender roles. We need to be careful that, despite our good intentions, we do not make gendered assumptions ourselves that might unwittingly send the message to children that all boys and girls are the same. Consider, for example, some of the ways in which some gendered issues have been approached. Mental health campaigns aimed at men, which utilise football terminology and imagery, may exclude the many men who have no interest in the sport. Incorporating competition into lessons will not meet the needs of all boys! We need to recognise that, among all the seemingly noisy, boisterous, competitive boys (remember that we often only notice what we expect to see), are quiet, sensitive, emotional boys. By tailoring our approach to the stereotype, we may be failing to meet the needs of these children as well as reinforcing the stereotype.

Throughout this book, particularly at the end of our "why" chapters, we have provided examples of ways in which you can take equitable approaches to the various issues discussed. Now that you have a greater understanding, and as you move forward with implementing equity into your practice based on what you have identified in your audit, you may wish to revisit these. However, here are some additional thoughts and ideas for inspiration. At the end of the day, you know your group of children, your families, your community and your setting best. You understand the barriers faced by certain children and the messages they may have grown up with, so you can tailor your approaches to ensure impact.

- If you are new to a setting, get to know your children, families and the local area. Talk to parents and carers about their children. Observe them and learn about their interests, what they gravitate towards or avoid, and what needs they might have that they have not been able to express. The more you know, the better you can tailor your approaches.
- Spend time increasing your awareness of the experiences of, and issues facing, different equality groups so you can be sensitive to the unique needs of different groups.
- An understanding of the dominant narratives within different areas, groups and cultures provides an opportunity to get in there early with the counter-messages. We know that as children get older the influences of peers and the media may mean that their views change and bias may increase or develop. Anticipating those messages and providing a solid base of positive values, tolerance and respect can only help!
- Provide encouragement to children who are stepping outside the gender boxes in subtle ways. This is not about saying, "Wow - look at you, a girl who does X!" as this may make it seem like they are doing something unusual, and may in turn reinforce the stereotype and induce stereotype threat. A better response might be, "Wow - that was hard but you showed determination and you learned how to do it."
- Remember we know that often when presented with a counter-stereotype, there is a tendency for people to misremember or forget it. For example, if you are reading a child a story where Mum is building a new bed, there is a good chance that many children will forget about this or remember it as being Dad who built the bed. This would suggest that it's not enough just to include the counter-stereotypes in our songs, stories and displays: we need to point them out, discuss them, celebrate them. Again, beware of introducing stereotype threat, but perhaps try a discussion: "Who built the bed? Has anyone here watched someone build furniture? Who did it? Can anyone build? Who builds things at nursery? What great things have you built?"
- While we are not advocating for gender-neutral approaches, doing equity in settings where gender difference is minimised can have a greater impact. That's what they did in the BBC *No More Boys and Girls* programme. As well as the proactive equitable approaches, they also stopped doing things like dividing the class by gender, having a girls' cloakroom area and a boys' one, using gendered pet names and saying "boys and girls" all the time - all of which continually reinforce difference, set girls and boys in opposition to each other and increase stereotypical ideas of what boys and girls can be and do.

Notes

1   We have used gender here as this is the term Margrét Pála uses.
2   Margret Pala uses "pink haze" and "blue haze" to describe what she calls the "safe zone" of gender stereotypical or gender-conforming behaviour, which can sometimes be quite extreme – for example, what some might describe as "bitchy", "tell-tale" girls or loud, unruly boys.
3   For a fuller description of the Egalia model, see T. Acar Edol, "Practicing Gender Pedagogy: The Case of Egalia". *Journal of Qualitative Research in Education* 7(4) (2019): 1365–85.
4   VICE, *Raised Without Gender* (2017). YouTube. Available at www.youtube.com/watch?v=4sPj8Hhb wHs (accessed 7 January 2022).
5   Again, it feels important to qualify these statements with the assurance that we know many boys and girls will have these skills and capabilities.

17 What Parents Can Do and How to Get Them on Board

Barbara Adzajlic and Susie Heywood

If you are a parent or carer, this chapter has lots for you to think about. If you're a practitioner, you may also be wondering what you can do to bring parents and carers along with you. When we deliver training, we very often hear comments, right at the start and continuing as we go on, around the issue of parents, carers and wider family members: "We might only see a child five mornings a week; their parents spend much more time with them and they need this training too."

It's a very fair point. Early years practitioners can't possibly be expected to right all the wrongs of society, or to educate every parent, or to change the communities in which they live. Nor should you. Most parents and carers, as you will know, are trying their very hardest to do their best for their children, and there is a bewildering amount of contradictory information, evidence, pseudo-science and opinion out there on how they should do that, in addition to the barriers of poverty, lack of time and lack of power. Many parents are already on board with gender equality, to a greater or lesser extent. Others might not be, and you may be worried about jeopardising those crucially important relationships you have with families by wading in and imposing your views where they are not welcome. So, just as there are bigger and smaller things you can do to change your practice right now and in the future, there are also simple things you can do to support parents to understand and support this important agenda.

Why is It Important to Engage Parents on This Issue?

As educators, you will know very well the importance of family engagement. You will also know that, while peer pressure becomes more important as children grow older, right now parents and carers are often the most powerful influence on their developing attitudes.[1] Please be reassured that if you are fighting a losing battle where some parents are concerned, you are still helping to make things better for the next generation by providing a safe space where children can be who they want to be. However, if you can bring parents, carers and family members with you, you can make even more of an impact by influencing what happens outside of nursery time, and once children leave you to go to school. Below are some of the questions or issues that practitioners have raised, and some suggestions for what you can do. Later on, we'll go through some questions parents and carers themselves might have and how you can respond. Or, if you are a parent or carer reading this, hopefully this section

DOI: 10.4324/9781003167921-21

will help you to think about the actions you can take. But first, some suggestions on how to engage generally with your families about gender equitable approaches.

Communicate

Once you have decided that you want to make some changes and work towards gender-friendly practice, you absolutely need to communicate this to your families. You might want to start with a general announcement, follow it up with bite size pieces of information to keep it on the agenda, and always offer opportunities for people to get involved or find out more. As people who work closely with families and get to know them well, you will know that communication is always key to introducing change. You know your families and the communities they live in much better than we ever could, so think about things like:

- What are the best ways to communicate with families generally: through newsletters? Social media? Posters and leaflets? A parent council or forum?
- What ways can you use to get through to specific families, thinking about language barriers and disability, family dynamics, work patterns. When is the best time for a chat?

You will have families that are keen to get on board, and others that are harder to reach for a variety of reasons. Offering different kinds of opportunities is important, as is continuing to communicate. Once you are established in what you are doing, you can add gender-equitable practice to your nursery handbook, talk to new families about it when you meet them and let them see your policies (and provide opportunities to be involved in developing and updating them). Keep the issue on the agenda with good news stories or short anecdotes in your newsletter or social media.

Offer Some Training and Awareness

Here are some ideas you can use if you are able to bring parents and carers in for an information session:

- Watch some film clips together. See Appendix 3 for ideas. Discuss: what do parents think? Do they agree with the messages? How can we address this together?
- Use the gender box activity in Chapter 5 (there is a link to the original activity with instructions on how to run it).
- Make your own media boards. Ask parents to bring in photos, printouts or magazine cuttings of the toys, games, books, films, songs and TV characters their children love. Paste them together in different areas according to whether the children are boys or girls. Once complete, look at the whole thing and talk about what messages children are getting from the media about what girls and boys do, like, look like and are good at - and what they aren't.
- Carry out a similar activity to the one above but using images aimed at adults, from TV, film, advertising, fashion and music. Talk about how men and women are represented in the media, and how this affects how we think about them.
- Do some of the unconscious bias activities described in Chapter 15. Be careful to be non-judgemental when people are caught out, but use it as a lead-in to talk about why we need to reduce our bias and how we can do that.

Help People to Find Their "Whys" ...

Training and awareness opportunities like those mentioned above will probably help with this, but if you don't have this opportunity, remember that nearly everyone has an interest in achieving gender equality – whether it's about their daughters growing up safe from gender-based violence, or their own experiences of barriers to following their chosen career, or because they have a friend or family member who is LGBT+, or because a man in their family refused to get help for a medical problem because of the tough guy stereotype, or because their great grandmother was a suffragette. Or simply because they have great ambitions for their child and don't want them to be in any way constrained from achieving great things. It is rare to find a parent who doesn't want the very best for their child. If you can work out where your interests align and you can explain that your approach is about making things better, you can start from a place of common understanding rather than conflict.

Lean In

Be curious about why people feel a certain way about an issue, and try to understand where they are coming from. Building good relationships with families is one of your superpowers as an early years practitioner or setting, so use this superpower to meet people where they are at and go forward together. Sometimes this is all it takes to recognise that there has been a misunderstanding, which can be easily corrected, or that they are holding on to a bias that, with a gentle challenge, they can be helped to let go of.

Walk a Mile in Their Shoes

If you are a parent (or grandparent, aunt, uncle ...) yourself, consider how you would feel and what would work for you. How has gender impacted on the way you parent? How aware are/were you of it? Did you go down the pink and blue route? Try to reflect on how, even when you are very aware of what you "should" do as a parent, it's very easy to forget or to slip up when you're busy trying to get everything done and your unconscious bias pops up in the middle of a stressful situation. Keeping this in mind can help you to empathise with parents who might be struggling.

Be Ready to Learn from Parents and Carers

Parents can also support you to stay on the right track. Encourage them to let you know if they notice anything that could be improved in the nursery. Tell them you are open to challenge yourself and that you can work together to improve things for their child.

Respect Individuals' Circumstances but Don't Accept the Unacceptable!

Sometimes you will have to make a choice between maintaining those all-important relationships with families and promoting aspects of this agenda. Sometimes you may choose to respect a family's beliefs and experiences, and not force things upon them with which they are not comfortable. However, keeping some people happy cannot mean allowing discrimination to take place. For example, you cannot accept homophobia or other forms of discrimination, and you may have to state that this is your nursery's policy – that families who join the nursery have been made aware of the policy, and that people who don't accept it might have to find another nursery.

... If All Else Fails

You have a wealth of legislation behind you to back you up. In the United Kingdom, most of these issues sit somewhere within the Equalities Act. Other policy and legislation in Scotland, such as the Curriculum for Excellence and Getting It Right for Every Child, mean we need to ensure that we are providing every child with a range of opportunities, so you can fall back on these when necessary. Check back to Chapter 2 for some other legislation and policy frameworks that support this agenda in the United Kingdom.

Frequently Asked Questions from Practitioners

Our relationships with our families are very important and are sometimes a bit precarious. They don't trust authority. How can we have conversations about this stuff and still keep them on board?
This is one of the fantastic things about early years settings: you are able to foster strong, trusting relationships with families that aren't always possible as children go through school and things become more formalised and authoritarian. So we would never suggest that you jeopardise these crucial relationships by forcing new ideas on people. You will have to decide what lines to draw and where to draw them, between keeping families on side and standing up for children's rights. We have seen many great examples where practitioners have encountered sceptical parents and managed to convince them gently and respectfully about this approach.

Sometimes it's about understanding what people's fears are. A dad who expressed concern about his son pushing a toy pram was completely won over by a practitioner who reminded him that was how he had got his son to nursery that day. Parents who express homophobic views can sometimes be brought round by being reminded that, at the end of the day, they just want their child to have a happy life. Others will be more difficult and you may have to be prepared to remind them of the nursery policies they signed up to when they registered their child, about equality and diversity and human rights, and about your legal duties. But finding the right time and place for those conversations will help to keep things calm and respectful.

Is this approach about making our kids and nurseries gender neutral, and ignoring the biological differences between girls and boys?
Ignoring or denying the physical differences between boys and girls is not what our approach is about. Some parents (see parents FAQs, below) and some early years settings (like the

Swedish model) go down this route, and it may well have its advantages: evaluation of the Swedish model shows that it has been successful in reducing the preference children have for same-gender playmates, and their tendency to make assumptions based on stereotypes.[2] However, our focus is on equity, which means taking action to compensate for the messages children have already absorbed, and continue to receive, in other parts of their lives. This means we have to recognise that boys are getting one set of messages and experiences, leading to one set of opportunities, and girls are getting another, very different, set. We don't deny that there are biological differences, but we believe these don't have to dictate what we do with our lives, aside from our reproductive functions. See Chapter 16 for more on equitable approaches, and the difference between this and complete gender neutrality.

How should we approach the families in our nursery who come from countries where women and men aren't treated equally? There are fathers who won't speak to the female staff.

First, we would always advocate care in the way we talk about other cultures. Sexism, misogyny and gender inequalities exist in some form in every culture and every society, but they manifest differently according to culture, religion, politics and history. Just because sexism isn't considered politically correct in the United Kingdom doesn't mean sexist attitudes aren't alive and well.

That said, there are cultures that are more conservative and countries where women don't have the same rights in law that they have in most of the Global North, and we have certainly heard examples like the one above, or of girls quite openly being treated very differently than their brothers, and their behaviour in school being monitored by their brothers.

You may be able to support some of these families to understand gender equity by helping them find their "why" – the issue with which they identify. Families who have come to Britain in search of a better life may be interested in career opportunities for their children. Some of the most gender unequal societies in the world have large numbers of women in engineering and science careers because it's a respectable career with prestige for the family, and a way out of poverty. Others may be acutely aware of other types of discrimination, injustice and human rights issues.

People who have left their home communities behind may live in fear of losing touch with their culture, language and customs. With the right support, they can find a balance between maintaining links with their old home and embracing aspects of the new one. A great example of this is a very short film made in Glasgow in 2015 called *A Strong Man*,[3] showing men from a range of cultural backgrounds getting involved in anti-violence against women work. The men talk about choosing to let go of aspects of their culture that are harmful, while keeping those that are good.

Ultimately, though, if you can't change the hearts and minds of adults, you are still making a huge contribution by telling children what is and isn't acceptable in your nursery and in this society, and by giving them that safe space where they can be free of stereotypes and prejudice.

Our nursery is in a deprived area with a lot of working-class families and "traditional" men. People want their children to do well but are scared about what will happen if their son is seen out in the community wearing a dress. How should I approach this?

This is a real issue for some people and an example of how class intersects with gender, leading to very specific ideas of what it means to be a man. You can help people in the community to become more comfortable with alternative ways to be a man by employing male staff, celebrating their involvement in all aspects of nursery life and being clear through your policy and communications about what families can expect from you. You can also help children to navigate this territory through critical thinking: people around here don't think boys should wear dresses/dance/play with dolls: is that fair? Why might that be? Why is it different here in the nursery?

The fear here, of course, is a fear of homophobic policing of masculinity, so perhaps you can support parents to think through how they can support their child's critical thinking and resilience to stereotypes. You can also remind them that gender equality is about much more than allowing boys to wear dresses, and go back to helping people find their "whys". If you are able to bring a group of parents together to talk about gender stereotypes, you might be able to start building a supportive community where it would be okay for boys and girls to be seen in the community not conforming to gender stereotypes.

Frequently Asked Questions That Parents May Ask You – or that Parents Reading This Might Ask

Should I raise my child gender neutral?

As you'll have gathered from previous questions, total gender neutrality isn't something we advocate in a nursery context, and in terms of gender-neutral parenting, we don't really know yet what the outcomes are. There is a growing movement out there using terms like "theybies" and "gender creative parenting", and hopefully, in time, research will start to emerge telling us what the impact is. Possible benefits include that strangers won't be able to automatically pigeonhole children and therefore to respond to them in gendered ways; and children themselves will have access to a wide range of experiences and opportunities, unhindered by knowledge of societal expectations on them, in their most formative years. A note of caution, though: whether or not children are assigned a gender, they still have a biological sex, and they need to know about their reproductive parts for health and safety reasons. If you do decide to go gender neutral, Cordelia Fine provides an interesting example of a couple who tried this, even to the extent of doctoring picture books so that the characters were all gender neutral; and ensuring that domestic responsibilities were equally divided between the (heterosexual) parents.[4] The choice is yours, but perhaps consider whether you want your child to be blissfully unaware of gendered expectations, or aware but equipped with critical thinking to challenge them.

I'm really up for this but my nursery isn't. What can I do?

If you aren't lucky enough to have a nursery that is already doing the work on this and want to bring it to their attention, feel free to show them this book! There are lots of resources and links to what others are doing at the end, where they can find out more.

What about when they go to school? Will all this good work be undone?

As children move up the education system, things become more formalised, which can mean that gender stereotypes become more entrenched. This is also the time when parental influence wanes in favour of peers and (to an extent) teachers. There is great work occurring on gender equality in many UK schools that you may be able to access (see p19). As a parent/carer, if you feel your child's school isn't really getting it, you could try raising the issue through your Parent Teacher Association or Parent Council. And keep up the good work at home! Your influence may have waned, but those positive messages can still get through!

I try, but their grandparents/my in-laws are old-fashioned and keep telling my son to man up/my daughter not to get mucky!

It's difficult when you feel your hard work is being undermined by others in your child's life (and this applies to many aspects of parenting). Try talking to relatives about why you feel this is so important, and help family members to find their own "whys" so they can support you in this. Even if you can't win them over, you can use this as a learning opportunity with your child: "There are some people that don't agree with us, maybe because they were brought up in a very different way. We don't have to agree with them but we still love them. Remember, you can be whatever you want to be ..."

I want my son to be kind, but we live in a community where he'll be ripped to shreds ...

Again, this one is about preparing your child for the reactions of others. Reinforce how important it is to be kind, or how much you love your son's dancing/your daughter's football playing. Talk about why others might see kindness as a weakness and why you disagree; counter the stereotype by continuing to show lots of examples of kind boys in books or films; and make sure your child knows who they can go to for help if they experience negative reactions.

Should I buy my daughter that 'make your own make-up' kit? Pink Lego?

It's definitely an improvement on just getting some ready-made (and probably cheap and nasty) make-up, or on not getting any Lego. But these attempts at making science and construction appeal to girls just reinforce the stereotypes that girls will only be interested in science if it's going to make them look good, or construction toys that are "girl"-themed. Try instead to seek out science and construction toys (or, equally, toys that promote nurturing and creativity for boys) that aren't geared towards a particular gender. Let Toys Be Toys can help you navigate your way through this territory (see Useful Organisations).

I've tried everything but my daughter just loves pink

That's okay! Whatever you do, don't let your daughter feel she's doing something wrong. She might have been influenced by friends, family, the media, into thinking that's what she "should" do; or she might actually just naturally love pink (it's a nice colour). And, with pink being so strongly associated with feminine characteristics, we don't want children thinking there's anything wrong with pink, and by extension with "girly" things and with girls. What you can do is make sure she has lots of other colours (or toys, or activities) in her life. You could talk about other colours and what's good about them, and you could show (or create) examples of pink being associated with masculinity. Rather than close it down as an option, use it as an opportunity to open up her world.

I've got it all wrong, I feel terrible, how can I turn it around?

It's never too late to make a difference. If we've learned anything from the neuroscience in Chapter 3, it's how amazing our brains are and how capable they are of learning, unlearning and relearning. Even if you feel you are swimming against a tide of gender stereotypes, remember that anything you do to disrupt that helps to chip away at those gender boxes.

What else can I do as a parent/carer?

Dr Christia Spears Brown reminds us that, although earlier is better, there is always something that parents and carers can do to help:

> I always encourage parents to start at birth. You really only have about three years of heavy influence. After that, the stereotypes are ingrained in our children's minds, and the best thing we can do is address them head-on. The next best option is to help children recognize a gender stereotype when they see one, in themselves and others.[5]

Here are some final tips for helping your children to navigate gender (and other) stereotypes:

- Do whatever you can to increase diversity of all kinds in children's lives. Find ways for children to meet all kinds of people, to learn about different ways of life, beliefs and identities.
- Minimise the stereotypes as much as possible. Think about the language you use, and try whenever possible to minimise the use of gendered language. Gender-neutral terms like firefighter, police officer and so on are important, but so is not always grouping or classifying people or children by their sex. We are not saying never use "boy" or "girl" – but think about other ways of referring to people and try to use them when you can – for example, "Wow – look at what that person is doing!"
- Be media savvy – really think about the media that your child is consuming and don't be afraid to make decisions about what is and what isn't suitable. If a programme is pretty poor when it comes to stereotypes and representation, cut it out. Look for positive examples and add them in. Learn about parental controls around online platforms.
- Point them out and correct stereotypes when you hear them! These things lodge themselves in children's minds very early on, and parents can play an active role in supporting children to recognise gender stereotypes when they see them or when they express them. Explicitly pointing these out when we come across them in things like books, stories or films can help draw children's attention to them, which is important because we know that when it comes to stereotypes, we very often misremember or forget counter-stereotypical examples when we do see them. If a child expresses a gender stereotype, we can provide a balance by giving an example of a person who doesn't fit the stereotype. This is a proactive approach.
- If you have a child who doesn't conform to gender stereotypes, you may – especially as they get older – want to talk to them about some of the negative comments or reactions they might receive from other children. You can help them to understand why people

might act like this, provide reassurance and help them to know what they could do or say when things like this happen. You might also need to work on your own subtle reactions - children pick up on these things really easily.

Notes

1 For example, a systematic review of body dissatisfaction and sociocultural messages related to the body among preschool children found that parental influence appears to be an important factor in the development of preschool children's body dissatisfaction and attitudes. See G. Tatangelo, M. McCabe, D. Mellor and A. Mealey, "A Systematic Review of Body Dissatisfaction and Sociocultural Messages Related to the Body Among Preschool Children". *Body Image*, 18 (2016): 86-95.
2 E. Barry, "In Sweden's Preschools, Boys Learn to Dance and Girls Learn to Yell". *New York Times*, 24 March 2018. Available at www.nytimes.com/2018/03/24/world/europe/sweden-gender-neutral-pre schools.html (accessed 7 January 2022).
3 *A Strong Man - Maryhill Integration Network*. YouTube. Available at www.youtube.com/watch?v= mwGEz3YhD6Y (accessed 7 January 2022).
4 C. Fine, *Delusions of Gender* (London: Icon Books, 2010), 14-16.
5 C. Spears Brown, *Parenting Beyond Pink and Blue* (Berkeley, CA: Ten Speed Press, 2014), 25.

18 Practice Scenarios

Barbara Adzajlic and Susie Heywood

So we've covered the what, the why and the how when it comes to tackling gender stereo-types in the early years. Hopefully by now you are already making changes to your practice and your settings (or at least planning them). While much of this seems straightforward and simple, we aren't kidding ourselves that it's always going to be easy. As we have already learned, this stuff can go against our own internalised ideas about gender roles and can involve completely changing the way things have always been done. Additionally, while we may be convinced of the why, and feel comfortable taking forward these approaches, others may disagree or not have the same level of knowledge or understanding, and we will inevit-ably face questions and situations that challenge us.

We've already discussed the importance of calling out instances of stereotyping and sexism (and all forms of discrimination or prejudice) in order to create safe and inclusive early years environments and a culture where things like this are not tolerated. As important adults in the worlds of the children in our care, it is also powerful for us to role-model respectful challenge, demonstrating to children the importance of leaning into issues and not being afraid to speak up. We know that sometimes challenging others can be difficult, and you should always exercise professional and personal judgement when approaching these kinds of situations. You will know when it's the right or wrong time and the best way to approach these conversations.

It has also become really apparent to us, in the course of our work, that the strength and quality of the relationship between early years staff and children and parents really facilitates gentle challenge and respectful discussion. Time and time again, we have heard practitioners describe the challenges they have faced, and the creative ways they were able to utilise their skills and the positive relationships they have with each other, and with parents and children, to conduct these tricky conversations and navigate difficult situations in respectful but effective ways. We have included some of these in the scenarios below, and are grateful for the learning we received from these brilliant practitioners.

Below we have provided some short challenge scenarios based on this learning and on our own reflections on the issues that may arise when embedding gender-equitable practice within early years settings. Some of these will be very familiar to you, some less so. We hope they will provide you with some guidance and confidence should you face similar scenarios.

One point to make in relation to all the scenarios concerns the importance of ensuring that the principles of gender equity are clear in your setting policies and materials. A key

DOI: 10.4324/9781003167921-22

reason for this is that when facing these moments of challenge, it allows you a starting point for discussion: "You should hopefully have read our policy on gender stereotyping ..." - that kind of thing - or an ending point: "I know that we disagree on this, but it's clear in our policy the approach that we need to take on this."

In each scenario, we have provided some discussion that unpicks some of the issues, possible motivations and pitfalls of each situation. We have then provided some possible responses, but it is important that in situations like this, you as a practitioner consider the wider context of each individual situation, including what you know about the people involved and where there may be intersections with other issues or inequalities. You are the expert when it comes to your setting, your colleagues, your children and families - and you should be confident in your ability to respond to these issues as you do with any other challenges that arise in your practice. We have also provided, where relevant, suggestions for further reading or links back to related parts of this book. We hope that you find this useful.

Scenario 1: The Boy in a Dress and an Unhappy Parent

Martin is usually collected by his mum at the end of the day, but one day his dad comes to take him home ... and stops dead when he sees Martin having the time of his life, twirling about in a princess dress. Dad looks disapprovingly at Martin, who stops twirling and asks to take the dress off.

Questions for Reflection

Why might dad be reacting like this? What could be the impact on Martin, right now and in future?

Discussion

This, or something like it, comes up regularly for practitioners with whom we speak. There's a lot going on here: the possible reasons for Dad's disapproval, the message this sends to Martin and the impact on his sense of self and his self-esteem, and what this could mean for the choices he makes in future. We don't know what conversation Martin will have with his dad on the way home and beyond, so we should do what we can to support this conversation to be a positive one.

Dad might just be surprised, having never seen Martin do this before (maybe he hasn't had the opportunity at home, or hasn't felt permitted). He could be fearful that Martin will become a target of others' gender policing, he could be worried that his son behaving in this way may somehow reflect badly on him as a parents or man, or he could be expressing his own homophobic or transphobic views.

Your response will depend on your knowledge of the context and your relationship with Martin's dad, but it's important to reinforce that this is perfectly acceptable behaviour; that it bears no relation to Martin's gender identity or sexuality (and that even if it did, it would still be okay); that children like to explore and be creative; and that policing this behaviour could instil a sense of shame in Martin and prevent him from being the person he wants to be, which can be harmful to his mental health. It could also lead to Martin gender-policing other children with similar negative effects.

Possible Responses

You could point out the many positives of the situation: "the children have been dressing up as all sorts of things this afternoon, we've had dinosaurs and unicorns too, they all have such great imaginations and we've had so much fun!" (This strategy also points out that, of all the things Martin could pretend to be, a princess is the least far-fetched.) You could point out what you've observed in Martin's dad: "You look a little surprised – would you like to ask me anything about what we've been doing today?" You could bring in a discussion about fairness: "We were talking earlier about how it's not fair that some children are allowed to do things that others aren't. We talked about things that we all like to do – read stories, play in the garden, wear different clothes and colours ..."

Hopefully one of these will allow you to have a discussion with Martin's dad to check how he feels about what he has seen and how he feels about it. You can then remind him about your policy and values, and gently correct him about any misconceptions he might have. If you aren't getting through, invite Martin's dad to come in and talk about it when he has more time. Ultimately, you can fall back on your nursery values and policies: all children can access all the resources; we don't tolerate homophobia; we promote gender equitable practice.

Further Reading

Chapter 10 looks at homophobia, transphobia and the gender policing of masculinity in more depth.

Scenario 2: Parental Concern Around LGBT+ Discussions

A parent calls to say they are unhappy that you are promoting same-sex relationships – which they say is not an age-appropriate topic – through the books you have been reading.

Questions for Reflection

What constitutes "age-appropriate"? What do children need to know at this stage? What might be the fears that lie behind this parent's view? How could you support them to reinforce your messages of inclusivity?

Discussion

A common misunderstanding is that talking about same-sex relationships means talking about sex (which would indeed be inappropriate in the early years!). By reading books with all kinds of families you are teaching children about the real world they live in, and helping them to see their lives reflected in your resources and therefore your values. Children will come across LGBT+ people in the community at some point in their lives, and we have a legal duty to protect those people from discrimination.

Possible Responses

Point out that it's totally appropriate to talk about mummies and daddies, whatever the family set-up is, and that all you are doing is reflecting the reality of many people in this world. Allay any fears based on misunderstandings that you are talking about sex.

If you have tried this and still encounter resistance, then it's hard to see this as anything other than homophobia, so you may have to remind the parent about your policy and values. Hopefully it will already be crystal clear that you are an inclusive setting that doesn't tolerate homophobia, and you can point out where your handbook, wall displays or other parent-facing materials state this.

Further Reading

Chapter 10 goes into homophobia, biphobia and transphobia in more detail, with lots of information on how you can be inclusive and why it's important to start this early.

Scenario 3: Boys Don't Cry

One of the little boys in your group has hurt himself in the playground. He's very clearly holding back tears and says "I'm not going to cry because my mummy told me that brave boys don't cry."

Questions for Reflection

How does this scenario relate to the "man box"? Why is it important that boys in particular are taught that it's okay to express their emotions? How would you handle a situation like this, which means contradicting the messages that a child is receiving at home?

Discussion

It is common for little boys to hear and absorb this message about not showing emotion, and we have already touched on some of the problematic outcomes associated with a culture that discourages certain emotional responses in men and that celebrates toughness and strength. As educators, we are in a position to provide a counter-narrative that lets boys know it's okay to show emotions and certainly okay to cry. We need to be careful not to send the message that there are only certain situations where it's okay to cry. This is an opportunity to provide those messages to this boy. It is also an opportunity to explore what is meant by bravery and to separate the concept of bravery from that of lack of emotion, fear or weakness.

Possible Responses

You could say something like, "Some people think that, but in this nursery we have a rule that everyone is allowed to feel sad, or upset and cry - it doesn't matter if you are a boy or a girl." You could reinforce this message at a later time using a story or book with positive messaging about emotions and crying. You may want to find examples to which he can relate of men who have been able to show their emotions - the counter-stereotype. If appropriate, you may also want to find an opportunity to chat to mum about what's happened. You could say something like, "He wasn't sure if he was allowed to cry so we spoke about how crying is important as it's about letting the bad feelings out and helping us to feel better." This is a way to gently challenge her views around this.

Further Reading

Chapter 7 goes into these issues in more detail.

Scenario 4: Responding to Conflict

A little girl is crying because a little boy has pulled her hair. You overhear a colleague say, "Ah, never mind, it's only because he likes you."

Questions for Reflection

What does this statement mean? Can you think of examples where you have heard this, or versions of it, in an early years setting or in wider society? What message does it give to the girl? What message does it give to the boy?

Discussion

Girls hear this kind of response frequently throughout their lives. On the surface, it seems like quite a nice thing to say to calm her and make her feel better, but dig a little deeper and we can see some problems.

For a start, this response frames the behaviour of young children in a heteronormative sexualised way. Children should understand that girls and boys can be just friends - that it doesn't have to mean anything else.

It also teaches children that mean and aggressive behaviour is acceptable if you "like" someone. What is this saying to children about what they can expect from relationships as they get older? Are we normalising unhealthy relationships? Excusing and minimising boys' and men's behaviour? Are we sowing the seeds of the sense of entitlement that some men can feel over women's bodies? It also minimises the girl's understandable reaction and teaches her that she may not get the support she needs when telling an adult about this sort of thing. It sets her up for more serious situations in future where she might not report a man's bad behaviour towards her out of pity or out of the belief that she is somehow responsible. It makes it harder for girls as they get older to negotiate tricky situations where they know something isn't right but "he likes you". By not addressing the violence, as well as sending messages that say this kind of behaviour is acceptable, we are missing an opportunity to talk to boys about healthy ways of expressing and demonstrating their emotions and showing respect to other children.

Would your colleague have said the same thing about a girl behaving badly towards a boy (unlikely), or a boy behaving badly towards another boy (even less likely)?

Possible Responses

If you overhear this, step in and make it clear that you will deal with any bad behaviour appropriately, whoever the child is. This sends an immediate message to the girl that her concerns are valid. Deal appropriately with the behaviour in a way that fits with your nursery's values, and have a conversation with your colleague about the interaction, making the points discussed here.

Further Reading

In Chapter 6, we looked at the harmful messages children get about the roles of men and women in relationships.

Scenario 5: Boys vs Girls

You've noticed in the course of your playroom observations that there is an ongoing boys vs girls theme in many of the interactions between the children. You've just overheard a group of girls chanting "girls are better than boys!"

Questions for Reflection

What's the problem with the boys vs girls narrative? Should we challenge this even though it's partly a normal developmental phase?

Discussion

As we touched on in Chapter 3, children begin to develop quite binary ideas around gender and what it means to be a boy or a girl at quite a young age. Along with this comes the tendency to hold the gender category of which you are a member in higher regard. At as young as three years of age, children show a preference for children of the same sex and attribute more positive characteristics and qualities to their own sex. We know that by the time they reach primary school, most children spend the majority of their time playing with children of the same sex. It's quite likely then that you will begin to see this kind of behaviour or hear phrases like this on a fairly regular basis, and while it might be to be expected, it doesn't mean we shouldn't take the opportunity to challenge it.

Possible Responses

It's important that you intervene in instances like this to correct the stereotype, which is clearly untrue and, while perhaps an apparently harmless bit of banter, is contributing to the idea of difference between boys and girls that sets them up in opposition to each other.

This is a great chance to have a conversation, and to establish some facts with the children. It's a chance to discuss respect for other people, and to begin to instil the skills of cooperation and respect for difference. You could plan activities that involve boys and girls working together to achieve a goal (finding an activity that you know everyone will find achievable is important here) or find examples of where boys and girls or men and women have worked together to achieve something inspirational.

Further Reading

The BBC Documentary *No More Boys and Girls* shows a teacher exploring with the children in his class the lack of difference in strengths and capabilities between boys and girls. It is interesting to see the reactions of some of the children! You may find some inspiration here.

Scenario 6: Concerns About Male Staff in the Nursery

You are showing parents around the nursery during their daughter's induction. You mention your male member of staff and how great it is to have a man among your staff. The parents agree that it's good to have a male role model, but then pause and say, "He won't be changing her nappy though, will he?"

Questions for Reflection

What fears or prejudice lie behind the parents' question? Why is it important that male staff members carry out all the duties expected of any member of staff?

Discussion

A male staff member is such a great opportunity to role-model caring and nurturing behaviour in men to children, their families and the community. Some people will still question why a man would be involved in intimate care, so it's important to take this opportunity to impress that all your staff are trusted to work with children; that they are all capable of performing all kinds of tasks; and that it's important for the children to see this. We wouldn't tolerate someone refusing intimate care from someone based on the colour of their skin, so we can't allow it in this case either.

Parents will naturally feel protective of their child, but they are choosing to trust you and this should extend to all your staff. Very occasionally, you might come across a family that has experienced some kind of trauma related to sexual abuse and you may decide in this instance to work with the family to help them gradually build trust, rather than throwing them in at the deep end.

Possible Responses

Reassure the family that all your staff are trusted with the children, explaining your child protection policy if necessary. Explain that you are a team and everyone has to muck in and do everything – men will also be found reading stories and giving cuddles, while women will be out playing ball games in the garden or leading IT activities. Explain why this matters and how it contributes to the dismantling of gender stereotypes that could be restricting what the children believe about themselves and their abilities.

Further Reading

In Chapter 11, we discuss with Shaddai Tembo some of the barriers that prevent more men from working in childcare, while in Chapter 13 we look in more detail about the importance of men in childcare roles and how we can support more men to be involved, both professionally and in their personal lives.

Scenario 7: Referring to Staff as "The Girls"

Your nursery has a new manager/headteacher who has loads of energy and experience, but who keeps on referring to the (all-female) staff as "the girls".

Questions for Reflection

Who in your life do you call "the girls"? Who in your life do you call "the boys"? Are there situations where this is okay and situations where it isn't?

Discussion

This one gets a variety of reactions from practitioners with whom we talk, ranging from, "What's wrong with calling your workmates the girls?" to "Absolutely no way!" There are several issues here:

- It diminishes the professionalism of the workforce to anyone who overhears it. Early years practitioners are often highly trained and the work they do is under-valued and under-paid. Staff are childcare development officers or whatever other term you would use on a job advert or a contract. They are not children!
- This is a person who has authority over the staff, and it probably wouldn't be okay for staff to refer to them as a "girl" or a "boy", so the fact that it's happening creates a power imbalance. The terms "houseboy" and "housegirl" are still used in post-colonial countries to describe fully grown adult servants, which shows us how words can be used to create and maintain power structures.
- In a profession that is trying to achieve better gender balance in its workforce, using a gendered term (whether "women", "ladies" or "girls") reinforces the idea, for staff, children, families and visitors, that this is a job for women.

- It's inaccurate (unless you employ females under the age of 18)! And it's therefore potentially confusing for the children.

If you struggle with this one, as some people do, think back to the Allport Scale in Chapter 5. It might not feel that important; you might feel completely comfortable with it, but it's one of those things at the bottom of the scale that, if we ignore them, contribute to some people's attitudes and behaviours escalating. Infantilisation, particularly of women, contributes to the idea that a group is less clever, or competent, or important. It can also affect women's confidence, influencing how they feel about their own capabilities.

Think also about whether your reaction would be different if the manager was male or female, and why?

Possible Responses

This is really difficult if you are the person with less power in this situation, particularly with a new manager. Depending on your relationship, you might feel able to just point out casually the issues with this and suggest that the staff are referred to by their job titles (except perhaps in the staffroom or on a night out, if people are comfortable with this - but certainly not in front of other people). "[Previous manager] tended to call us the CDOs or sometimes 'folks' since we started doing all this work on gender equity ..." To avoid it happening in the first place, of course, a good management handover would cover this topic, as would the interview process that brought this person into the post!

Further Reading

There are many articles online about this topic - although not all agree with our position! This is a good one to get you thinking.[1]

Scenario 8: It's Not for Girls

You observe a girl watching a group of boys playing with toy trucks and vehicles in the sand. She approaches and tries to join in, but they tell her "You can't play because it's only for boys."

Questions for Reflection

Would you respond right away, or later? Are there things you could do to try to prevent things like this happening?

Discussion

This is prejudice/discrimination, so it needs to be addressed. The children are acting out stereotypes they have learned, and are reinforcing them by teaching them to another child. Getting in there quickly is a great opportunity to challenge the stereotype and support children's critical thinking. It's also an important opportunity to promote inclusion and empathy. So your immediate response matters, but so does what you do afterwards to make it less likely to happen again.

We also know that children tend to gravitate to same-sex friendship groups as they get older. They have absorbed the idea that boys and girls are different, but we have also socialised them to act similarly and share similar interests to children of the same sex, so in many ways it's hardly suprising! We have already touched on the idea that gender is policed more strictly both by and for boys, and that we often see boys rejecting anything considered feminine. This may be what we are seeing being played out in this scenario.

Possible Responses

Question why anything could possibly be only for half the children. If you have already talked about fairness or gender stereotypes, bring it back to this and remind children what you talked about.

Take care, though! Probably no one will be able to think of a reason why the activity is "for boys" and once you have addressed the stereotype it might come down to in-group play preferences, so the boys might resent being "made" to include the girl, which will be no fun for anyone. Also, jumping in as the saviour for this little girl could result in her looking for help in future rather than feeling able to deal with situations herself. So try to structure the conversation in a way that empowers her – asking her what she thinks about the situation and what should happen. And make it fun – point out interesting and creative ways that they can play together.

Taking time to work with the children on rules for fair play will help prevent this scenario happening, and could benefit children who might otherwise be excluded for other reasons. You could also create opportunities for all the children to create or achieve something together, where they can recognise everyone's contribution as important and valuable, and realise that working together is good for everyone.

Further Reading

Remind yourself about the ways children learn and absorb messages about gender by revisiting Chapter 3.

Scenario 9: Sword and Gun Play

During outdoor playtime, you notice that almost all the boys spend the majority of the time pretending that sticks are guns or swords.

Questions for Reflection

How do you feel about this kind of "violent play"? Would this impact the way you respond? How do you balance responding to something like this with the importance of child-led play?

Discussion

This is an interesting one, and we are pretty sure you will already be quite adept at knowing the most appropriate response to this, but we've added it in as it's a chance to reflect on when it might be appropriate to intervene in children's play and how. We know how important intrinsic child-led play is, but it's interesting to consider whether this type of stereotypical gendered play is truly intrinsic or is led by the suggestions of a society that primes boys for certain types of activities and play. Is this children exploring the things they have seen in the world, making sense of it, having fun, or is it boys beginning to personify the "tough guy" persona that they quickly learn is what is expected of them?

While there may be people who morally object to this kind of play, or whose worries are around the potential for injury, we are not suggesting that any intervention should occur in an attempt to stamp out this type of play altogether. Free play is important, as it is allowing children to manage their own risks. If there are other children, particularly boys, who don't want to join in the rough play then keep an eye to ensure that they aren't being pressured into it. One practitioner also told us about a boy who had arrived in the United Kingdom as a refugee and whose parents regularly watched news items depicting gun violence or its aftermath. There may be children who need to act out what they are seeing in order to help them process it.

At the end of the day, even is the chosen game is swords, it's likely that the play is bringing with it opportunities for other types of experiences and learning: sharing, cooperation, team-work, role-play, empathy, so rather than focus on the play, focus and comment on these when you notice them.

Possible Responses

Rather than intervene in a way that suggests there is something wrong with what they are doing, an equitable approach to this could be to attempt to gently introduce other scenarios and suggestions for how the children could use the sticks. You could consider modelling these yourself alongside the children. Expose them to other ideas and stimulate their imaginations. If the children wish to continue in their game, it may be useful to ensure that they are aware of other children and if needed show them ways of keeping safe while they play.

Further Reading

Chapter 7 looks more at male violence and discusses the learned expectations of the tough guy persona. There's a really interesting case study of how Shaw Mhor Nursery in Glasgow handled a similar situation with aggressive play among boys in the Gender Equal Play document from The Care Inspectorate and Zero Tolerance.[2]

Scenario 10: Addressing Racism in the Nursery

Taylor, a young Black boy, approaches you upset because he is always made to be "the baddie" in the game with the other children.

Questions for Reflection

Why might we have included this scenario in a book about gender stereotypes? How alert are you to racism within the nursery?

Discussion

It is important that any potential discriminatory behaviour is challenged and discussed, so this situation needs a response that both offers comfort and reassurance to Taylor, and that challenges and calls out the behaviour and bias of the other children. The roots of racism are laid down early – we cannot gloss over this. However as practitioners we need to handle this sensitively and from a place of respect, knowledge and understanding, which acknowledges our own privileges and bias.

We know there is a lack of racial diversity across children's media,[3] but children may also be receiving additional messages about race through what is and is not represented. For example Pragya Agarwal describes how "there is a power imbalance about how blond hair is depicted and perceived in children's books, cartoons and toys as being better and superior. White, fair-skinned, blond-haired, blue-eyed becomes the norm as children see this all around them."[4] She goes on to explain the association of whiteness with goodness and purity, and blackness with evil and dirtiness. It may be very likely, then, that these racist ideas are fuelling this scenario, so it needs to be challenged and discussed. There is also a possible gendered component which it's worth touching on here. We know that Black boys in particular can face racial stereotypes, which see behaviour being labelled as problematic and more aggressive.

While Taylor may not be aware of all this, his experience is that he is being treated unfairly and there is a risk of an impact on his self-worth, perhaps compounded by and reinforcing experiences of racism and prejudice in other areas of his life, or which he has observed happen to his family or friends. It is important to offer comfort and reassurance to Taylor, acknowledging his experience and validating his sense of unfairness.

In the longer term, you should keep a close eye on the children to ensure this incident and others like it are not repeated. Instances of discrimination or prejudice may not always be clear, so practitioners need to be observant. We have a responsibility to foster positive racial attitudes in children and to help children to understand privilege. The best way to overcome prejudice is to spend time with those people, get to know them and build understanding, shared interests and empathy. Consider ways in which you can support the children to do this.

Possible Responses

Depending on your knowledge of Taylor and his family, as well as your experience and confidence in dealing with issues about this subject, you may wish to discuss what happened with Taylor's family and possibly Taylor himself about the best way to respond. We can't assume that all Black children will have had the same experiences; we can't assume we know what they need; and so having these discussions will help you to understand more. They will likely have suggestions based on their own experience, which you may not have considered.

Be careful – you do not want to compound Taylor's feeling of being singled out, but you do want him to know that you are serious about dealing with it should he want you to. Stepping into the game as an adult and directing the play to ensure that children take turns with the different roles could be a useful immediate response, explaining how it is only fair that everyone gets a turn at each role.

Depending on your discussions with Taylor's family, as well as discussions with your team, there may be other things you could consider at a later date, particularly when it comes to discussions with the other children in the nursery. For example, circle time could be used to have conversations about race, difference, privilege and prejudice. If you feel you lack the knowledge and confidence around this, then seek the help of experts who may help you to really consider the work that you may need to do to ensure that anti-racist practice is embedded across your whole setting.

Further Reading

We have done our best to provide some suggestions here, but we are aware that these are limited by our narrow experience as White women who are trying our best to understand these issues. For more nuanced and in-depth understanding, we would recommend Pragya Agarwal, *Wish We Knew What to Say: Talking with Children About Race* and Jane Lane, *Young Children and Racial Justice*, both of which were really helpful in formulating our thinking and response to this scenario. You may also find it useful to revisit Chapter 15, which looks at bias and includes some suggestions for how we can tackle and reduce bias in young children.

Scenario 11: The Focus on Girls' Appearance

You constantly catch yourself greeting little girls as they arrive at nursery by commenting on their hair or their clothes. You know the harm this does and want to do better.

Questions for Reflection

Why do we respond to little girls in this way? How do you greet boys on their arrival? Why is the answer not to ensure you compliment boys too?

Discussion

We have discussed body image and the pressures on females in particular to look a certain way. The way we talk to and describe little girls very often reinforces the idea that their value lies in the way that they look. Often this stuff rolls off our tongues before we have even had a chance to think about it, particularly if it's clear that a child has made a special effort that day, done something nice with their hair, or is looking at you with the expectation of some sort of comment (you'll know the look!). We all want to feel noticed, and it's important that the children in your nursery feel that way as they arrive; however, there are so many ways we can do this without focusing on appearance.

Thinking "equity", you might want to look for stories you could use where the characters learn why appearance is not what really matters, or stories that feature smart, adventurous girls and boys. And remember, it's about more than just reading the story - we need to point this stuff out and discuss it with the children to reinforce the counter-stereotype.

Possible Responses

You can still show you notice their appearance and provide that bit of validation to a child without including a value judgement. Rather than say "Don't you look pretty today!", point out something specific to show you have noticed or ask them a question about it: "Oh look - you've got a plait in your hair! Who did that for you? It must have taken ages!" or "Is that a new jumper you have on? It's got a cool picture of a unicorn on it!"

Further Reading

Chapter 8 on body image is relevant here.

Scenario 12: Use of Pet Names

One of your colleagues uses different pet names for the boys and girls - "sweetie" for the girls and "pal" for the boys.

Questions for Reflection

Why do we use pet names? How comfortable do you feel about challenging the practice of your colleagues?

Discussion

We want our children to feel noticed and special. We also want to build relationships and a personal connection with them. Pet names are one way we do this with many people in our lives, particularly children, so it's quite common to hear them being used in nursery and education settings, and they might not always be problematic. However, pet names can be inherently gendered and can send messages about what we expect from, or how we relate to, boys and girls. I have heard a male teacher reflect on how he and other male colleagues used certain pet names with girls as an attempt to make himself appear softer, and with the boys to build a kind of buddy relationship.

Using different names for boys and girls also reinforces difference, which as we know can increase stereotypical beliefs. It is also important to consider whether there may be any cultural or regional variations in how certain words are used, understood or interpreted. What might be a term of endearment to one person could feel quite different or even offensive to another.

Possible Responses

When you get the chance, explain what you have noticed, comment on how difficult it can be to change these things but how important it is to do so, and ask whether there is anything you can do to support this. You could undertake some peer observation and feedback around pet name use as a way of reflecting on current practice – very often we don't even notice we are doing it! Perhaps you could agree on a list of terms that you are all happy to use; however, be careful, as any use of different names for boys and for girls will continue to reinforce difference, regardless of what words you choose.

Further Reading

In the BBC documentary *No More Boys and Girls*, the teacher, Mr Andre, had a similar habit and the children were enlisted to help break his habit by noting on a chart the times when he used the names. He was motivated to change his practice going forward. You could suggest watching it together as a team and hold a discussion about practice.

Scenario 13: Gender Non-conforming Children

A parent says their child has identified as "trans" and wants to discuss how the nursery will handle this. They ask that all children are referred to as "they".

Questions for Reflection

What do you think the parent means when they say their child identifies as "trans"? How can you ensure your setting is inclusive and welcoming to all children, regardless of how they view their gender?

Discussion

Childcare settings need to be ready to welcome, include and value children, whatever their gender identity. Many parents are working hard to support their children through this and it can be very difficult, for them and for you, to know what is the right thing to do. It can also be a challenge to find a balance between respecting the parents' views and managing their expectations, while also catering to the other children and families in the nursery and, of course, making sure the child's own views are heard and their needs are met. Here are some things to consider.

That a child rejects binary gender categories does not automatically mean they are transgender. Children go through phases of believing they are all sorts of things, so being another gender doesn't have to be a big deal at this stage. They may well continue to reject their given gender, or they may not. So labelling a child as "trans" may not be helpful (especially within the child's hearing). "Gender non-conforming" might be more accurate (but again, discussing this in the child's hearing might not be either advisable or necessary).

Parents, as mentioned, may be struggling to find the best way to support their child, and may not have all the information they need to make this decision. Remember that rejecting gender stereotypes about being a boy, and even saying you want to be a girl can also be a symptom of just not being happy about what society tells you it means to be a boy. In another scenario, we heard of a parent whose son was identifying as a girl. The parent therefore decided to go hyper-"girly" to accommodate this, with dresses, unicorns and lots and lots of pink. The result of this is to reinforce gender stereotypes with the idea that, as a girl, you can have all these things that, as a boy, you couldn't. You might be able to help this parent find other ways of supporting their child not to conform to gender stereotypes, without going as far as changing pronouns. Checking what the child actually wants is a really important part of this.

Changing everyone's gender pronouns, unless you are doing this as part of a carefully thought-out strategy (see the Swedish example in Chapter 16), risks getting into complicated situations that staff, parents and children are unprepared for and uncomfortable with, and you could face a backlash. For the biological boy who is identifying as a girl, or the biological girl identifying as a boy, being referred to as "they" isn't necessarily what the child has asked for.

Again, let's bring it back to the child, and the other children. If the child wants to be known by another name and given another gender, is it really a big deal right now? Chances are if you go with what the child wants without making a fuss, they will settle into their new role quickly, for however long they might need to, and the other children will just accept it.

Possible Responses

If a child wants to be referred to as another gender and by a different name (and if you are sure that this is what the child, not just the parent, wants), then do this with as little fuss as possible. Let the children know that Jennifer is now going to be called Jason, and start using he/him pronouns. You will probably find that the children in the nursery are far more accepting of these things than you think.

Further Reading

Chapter 10 looks at how gender stereotypes impact the way we think about gender identity, and how we can make early years more inclusive and comfortable for people who don't conform to their given gender.

Scenario 14: Marriage Talk

At the end of the day, two little girls who are best friends are leaving with their parents. They are chatting away and one of them says to the other, "When we grow up we should get married!" A parent overhears and laughingly says, "You two are ridiculous! One day you'll meet a handsome prince and change your mind!"

Questions for Reflection

Would you let this go as a harmless and well-meant comment? Would the situation be different if it were a boy and a girl having this conversation? What if it were two boys? Why?

Discussion

Anyone who has been around children will know they sometimes talk about being in love with or wanting to marry their best friends, without of course really understanding what romantic love and marriage are all about. But quashing this kind of talk (even with a light-hearted use of the word "ridiculous") at this stage closes down the opportunity children have to be open-minded about different kinds of relationships.

There's also a chance the comment could be overheard by someone who is part of a family with a same-sex relationship. You would be much more likely to hear parents talk positively and even encouragingly about a boy and a girl growing up and getting married one day, and thinking this is very cute. This just reinforces heteronormativity, and therefore also homophobia. It also reinforces that idea that children of different sexes can't just be friends (while those of the same sex should) – that there must be a romantic element to it. Finally, the handsome prince comment does even more: it gets into the idea that girls are waiting around for a rich, handsome man to sort them out!

There's another possible scenario here that has similar but also quite different connotations. What if it were two boys? There would be no handsome prince, or indeed probably beautiful princess, coming to "rescue" them from being "ridiculous", but there would probably be more alarm at the prospect of two boys in a close relationship. This is one of the really heartbreaking aspects of the "masculinity straitjacket" – the way boys' relationships are policed so that, beyond a certain age, there can be no close companionship the way there can be between girls, with all the benefits those relationships bring.

Possible Responses

This is one of those situations where parachuting in with an unsolicited response could be detrimental, so you might need to think about tone and timing. Having a suite of ready responses will be handy: "I don't think these two need any handsome princes in their lives, they seem pretty strong and capable by themselves!" or "I think that's a lovely idea! Being good friends is the best start to any relationship" or, for boys in particular, "It's lovely to see boys talking about love and friendship. We've been talking about how everyone can be kind and caring. It's so important boys can have close friendships with each other just the same way girls can. It's good for their mental health."

To support these conversations, you will also hopefully be finding lots of ways of normalising different kinds of relationships and families, and of highlighting this to your families. Also consider the situations in the nursery where marriage and relationships come up. Do Mary and Joseph always have to be played by a girl and a boy (we're not saying they should or shouldn't, but if a girl desperately wants to be Joseph, is it that much more bizarre than being a camel or a star?)

Further Reading

In Chapter 10, we talk about ways of introducing and normalising conversations about different family set-ups and making your setting inclusive and welcoming to all.

Notes

1 S. Madsen, "Why Calling Women 'Girls' is A Bigger Deal Than You May Think", *Forbes*. 9 August 2021. Available at www.forbes.com/sites/forbescoachescouncil/2021/08/09/why-calling-women-girls-is-a-bigger-deal-than-you-may-think/?sh=99d6bad2fda5 (accessed 7 January 2022).
2 The Care Inspectorate and Zero Tolerance, *Gender Equal Play in Early Learning & Childcare* (2018). Available at https://hub.careinspectorate.com/media/3466/gender-equal-play-in-early-learning-and-childcare.pdf (accessed 7 January 2022).
3 The 2019 report from Hopster TV titled *Is Kids' TV Making Your Child Prejudiced?* found that ethnic minorities were only included in around half of the content examined, and often in the background. Only six shows (out of 50) had BAME characters as the "stars" of the shows.
4 Pragya Agarwal, *Wish We Knew What to Say* (Boston: Little, Brown, 2020), 68.

19 A Call to Action

Barbara Adzajlic and Susie Heywood

So there you have it! Our approach: reduce the stereotypes and ensure that children are exposed to messages that provide a counter balance to them. Provide all children with the opportunities and experiences that will allow them to develop the knowledge, the skills and the emotional capabilities to believe it is possible for them to achieve whatever they put their minds to, unlimited by the expectations the world places on them because of their gender. Help them to believe and accept that there is no one way to be a boy and no one way to be a girl. Look out for and encourage those children who are pushing against the norms.

It's pretty simple: we can choose to be part of the problem, or we can choose to try to provide something different. We can continue to grow gender bias within our children, or we can choose to implement strategies that just might make a difference.

It is now over to you to decide how to incorporate some of our suggestions into your practice and interactions with the children in your care. We hope that reading this has both convinced you of the need to take action (the "why?") and also given you clear ideas and suggestions for the "what?" and the "how?". We hope you use the tools and suggestions we have provided, or develop tools and ideas of your own - find your own approach. We know it's a lot, so take some time to digest and reflect on what you have read. Talk to other people about it. Share your thoughts and ideas.

Making changes is always easier when we aren't working alone. A whole setting approach that involves all staff in the nursery is preferable, but if that's not possible then try to find someone in your setting who can support you with this. We have certainly benefited from having each other to bounce ideas off, chew over issues, and motivate each other to keep going when sometimes it felt like nobody else really understood why we were so passionate about this stuff.

One of the things that we think is useful in our approach, which sees gender stereotypes and inequality at the root of a wide variety of issues that affect a wide variety of people, is that it can become a home for a variety of (sometimes competing) agendas. It may be that the thing that drives you to take action is not the same as someone else's, but you can find commonality of purpose - namely the desire to ensure that young children are not limited in any way by outdated and unrealistic gender stereotypes. So whether the reason is a desire to see an end to violence against women, a concern for poor educational outcomes among certain boys, a worry about the links between idealised body images and eating disorders among young people, or many of the other health and social issues where gender inequality

DOI: 10.4324/9781003167921-23

and rigid gender roles are having an impact, we can gather together under a shared goal of early years spaces free from gender stereotypes with equality and equity at their heart, where children's rights and needs are at the centre.

Remember too that learning never stops. We would encourage you to seek out relevant training for you and your colleagues. Read some of the brilliant books that we've recommended at the end of ours. If you are active on social media, you may want to seek out accounts or hashtags to follow that talk about some of these issues, to help you stay up to date and in touch with some of the latest research or thinking. We have seen loads of brilliant examples of practice from practitioners and settings up and down the country. We've also seen an increase in people sharing the stereotypes and gendered messages when they come across them – challenging and calling them out. We have certainly seen this agenda catching on, becoming more mainstream and understood.

It's also useful to find people to follow that are not like you, who may have different experiences and perspectives, who may not have the same privileges you do, or who have faced bias and discrimination. Listen, listen and listen some more. As White women, we have learned so much from listening to and reading the views of some of the practitioners and academics who were involved in creating The Early Years Black List, for example. We learned about racism in the sector affecting staff and specific issues for Black children and parents. We found books written by Black authors to help us deepen our understanding. It really helped us to reconsider, refine and improve our approach. Look for further training from experts in specific topic areas if you identify a learning need, or seek out someone who can help you understand better.

We would encourage you to have conversations whenever opportunities arise. You'll probably find that there are lots of opportunities, particularly to challenge stereotypes. Our experience is that once you are tuned into this stuff, you will see it and hear it everywhere. It can be easy to be disheartened by the sheer volume of the stuff you might come across – to feel like you are alone in pushing a heavy stone up a very steep hill, and feel like your actions alone can't make much difference. But they can! And you aren't alone – there are many of us championing this agenda within the early years, and in education and beyond. And there also are plenty of positive examples when you look for them – really good examples of the counter-stereotypes that show anything is possible. We now see these all the time too! Rather than focus on the negative too much, try to point these out and talk about them with the children and your colleagues – help people to notice and remember them. Your role with children in the early years is powerful, vital and can make a huge difference – you can help dismantle the gender boxes!

If you have found this book helpful, please do recommend it to colleagues and friends – or pass it on. It won't do much good gathering dust on a shelf! You will also have ideas and suggestions of your own – things you have done that you feel worked well. Share these! Let us know about them and we will share them too – we would love to hear from you! Let us know how we can improve on our approach, your own reflections and ideas. We are keen to continue listening and learning. Together we can help create a community of practice that can be supportive and grow stronger through the sharing of ideas and experiences.

It's been no mean feat writing this book – especially during a global pandemic when, as working mothers, we also had home schooling, childcare, exam pressures and pretty much full-time jobs to contend with. The fact that you are reading this means so much to us, so thank you!

We think our message is a simple one, a powerful one, and one worth ending on: gender stereotypes are limiting our children – but together we can change the narrative.

Good luck!

Susie and Barbara

Gender Friendly Scotland: www.genderfriendly.co.uk

Twitter handle: @GFNScotland (Gender Friendly Scotland)

Appendix 1: Action Checklist

You can use this as you read through this book to note any ideas or actions that feel useful for you, your practice and your setting. Along with the findings of your audit, these may form the basis of an action plan for how you will take a gender-equitable approach going forward.

My Action Checklist	
Idea for action	Page number

Appendix 2: Audit Table

	Celebrating success: What's going well?	Areas for action: What do I want to develop further?
People This section looks at the people we come across and interact with, and how we ensure we are being fair and inclusive and helping others to do the same.		
How do I use my knowledge of each child and their family context to consider whether they are fully included in nursery life? Do I actively make the effort to understand the circumstances of each family?		
Is my setting visibly inclusive of LGBT+ families?		
Am I confident about actively challenging any discrimination I come across?		
Do I interact differently with family members depending on their gender? Are there differences in what information I give them or what I ask of them?		
Does my setting ensure that our communications are free from assumptions about sexuality and gender identity? Are they inclusive of dads, single-parent families and kinship care arrangements?		
Do communications (website, social media, newsletters, handbook, etc.) make a gender equitable ethos clear? Do families know what to expect? Are regular reminders and updates provided?		

As well as families, does my setting make a gender-equitable ethos clear to the wider community and stakeholders? Am I confident in explaining/challenging when necessary?		
Are there any social or cultural issues within my community that I need to consider when developing gender equitable practice?		
Do I proactively seek to find ways of involving dads in aspects of nursery life?		
Do I invite people to visit the nursery who can help to demonstrate counter-stereotypical examples of the types of people who do different jobs, hobbies or sports?		
Place This section looks at our physical space, indoors and outdoors: play areas, toilets and cloakrooms, waiting areas, staff rooms and what we have in them.		
Do I understand how different groups of children use the different play spaces? Are there sex/gender or other differences in where children play and who and what they play with?		
Are spaces, and the resources in them, set up in ways that encourage all children to try out a range of experiences? Are there changes I could make to improve this? Are there deliberately gendered spaces like cloak rooms and toilets? Is this necessary?		
Do play resources reflect gendered marketing of toys or are they more open-ended?		
Do colour schemes suggest that certain spaces or resources are "for girls" or "for boys"?		

Are books inclusive? Do they reflect a range of people in different roles and with different talents and interests; different types of families; different skin colours and different abilities? Do I use them to counteract stereotypes?		
Do I actively seek diverse and inclusive programmes and films to show the children? Do I seek to understand the stereotypes and biases that may be included in those that I show or those that I know the children consume? Do I discuss these with the children?		
Do displays reflect a range of different people in different roles (e.g. dads reading stories; mums working in the garden; people in non-gender-stereotypical careers; celebrating children's success in a range of areas)? How can I draw the children's attention to these?		
Is the layout and look of staff rooms and spaces inclusive of all people who may work in the setting (now and in the future)?		
Is the layout and look of waiting areas inclusive of all types of family members and other people who may visit?		
Practice This section is about what we do, how we use our resources and our knowledge and understanding.		
How do I ensure role-modelling supports gender equity? Do children and their families see a range of staff (and visitors) carrying out a range of tasks?		

Do I consider the language I use with and in front of children, and how it supports gender equity? Do I use gendered pet names? Do I use gender-neutral terms like police *officers* instead of police *men*? Do I speak to some children differently than others, and have I considered why and what effect it might have?		
Do I ensure that the way I speak and teach about bodies and food is inclusive of all types of bodies and does not focus on appearance or weight?		
Do I ensure that I give boys and girls equal attention within the nursery?		
How consistent is my behaviour management and use of praise? Do I have different expectations of, and responses to, girls and boys? Do I actively counteract the gendered expectations society has?		
Do I promote good mental health in children? Do I consider specific areas where some children may need more support (e.g. encouraging girls to speak up about problems, and boys to describe their emotions)?		
How do I use resources? If I use books, songs or toys that are gendered, or reflect old-fashioned attitudes, do I use them to promote discussion and critical thinking? Do I point out the stereotypes and the counter-stereotypes?		

How do I respond to challenges in play scenarios - for example, children excluding other children, or assigning them roles, based on their gender, skin colour, language or physical ability or other characteristics?		
If I am involved in special needs assessment referrals, am I aware of the gendered differences in referrals of boys and girls? Do I strive to avoid gendered assumptions in my assessments of children?		
How do I respond to "gender policing" between the children? Do I challenge bias and prejudice of all kinds between children?		
Do I ever group children by gender? If so, is this done in a planned and considered way to counter dominant narratives and promote equity? How can I do this in ways that do not draw attention to differences or stereotypes?		
Do I plan for opportunities to promote gender equity or challenge stereotypes - for example, birthdays and celebrations, campaigns, transitions to primary school?		
How do I ensure that my interactions with grown-ups promote gender equity, model healthy relationships and respect, support learning and development and challenge discrimination?		
Do I create opportunities to share, reflect on and support other staff with their gender equitable practice?		

Do I consider how gender equity intersects with anti-racism and other anti-discriminatory practice? Do I need to seek additional training with experts in these areas?		
Planning and policy This section looks at our overall ethos, how our planning and policy support gender-equitable practice, and the role and development needs of our leadership, management and staff.		
Do policies reflect a commitment to gender equity? Is there a specific gender equity policy? Are diverse children and families involved in developing and updating policy?		
Do uniform policies encourage equal opportunities for play and exploration? Do they reinforce difference? Are girls, in particular, encouraged to wear clothing that allows them to participate fully? If there is no uniform policy, how can clothing and footwear be prevented from being a barrier to participation?		
Do leadership and management demonstrate a commitment to gender equitable practice? Is management visibly supportive when staff are challenged?		
Do my colleagues understand and support a commitment to gender equitable practice? How could I support staff to develop their knowledge, understanding and confidence? How can I ensure that support and ancillary staff are involved?		
How can my setting ensure new staff are aware and supportive of a gender-equitable ethos?		

How can my setting identify and overcome barriers to recruiting a diverse range of staff members?		
How can my setting support staff who are in a minority (e.g. men, LGBT+, BME staff) to feel welcome, and support them to overcome challenges to remaining in post?		
Does my setting understand and consider gendered issues in the retention and promotion of staff (e.g. equal pay issues; the glass escalator; maternity/paternity, parental and other carers' leave; the needs of menopausal women)?		
How do I and my setting ensure that good practice is sustainable? If there is a change of management, does handover include a continuing ethos of gender equitable practice? How are new staff introduced to the concept so that they know what to expect?		

Appendix 3: Further Information

Safety and Support Information

Mental Health

If you are having a difficult time of struggling with difficult feelings, then talking helps. The Samaritans UK can be contacted by freephone 24 hours a day on 116 123. You can also visit www.samaritans.org.

If you are having thoughts of suicide and need help right now, dial 999 right away – do not try to cope alone.

For support around the mental health of a child or young person, contact Young Minds on 0808 802 5544 or visit www.youngminds.org.uk.

Gender-based violence

For anyone needing support for domestic abuse for yourself as well as family members, Refuge provides a free, confidential, 24-hour helpline with BSL and language interpreting, and will also link you to local supports. Call 0808 2000 247 or visit www.nationaldahelpline.org.uk.

Rape Crisis Scotland: Call 08088 01 03 02 or visit: www.rapecrisisscotland.org.uk

Rape Crisis England & Wales: Call 0808 802 9999 or visit: www.rapecrisis.org.uk

Rape Crisis NI: Call 08000246991 or visit: www.rapecrisisni.org.uk

Ireland: Dublin Rape Crisis Centre: Call 1800 778888

Support for men: Some Rape Crisis centres offer support to men and boys. You can also call 0808 8010327 or visit: www.mensadviceline.org.uk.

Eating disorders

Beat: visit: www.beateatingdisorders.org.uk (individual helplines for UK 4 nations).

LGBT+ support

Stonewall: Call 0800 0502020 or visit: www.stonewall.org.uk.

LGBT Youth Scotland: Call 07984 356 512 or visit: www.lgbtyouth.org.uk.

Parenting helplines

Many organisations that support children and young people also offer support and helplines for parents and carers. Here are a couple:

Family Line: Call 0808 802 6666 or visit: www.family-action.org.uk/what-we-do/children-families/familyline.

Parentline Children 1st (Scotland): Call 08000 28 22 33 or visit: awww.children1st.org.uk/help-for-families/parentline-scotland

Useful Organisations

Beat Eating Disorders: www.beateatingdisorders.org.uk
Changing Faces: www.changingfaces.org.uk
The Early Years Blacklist: www.theearlyyearsblacklist.com
Fatherhood Institute: www.fatherhoodinstitute.org
Fathers Network Scotland: www.fathersnetwork.org.uk
Fight The New Drug: www.fightthenewdrug.org
Gender Action in Schools: www.genderaction.co.uk
Gender Friendly Scotland: www.genderfriendly.co.uk Twitter handle: @GFNScotland (Gender Friendly Scotland)
Gina Davis Institute on Gender in Media: www.seejane.org
Global Equality Collective: www.thegec.org
Improving Gender Balance in Education Scotland: https://education.gov.scot/improvement/learning-resources/improving-gender-balance-3-18
Improving Gender Balance Ireland: http://stimulatingphysics.ie/
Institute of Physics: www.iop.org
Let Clothes Be Clothes: www.letclothesbeclothes.co.uk
Let Toys Be Toys/Let Books Be Books: www.lettoysbetoys.co.uk
Lifting Limits: www.liftinglimits.org.uk
Men in the Early Years (MITEY): www.miteyuk.org
Mental Health Foundation: www.metalhealth.org.uk
National Parent Forum of Scotland: www.npfs.org.uk
White Ribbon UK: www.whiteribbon.org.uk and White Ribbon Scotland: www.whiteribbonscotland.org.uk
Zero Tolerance: www.zerotolerance.org.uk

Useful Film Clips

Some of the following films, or film clips, have been mentioned in the book. We have also included some others that might be useful to further your understanding of some of the issues or to generate and support conversations with others.

Children and gender stereotypes

NHS Greater Glasgow & Clyde's ten-minute film demonstrating children's understanding of sex and gender. NHS Greater Glasgow & Clyde (2020) *Young Children and Gender: NHSGGC - Early Years & Gender*, 3 July 2020. Available at www.youtube.com/watch?v=Ak4p8y2CxDU accessed 1 February2022).

No More Boys and Girls: Can our Kids go Gender Free? – two-part BBC documentary on a gender equality drive in an English primary school. The full programme is sometimes available on BBC iPlayer and parts can be viewed on YouTube.

A short (three minutes 25 seconds) clip from *No More Boys and Girls* demonstrating gendered toy choices by adults can be viewed here: BBC Stories (2017) *Girl Toys vs Boy Toys: The Experiment*, 16 August 2017. Available at www.youtube.com/watch?v=nWu44AqF OiI (accessed 1 February2022).

Gender-based violence

Two short animations demonstrating the links between gender stereotypes, gender inequality and gender-based violence:

A (two minute 20 seconds) film by Zero Tolerance (2020): *It's Time for Prevention*, 7 October 2020. Available at www.youtube.com/watch?v=reOFiNX2EfI&feature=emb_logo (accessed 1 February2022).

Australian (four-minute, 30 second) film from Our Watch (2017): *Let's Change the Story: Violence Against Women in Australia*, 30 March 2017. Available at: www.youtube.com/watch?v=fLUVWZvVZXw (accessed 1 February2022).

Masculinity, Violence and Men's Mental Health

Brothers in Arms Scotland, a men's mental health charity, produced a two-minute film about masculinity and men's mental health: Brothers in Arms Scotland (2018) *Brothers in Arms – Real Men*, 29 October 2018. Available at https://youtu.be/vpqSVSRwO7Y (accessed 1 February2022).

Tony Porter TED Talk on how the "man box" and masculinity influenced various parts of his life: TEDWomen (2010): *A Call to Men*, December 2010. Available at www.ted.com/talks/tony_porter_a_call_to_men?language=en (accessed 1 February2022).

Jackson Katz has produced films about the harmful impacts of masculinity. This short clip is free to use and gives an idea of the themes covered in the full, paid-for versions: Media Education Foundation PRO (2021): *Tough Guise 2 – Home-use*, 19 May 2021. Available at: https://vimeo.com/ondemand/toughguise2homeuse (accessed 1 February2022).

Femininity

A short (three minutes, 30 seconds) film challenging the derogatory language we often hear about doing things "like a girl": Always (2014): *#LikeAGirl*, 26 Jun 2014. Available at: www.youtube.com/watch?v=XjJQBjWYDTs (accessed 1 February2022).

Two minutes 30 seconds of actor Cynthia Nixon talking about some of the negative impacts of the "woman" gender box: Girls. Girls. Girls. Magazine (2020): *Be a Lady They Said*, 24 Feb 2020. Available at www.youtube.com/watch?v=z8ZSDS7zVdU (accessed 1 February2022).

Body Image

Dove has produced a number of short films linked to its Real Beauty Campaign, which show how ideas about beauty have been influenced and distorted by the media, and aim to challenge this. A recent example is this one: Dove US (2021): *Reverse Selfie*, 20 April 2021. Available at www.youtube.com/watch?v=knEIM16NuPg (accessed 1 February2022).

LGBT+

A seven-minute film about the importance of calling out homophobic language and behaviour. LGBT Youth Scotland (2014): *Shh! Silence Helps Homophobia*, 4 March 2014. Available at: www.youtube.com/watch?v=XQKGigb5I28 (accessed 1 February2022).

Education and Career pathways

Inspiring the Future, a two-minute film demonstrating what happens when children are asked to draw a pilot, a surgeon and a firefighter, and how children can be inspired to think "outside the box": MullenLowe Group (2016): *Inspiring the Future – Redraw the Balance*, 15 March 2016. Available at www.youtube.com/watch?v=qv8VZVP5csA (accessed 1 February2022).

RECOMMENDED READING

Books for Adults

Note: Not all of these books have been referenced in the chapters of this book, but all have
provided us with some sort of inspiration and a huge amount of learning and enjoyment.
We hope you enjoy reading them as much as we have!

Agarwal, Pragya 2020. *Wish We Knew What To Say: Talking with Children About Race*. Boston:
Little, Brown.

Asher, Rebecca 2016. *Man Up: How Do Boys Become Better Men?* New York: Vintage.

Ball, Ros and Millar, James 2017. *The Gender Agenda: A First-hand Account of How Girls and
Boys are Treated Differently*. London: Jessica Kingsley.

Bates, Laura 2020. *Men Who Hate Women*. London: Simon & Schuster.

Brearley, Joeli 2021. *Pregnant Then Screwed: The Truth About the Motherhood Penalty*.
New York: Simon & Schuster.

Connell, R.W. 2000. *The Men and the Boys*. Cambridge: Polity Press.

Cooper, Yvette 2019. *She Speaks: The Power of Women's Voices*. London: Atlantic Books.

Crabbe, Megan Jayne 2017. *Body Positive Power: How to Stop Dieting, Make Peace with Your
Body and Live* . London: Vermillion.

Criado Perez, Caroline 2019. *Invisible Women: Exposing Data Bias in a World Designed for
Men*. London: Chatto & Windus.

Eddo-Lodge, Reni 2017. *Why I'm No Longer Talking to White People About Race*. London:
Bloomsbury.

Eliot, Lise 2009. *Pink Brain Blue Brain: How small differences grow into troublesome gaps
- and what we can do about it*. London: Oneworld.

Fine, Cordelia 2010. *Delusions of Gender: The Real Science Behind Sex Differences*. London:
Icon Books.

Fine, Cordelia 2017. *Testosterone Rex: Unmaking the myths of our gendered brains*. London:
Icon Books.

Forbes, Molly 2021. *Body Happy Kids: How to Help Children and Teens Love the Skin They are
In*. London: Vermillion.

Gillan, James 1997. *Violence: Reflections on a National Epidemic*. New York: Vintage Books.

Kaufman, Michael 2019. *The Time Has Come: Why Men Must Join the Gender Equality
Revolution*. Berkeley, CA: Counterpoint.

Kimmel, Michael 2013. *Angry White Men: American Masculinity at the End of an Era*. London:
Bold Type Books

Lane, Jane 2008. *Young Children and Racial Justice: Taking Action for Racial Equality in
the Early Years - Understanding the Past, Thinking About the Present, Planning for the
Future*. London: National Children's Bureau.

Lewis, Helen 2020. *Difficult Women: A History of Feminism in 11 Fights*. New York: Vintage Books.

Manne, Kate 2018. *Down Girl: The Logic of Misogyny*. Harmondsworth: Penguin.

Manne, Kate 2021. *Entitled: How Male Privilege Hurts Women*. Harmondsworth: Penguin.

Muir, Robyn forthcoming. *The Princess as the Political: A Feminist Analysis of the Disney Princess Phenomenon*. Bristol: Bristol University Press.

Palmer, Sue, ed. 2020. *Play is the Way: Child Development, Early Years and the Future of Scottish Education*. Edinburgh: CCWB Press.

Pinkett, Matt and Roberts, Mark 2019. *Boys Don't Try: Rethinking Masculinity in Schools*. London: Routledge.

Rippon, Gina 2019. *The Gendered Brain: The New Neuroscience That Shatters the Myth of the Female Brain*. London: The Bodley Head.

Rudd, Matt 2020. *Man Down: Why Men are Unhappy and What We Can Do About It*. London: Piatkus Books.

Sanderson, Catherine A. 2020. *Why We Act: Turning Bystanders into Moral Rebels*. Cambridge, MA: Belknap Press.

Schulte, Brigid 2014. *Overwhelmed: Work, Love and Play When No One Has the Time*. New York: Sarah Crichton Books.

Spears Brown, Christia 2014. *Parenting Beyond Pink & Blue: How to Raise Your Kids Free of Gender Stereotypes*. Berkeley, CA: Ten Speed Press.

Spears Brown, Christia 2021. *Unravelling Bias: How Prejudice has Shaped Children for Generations and Why It's Time to Break the Cycle*. Dallas, TX: BenBella Books.

Taylor, Jessica 2020. *Why Women are Blamed for Everything: Exploring Victim Blaming of Women Subjected to Violence and Trauma*. London: Victim Focus.

Webb, Robert 2018. *How Not to Be a Boy*. Edinburgh: Canongate Books.

Williams, Sophie 2020. *Anti-Racist Ally: An Introduction to Action and Activism*. New York: HarperCollins.

Wolf, Naomi 1990. *The Beauty Myth*. New York: Chatto & Windus.

Books for Children

New picture and story books are coming out all the time, but we wanted to share a few of our favourites with you here. The Global Equality Collective and Let Books Be Books (see Useful Organisations above) maintain up-to-date lists and provide guidance.

Adrea, Giles and Parker-Rees, Guy. *Giraffes Can't Dance*.

Best, Elanor, *Sophia Sparks – A Little Inventor with Incredible Ideas!*

Bright, Rachel and Field, Jim, *The Lion Inside*.

Cherry, Matthew A. *Hair Love*.

de Haan, Linda and Nijland, Stern, *King and King*.

De La Mare, Annahita and Kirkham, Jennifer, *The Start of Something Big*.

Donaldson, Julia and Ogilvie, Sara, *The Detective Dog*.

Donaldson, Julie and Scheffler, Axel, *Zog and the Flying Doctors*.

Garson, Sarah, *Alfie's Angels*.

Hoffman, Mary. *The Great Big Book of Families*.

Kemp, Anna and Ogilvie, Sara, *The Worst Princess*.

Kemp, Anna, *Dogs Don't Do Ballet*.

Lee, Hannah, *My Hair*.

Love, Jessica. *Julian is a Mermaid*.

Merino, Gemma, *The Crocodile Who Didn't Like Water*.

Milner, Kate, *It's a No Money Day*.
Percival, Tom, *The Invisible*.
Richardson, Justin and Parnell, Peter. *And Tango Makes Three*.
Rowland, Lucy and Hindley, Kate, *The Knight Who Said No*.
Thomas, Pat, *Why Do I Feel Scared? A First Look at Being Brave*.
Verde, Susan, *I am Human. A Book of Empathy*.

GLOSSARY

Cognitive dissonance: The tension or discomfort that people experience when they want to stand up for what they believe in, but societal pressure or inconvenience makes this difficult.

Equity: The quality of being fair and impartial. Different from equality in that it entails not treating everyone the same, but rather providing what people need in order to have the same access/opportunities.

Gender: A spectrum within which a person identifies as boy/man, girl/woman, anywhere in between or neither. Refers to social and cultural rather than biological differences.

Gender-based violence: The spectrum of violence and abuse directed against a person because of their gender or violence, which affects people of a particular gender disproportionately. It is committed primarily but not exclusively against women by men. It includes, but is not limited to, domestic abuse, rape and sexual assault, stalking and harassment, commercial sexual exploitation, child abuse and harmful traditional practices including forced marriage and female genital mutilation.

Gender Equality: The state in which the access to rights or opportunity is not affected by gender.

Heteronormative: The assumption that heterosexuality is the normal and preferred sexual orientation.

Intersectionality: The crossover or "intersection" between different types of discrimination, which can compound the disadvantages faced by people or groups who are affected.

LGBT+: An "umbrella term" that is used to cover the range of identities associated with non-heterosexuality and gender non-conformity. It includes, but is not limited to, Lesbian, Gay, Bisexual, Transgender, Queer, Intersex, Asexual/Agender.

Microaggression: The small, often unrecognised and unremarked-on incidents of discrimination that can be experienced on a daily basis by women, people from minority ethnic groups, people with disabilities and others.

Sex: Either of the two main categories (male and female) into which humans and most other living things are divided on the basis of their reproductive functions.

Sexuality: The sexual feelings and attractions that we have towards other people (Note: Sexuality is different from and separate to gender identity)

Stereotype: A widely held but fixed and over-simplified image or idea of a particular type of person or thing.

Stereotype threat: The phenomenon whereby mention of a negative stereotype can influence people belonging to the group that is negatively represented, and can negatively impact their performance or ability.

Unconscious bias: A bias is a preference or inclination for or against a particular group that is so deeply entrenched we aren't even aware of it, even when we act upon it and it affects our ability to treat people fairly. Unconscious, or implicit, bias is a mental short-cut to quickly process information and make a decision. Unconscious bias is what happens when we act upon deeply ingrained social stereotypes.

INDEX

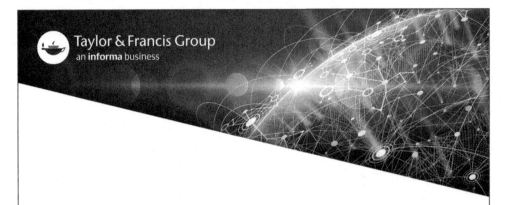

Printed in the United States
by Baker & Taylor Publisher Services